Reading Ancient Slavery

READING
ANCIENT SLAVERY

Edited by
Richard Alston, Edith Hall
and Laura Proffitt

Bristol Classical Press

First published in 2011 by
Bristol Classical Press
an imprint of
Bloomsbury Academic
Bloomsbury Publishing Plc
36 Soho Square,
London W1D 3QY, UK
&
175 Fifth Avenue,
New York, NY 10010, USA

Editorial arrangement © 2011 by
Richard Alston, Edith Hall and Laura Proffitt

CIP records for this book are available from the
British Library and the Library of Congress

ISBN 978 0 7156 3868 2

Photo credits

Fig. 4.1: Museum of Fine Arts, Boston, Gift of Thomas Gold Appleton.
Figs 4.2, 4.6, 5.4: Bildarchiv Preussischer Kulturbesitz / Art Resource, NY.
Figs 4.3, 4.5, 4.7, 4.8: Réunion des Musées Nationaux / Art Resource, NY.
Fig. 4.4: Scala / Art Resource, NY. Fig. 5.1: Vanni / Art Resource, NY.
Figs 5.2, 5.5: J. Paul Getty Museum, Los Angeles, CA.
Fig. 5.3: Hearst Castle, San Simeon, CA.

Typeset by Ray Davies
Printed and bound in Great Britain by
CPI Antony Rowe, Chippenham and Eastbourne

www.bloomsburyacademic.com

Contents

Contributors

Richard Alston is Professor of Roman History, Royal Holloway. Richard has worked extensively on social and economic history of the Roman imperial period and is the author of *Aspects of Roman History: AD 14-117* (1998) and *The City in Roman and Byzantine Egypt* (2002). His work is at the interface of ancient history and modern social theory. His current project is a comparative history of imperial formation of selves and his interest in Reception is in political philosophy.

William Fitzgerald is Professor of Latin at King's College London and has taught at the University of California and Cambridge University. He has published on Latin literature and comparative literature and his books include *Martial: The World of the Epigram* (2007), *Slavery and the Roman Literary Imagination* (2000) and *Catullan Provocations: Lyric Poetry and the Drama of Position* (1995).

Edith Hall holds a joint Research Chair at Royal Holloway, University of London, where she is Director of the Centre for the Reception of Greece and Rome. She has previously held appointments at the Universities of Cambridge, Reading, Oxford, and Durham. She is also co-founder and Consultant Director of the Archive of Performances of Greek and Roman Drama at Oxford University, and author, co-author or editor of *Inventing the Barbarian* (1989), *Dionysus since 69* (2004), *Greek Tragedy and the British Stage* (2005, with Fiona Macintosh), *The Theatrical Cast of Athens* (2006), *The Return of Ulysses: A Cultural History of Homer's Odyssey* (2008), and *Greek Tragedy: Suffering under the Sun* (2010).

Leanne Hunnings was awarded her doctorate at Royal Holloway University of London in 2008 for her AHRC-funded thesis 'Imagining the Ancient Greek slave: Death, Social Death, and Resurrection', which examined the links between the representation of slavery and death in archaic and classical Greek literature and its reception during the Abolition debates in English literature, 1780-1840. Her academic interests include the role of women, ethnicity, human rights, and slavery as an ancient and modern social phenomenon. She has taught in Ireland and Spain, and in 2010 contributed to human rights, global citizenship, and social justice education in the UK secondary school sector.

Contributors

Deborah Kamen is an Assistant Professor of Classics at the University of Washington, Seattle. She has written a number of articles on both Greek and Roman slavery, and has recently completed a monograph entitled 'Manumission in Ancient Greece: Modes, Meanings, and Metaphors', which is under review at Cambridge University Press. She is currently writing a book on social and legal status in Classical Athens.

S. Sara Monoson is Associate Professor of Political Science and Classics at Northwestern University and the author of *Plato's Democratic Entanglements: Athenian Politics and the Practice of Philosophy* (2000), which was awarded the 2001 American Political Science Association's Foundations Book Prize for Best First Book in Political Theory. She has also written articles on Athenian democratic thought, Thucydides, and international relations theory. Her current project examines creative appropriations of Socrates in post-war American popular media.

Boris Nikolsky graduated from Moscow State University in 1992 and completed his PhD at the Russian Academy of Sciences, Moscow, in 1995. Since 1995, he has been teaching Greek at the Russian State University for the Humanities in Moscow. His research interests lie mainly in the spheres of ancient philosophy and drama. He has published a commentary on Cicero's *De finibus* (2000, in Russian), and now he is working on an interpretation of Euripides' *Hippolytus*.

Laura Proffitt received her BA and MA degrees from the University of Durham, before completing an AHRC-funded PhD at Royal Holloway, University of London, where her thesis examined the relationships between discourses of family and slavery in Sophocles' *Ajax*, Euripides' *Ion* and *Andromache*, and Menander's *Epitrepontes*, as well as the history of scholarship on ancient slavery from 1800 onwards. Having taught at both Royal Holloway and the University of Reading during her PhD, she is now teaching Greek history and drama at Birkbeck College, University of London.

Patrice Rankine is Associate Professor of Classics at Purdue University, Indiana. He graduated from Yale University in 1998, after completing a dissertation on Seneca. He has developed interdisciplinary interests in African American literature and the reception of the classics among black American authors. His book, *Ulysses in Black: Ralph Ellison, Classicism, and African American Literature* (2006) was a Choice Magazine Outstanding Academic Book in 2007. He is currently expanding his studies in black literature beyond the borders of the United States, with research into the reception of Greek and Roman themes in the works of Ralph Ellison, Derek Walcott, and Wole Soyinka. Professor Rankine is also working on a book on the reception of Aristotle's *Poetics* in classical and modern literature, which includes a chapter on Shakespeare's *Othello*.

William G. Thalmann is Professor of Classics at the University of Southern California. He was educated at Amherst College and Yale University, where he received his PhD in Classics in 1975. He also studied at the University of Texas in Austin and at the American School of Classical Studies in Athens. He has been teaching at the University of Southern California since 1987 and has published articles and books on Greek tragedy and epic poetry. He is especially interested in the role of poetry within social and political developments in ancient Greece. His books include *Conventions of Form and Thought in Early Greek Epic Poetry* (1984), *The Odyssey: An Epic of Return* (1992) and *The Swineherd and the Bow: Representations of Class in the Odyssey* (1998).

Kelly L. Wrenhaven is Assistant Professor of Classics at Cleveland State University, Ohio. She has previously held posts at Trinity College Dublin and the University of Victoria, after studying at the Universities of British Columbia, Cambridge and St Andrews, where she received her PhD. Her research interests include ancient Greek slavery; epigraphy, especially manumission documents; the construction of civic and cultural identity through opposition; the use of language to construct identity; the use of evidential torture in Greek law courts; ancient sepulchral inscriptions and relief sculpture; depictions of courtesans in art and literature and, more broadly, ancient ideas about prostitution and sexuality. She is the author of *Reconstructing the Slave*, an examination of slave representation in the Greek *polis* (forthcoming, Bristol Classical Press, 2011).

Acknowledgements

This is the third book to have been produced by the Centre for the Reception of Greece and Rome at Royal Holloway, University of London. The essays it includes began life as some of the papers delivered at an international conference at Royal Holloway and the British Library in December 2007, held to celebrate the bicentenary of the parliamentary act which abolished the slave trade in the British colonies in 1807; some of the other talks delivered at the conference are being published separately in a companion volume entitled *Ancient Slavery and Abolition*. Many individuals have contributed to the emergence of this work. We are particularly grateful to Leanne Hunnings, whose idea the conference was and who worked so determinedly to ensure that it ran smoothly; Ahuvia Kahane, Justine McConnell, Lorna Hardwick, whose contributions at the conference were invaluable, and Sandra Joshel. Deborah Blake at Bristol Classical Press has been a staunch supporter of the project. Generous financial support was forthcoming from the Gilbert Murray Trust, the Society for the Promotion of Hellenic Studies, and the Classical Association. But without the extraordinary generosity of one remarkable individual the conference could never have been held at all, and that individual is a lifelong campaigner against social injustice, Professor Marianne McDonald. We are extremely grateful to her.

Rereading Ancient Slavery

Richard Alston

This volume emerged from a conference held at Royal Holloway and the British Library in 2007 to celebrate the bicentenary of the Abolition of the slave trade. The conference considered the nature and legacy of Classical slavery; the papers were divided between those which looked at the direct influence of knowledge of ancient slavery on debates on Black emancipation in the Abolition period and later,[1] and the papers on ancient slavery and its ideologies, which are collected in this volume. Yet the unity of theme within the original conference crossed the divide between these two volumes, in part since there is both an obvious integration of the understanding of slavery in modernity with the institutions of ancient slavery, and in part because the intellectual and moral location of our authors in a post-Abolition world largely determines their approaches. The historical experience of Atlantic slavery has hung over all studies of ancient slavery.[2] That tradition has tended to generate an often implicit but frequently explicit comparative agenda unusual in ancient historical studies.[3] This comparative agenda reflects to a greater or lesser extent the urge of nineteenth- and early twentieth-century theorists to categorise societies and thus the issue of a 'slave society' has been to the fore in debates.

Recently the academic focus has shifted towards representation (part of the 'cultural turn' in critical thinking), and our volume furthers this trend. This collection looks at representations of slavery in the ancient world from Homer to the second century CE, focusing mainly on literary material, but with some discussion of pictorial representations. Many of the representations studied are fictional and this, in part, reflects the fact the most antique representations of slavery are within fictional narratives.[4] In moving away from the traditional foci of social historians on juridico-philosophical material to 'soft' historical sources (ones in which the normative or factual value of the source is not easily established), our collection encounters methodological problems as to the 'truth value' of these fictional discourses and whether these sources are in any way normative, as well as broader issues of how we understand the ancient world.

The sharp distinction between 'factual' and 'fictional' sources for social history, inbuilt into the traditional boundaries of the Classical sub-disciplines of 'literature', 'history', and 'philosophy', remains conspicuous in the narrow range of genres to which de Ste Croix limited his discussion of the 'ideological plane' in 1981. The interdisciplinary challenge made to this separation of ancient sources by the French anthropological structuralism of Vernant and Vidal-Naquet soon afterwards began to encourage scholars towards a more synthetic approach to studying ancient society, although the initial trend almost always entailed historians simply mining for 'facts' about slavery the type of source, especially the ancient novel, that had hitherto been regarded by their colleagues as too 'literary' to be reliable.[5] It was not until the mid-1990s that energy began to flow in the other direction, as a handful of more literary-minded scholars began to develop techniques for reading the representations of slaves and slavery in ancient poetry and fiction in ways that resisted the class-bound as well as the patriarchal and ethnocentric ideologies that they produced and maintained, arguing that aesthetic protocols in literature, although often working to obscure the reality of slavery, do so according to codes which are nevertheless revealing. These techniques were developed in studies of the Greek novel and Greek drama,[6] along with innovative contributions on love elegy, oratory, and St Augustine in an important North American collection of essays published in 1998.[7] The same year saw the first of a spate of four major studies by scholars working closely together in California, on slavery and its representations in Homer's *Odyssey* by William G. Thalmann (1998), Plautine comedy by Kathleen McCarthy (2000), Roman literature more widely by William Fitzgerald (2000), and Greek authors including Plato and Aesop by Page duBois (2003). Yet this work did not evoke the response that it deserved, especially outside North America, and one of the aims of the conference which gave rise to this volume was to further discussion of the way to handle 'representations' of slavery.

In what follows, I will argue that the representational approach to slavery offers considerable benefits and in particular it allows us to understand better the 'alterity' of ancient slaves and thus the processes by which the citizen community was constructed and conceived. The perspective of the slave offers us a radical position from which we can understand and critique ancient societies. This stands in contrast to the systemic approaches, upon which I will focus initially and from which my historiographic analysis emerges.[8] I argue that the problems that we have encountered in our attempts to understand ancient slavery are such that we need to revise traditional ways of understanding society and develop social theory and methodologies which are flexible and robust. The challenge presented by ancient slavery is considerable.

Twentieth-century approaches to slavery have been dominated by the Marxist tradition.[9] Marx himself, in spite of his Classical education and his extended study of Classical philosophy, had little to say about antiquity and even less to say about slaves (see below). Nevertheless, Marx suggested the slave created a unity within the citizen body of the *polis* since citizens co-operated in part because of their fear of and need to secure their property rights over the slaves.[10] Moses Finley similarly argued that

a primary determining element in political culture was the division between slave and free, and that this prevented the evolution of class politics
within antiquity.[11] Instead, politics was a matter of social orders, carried
out within the citizen body. Slaves could be seen to stand external to the
political system, but within the economic system, their role being not as
agents, but as 'others', who helped define and cement identities within the
free political community. As such they were internal barbarians, an enemy
within, but an enemy that helped define the free community. This idea can
be developed to suggest that the origins of Western liberty lie in slavery; the
creation of the anti-type of the unfree allows the valorisation of freedom, but
also the creation of freedom as an absolute category and moral quality.[12]

For Finley and Marx ancient society was a slave society. Although Marx
himself never elaborated on this issue, slavery has had considerable
rhetorical importance in the later Marxist tradition, and as a result
arguments about Marxism have been fought out around issues of ancient
slavery.[13] Three related issues lie behind this debate: whether slaves can
be conceived as forming a class with class consciousness, whether slaves
manifest resistance to slavery,[14] and whether slavery was a 'determining
factor' within ancient society. Yet, as I shall argue, these issues have been
elevated far beyond their importance in the original Marxist analysis, and
the continued pursuit of these issues outside the Marxist paradigm dis-
torts our understanding of slavery.[15]

Famously, there is no definition of class within Marx, but conventionally class is understood in relation to the modes of production. A class is
thus formed of members who have a particular relationship to the mode of
production (primary labourers, landowners, etc.). Class is inevitably a
porous concept, with considerable room for variation in categorical definition alongside the issue of 'relationship to the mode of production' and
when it comes to particular individuals. The translation of a primarily
economic category into a social and political category is inevitably inexact.
It is obvious to all who engage with the ancient sources that not all slaves
were in the same economic or social position. They may have been owned,
but slaves in chain gangs on Roman estates, slaves working as shepherds
in the hills, slaves working alongside masters or peasant tenants on the
small farms that were the norm within the Mediterranean, slaves in craft
production, working in mines, performing domestic labour, working as
prostitutes and courtesans, or engaged in administrative or educational
labours within the households of the elite, and later within the *familia
Caesaris* (working as officials of the emperor) could hardly be described as
having the same experiences or life-prospects. Primarily, as all would
surely agree, slaves formed an order (a defined status group) within
society.[16] Yet, I would like to defend the notion that slaves constituted a
social class. Many or most slaves did not own the product of their own
labour, nor the means of their labour, nor their own persons, nor have the
means to reproduce themselves socially; many or most slaves had a

distinctive part in the economic system.[17] Although there was no exact match between order (the primary category) and class (the secondary category), one could argue that a large proportion of the slave population had a particular relationship to the mode of production and thus formed a class. One could further conventionally refer to slaves as a class, allowing for exceptions in which some slaves had a different relationship to the modes of production.

But to establish that we might conventionally describe slaves as a class creates a further series of problems, notably the issues of ideology and of the character of the ancient economy. The former problem is central to the historiographic tradition. Opponents of Marxism tend to argue that since we cannot detect slaves attempting a social revolution (attempting to overthrow the slave-system itself) nor identify a unity of sympathy within the slave communities of antiquity, there was no class consciousness, and from this negative position a whole series of analytical assumptions flow. Yet, this focus on class consciousness depends on a perceived requirement for each social class to have consciousness and ideology, which is in itself a confusion. It is a crude rendition of the Marxist perception that history tends to result from class struggle into an indefensible assumption that actions of agents are determined by their class position.[18] There is no requirement in Marx or in his major successors for classes to operate with class consciousness or for classes to develop distinctive ideologies.[19] Thus, the lack a revolutionary servile manifesto from antiquity is unsurprising and of very limited significance to mainstream Marxist analysis.[20] The conventional Marxist argument runs in a different direction: the relationship between political agency and class structure is problematic and not deterministic.[21] Class struggle operates through the political and social system, and has a central role in determining that system, but the actions of individual actors are not necessarily determined by their class position. Thus, a series of actions will tend to produce a society in a certain form even if those actions are in themselves not primarily motivated by class factors. Political and ideological debate will often occur in semi-autonomous zones in which class struggle will be manifested, but the rhetoric of those debates and the motivations of actors will appear to be autonomous from issues of class struggle.

The second issue relates to the issue of the mode of production. At least some Marxists argue that there was a distinctive slave mode of production in Greek and Roman antiquity.[22] This is in part a categorical question: it allows the categorisation of ancient society within a comparative history. Further, if Greek and Roman antiquity operated a hegemonic slave mode of production, then the societies could be classified as 'slave societies'. The slave mode of production is, thus, analytically prior to the question of ideology and, for at least some Marxists, the slave mode of production would generate a 'slave society', irrespective of the contemporary understanding of society on the ideological plane.

4

1. Rereading Ancient Slavery

Even if one does not accept the Marxist dynamic of history, as many, of course, do not, Marxist analysis renders complex the relationship between class (as an objective rather than a subjective category), status, political acts, the economy, and the formation of society. For our purposes, a more complete understanding of the Marxist tradition affects our understanding of the relationship between ancient slavery and ancient society, especially as it has been discussed within the historiographic tradition, and questions the significance of issues of resistance and servile ideology to our understanding of slavery. It raises the question of whether and, indeed, how the ideology of the slave matters, beyond a merely sentimental commitment to past generations.

The preliminary questions, however, are whether there was a slave mode of production in Classical antiquity, and whether that slave mode of production generated a slave society. Within Marxist theory, for this to happen, the slave mode of production would have to become hegemonic: that is, it generates the class relations within society. This condition reflects the reality that any economy will display multiple modes of production and that an economy in transition (as all economies are to some extent) will have aspects of new and old economic forms co-existing. Within Marxist writing on antiquity, there is no agreement as to whether the slave mode was hegemonic, or even of great importance.[23] It seems likely that in every period of antiquity a substantial part of the production of a society stemmed from free labour, either on the land or in trade or industrial production. In 1968, Finley, who although not a Marxist was committed to the idea that Classical Athens and Classical Rome were slave societies, attempted to find a way out of this problem in arguing that slave societies were those in which slavery was the major mode of production for the elite.[24] In similar fashion, in 1975, de Ste Croix argued, with a Greek focus, that peasants were not a class since they were not part of the productive economy.[25] Such a move replicated a traditional Marxist denigration of peasant economies as pre-political or pre-economic.[26]

De Ste Croix was hardly the first to make this move. Meyer argued a similar position in 1910, and Toynbee's influential study of Roman Italy in the second and first centuries BCE also saw peasant economies as essentially ahistorical.[27] For Meyer and Toynbee, the importation of large numbers of slaves allowed the development of a new 'stage' in ancient economic progression, a proto-capitalist 'stage' based on estate agriculture. The accession of slaves into the economy allowed the productive exploitation of the surplus labour within a peasant mode (it is axiomatic within classical economics that the peasantry were underemployed or inefficiently employed), which in turn generated significant surpluses that were invested in the development of Classical culture. Slaves were thus central to the economy that mattered, in the sense that the peasant economy was maintained in unchanging balance. By ignoring other forms of production, one could argue for the hegemonic status of the slave mode.

5

If the 'slave economy' could be seen as the hegemonic productive mode of antiquity, then one would expect a particular class structure to result, and thus class struggle would manifest itself in particular ways. Yet, and this is surely a crucial issue, the co-existence of the slave mode with other earlier modes of production would inevitably lead to a confusion of modalities and class structures.[28] With Toynbee, and indeed later Italian Marxists, the development of the slave system is associated with the rise of *latifondiste* agriculture, partly in the wake of the devastation of Italy in the Punic war. It is, however, very difficult to detect such a development in the archaeology of Roman Italy. Instead, even in imperial Italy the predominant form of agricultural exploitation appears to have been via relatively small farms managed through tenants or directly, and with a mix of free and servile labour. Earlier analyses relied on the highly questionable assumption that smallholders were engaged mainly or only in subsistence production. In a world of small farms and mixed labour forces, it is difficult to postulate a 'two-economies' model, with a peasant subsistence economy and a proto-capitalist economy based on the labour of slaves. The distribution of high quality pottery within the Italian countryside, for instance, points to rural residents being integrated into the market. Although one cannot know the status of rural populations, it seems very likely that the countryside remained home to substantial numbers of the free, and further that servile labourers would not have been using high quality pottery. This would effectively disallow any attempt to alienate smallholders from the economy.[29] If we cannot maintain a plantation model of agriculture for Roman Italy, then the Marxist model of the slave mode as hegemonic and Finley's argument that slavery was the major productive institution for the elite becomes difficult to support and consequently questions arise as to whether Roman society was a slave society. Still less can we maintain a slave mode for Athenian society.[30]

Yet if we dismiss the slave mode of production as it is traditionally conceived, we are faced with a somewhat more complex problem. For although the agricultural and industrial economy depended on labour in many different forms and organised in different ways, the focus on certain forms of 'economic' production ignores the broader role of slave labour in social reproduction. The focus on agricultural production works within a more or less explicitly commercial and market-oriented vision of economic and productive life, and may well owe much to Atlantic plantation slavery. Nevertheless, slave-ownership was distributed widely within Greek and Roman society and many households and enterprises supplemented the labour of the family or paid free labour with servile labour. Given the prevalence of slavery within urban and household production, the analytical concentration on the agricultural slave is hardly defensible, and certainly does not reflect the interests of our Classical sources. If we shift the focus away from agricultural production to all labour (including household labour), it would seem that servile labour was likely crucial to maintaining (and reproducing) many households, both elite and non-elite. In so doing, we give more weight to female and domestic labour, labour traditionally seen as non-economic.[31]

Nevertheless, if we conceive of class as a feature of one's social relation to the productive system rather than as a feature of one's role within that system (as suggested above), and thus offer a less economist reading, then we can employ a more dynamic and subtle understanding of class and slavery that helps us both with the relationship between class and order, and with certain features of Greek and Roman slavery that have caused analytical problems for all traditions. For instance, one of oddities of Classical slavery is the tendency to free slaves. If slaves *qua* slaves were the hegemonic labour force in Roman society, this would not only represent a damaging outflow of capital from the richer households, but would seem to undermine the economic system itself. Yet, if there was no hegemonic slave mode of production, and, in fact, limited distinction between servile and free occupations, the transformation of status that came with being freed would not represent a transformation of position within the productive economy, but of the relationship of the individual to that economy.

This feature explains the autonomy of at least some slaves within the Athenian and Roman systems. Slaves could run enterprises as quasi-autonomous individuals, receiving a 'wage' which, whatever the legal status of the money, allowed the accumulation of private wealth. Salmeri's recent discussion of a slave prostitute at Pompeii argues that servile prostitutes not only worked alongside free prostitutes but that distinguishing between slave and free prostitutes would have been difficult. The slave woman in Salmeri's case study bore adornments (one of which had an inscription that identified her as a slave) that can be paralleled in depictions of free women from the same period.[32] Since a slave could operate as if a free-worker, persons outside the household might have been unsure of the legal status of the worker. And it is of just this confusion that the 'Old Oligarch' complains in Classical Athens.[33] In such circumstances, we are allowed to wonder whether the slave experience would have been so much worse than that of other free workers and within the traditions of contemporary historiography (Weberian, Marxist, or other) such an absence of distinction would mean that the slave could hardly be distinguished from his or her free counterpart as being part of a separate class, order, or group.[34] Yet, taking the part of the 'Old Oligarch' and social conservatives in obfuscating the distinctions between slavery and citizens for their own particular ideological reasons seems somewhat contentious: it is demonstrable that slave status did matter and mattered considerably to ancients.

We are left, then, with a paradox and a problem that form something of a crux in slavery studies: we have a society in which slavery was crucial to social reproduction, but was not a distinctive mode of production. But without a slave mode of production, can antiquity be seen as a slave society? Turley argues that there is a fundamental difference between societies with slaves and slave societies, which depends on the economic function of slaves.[35] Although it seems to me that this entangles the debate on slavery within an unhelpful functionalism, on this model Greek and Roman society would be societies with slaves (many of them) and not slave societies. But if Roman society was not a slave society (an archetypal slave-owning culture), it leaves open the question of which world societies could be classified as slave societies. The problem would seem to be in part (as we shall see below) that Atlantic slavery, incorporated as it was into the particular circumstances of incipient capitalism and colonial expansion, is adopted as a paradigmatic form, and this adoption allows the importation of certain modes of societal analysis more suitable for modern societies into other social situations.

The issue has become one of definition. Divorced from the analytical perspective offered by Marxism, recent accounts of slave systems have tended to be vague. Dal Lago and Katsari suggest that a slave system exists when slavery forms 'the foundation of an economy', and is 'pervasive' within society, but there is, perhaps inevitably, little detail as to how that is judged.[36] Scheidel in the same volume treats a slave system as the means by which slaves appear in the workforce, and leaves open the question of a 'slave society'.[37] Hopkins relied on numbers. He suggested that a slave society is one in which slaves amount to 20% of the population.[38] As Hopkins admitted, the figure of 20% has little value in itself and one of the reasons for choosing such a percentage is to allow comparison with Atlantic slave systems (with its assumption of plantation agriculture). More fundamentally, such a figure supports Hopkins' model of imperial conquest, peasant deracination, and enslavement as complementary elements within the Roman Republican system. If one rejects that model, as I am inclined to do, then the value of the 20% figure becomes negligible.[39] One might argue that a 5% or 10% proportion of slaves in the population would suggest that slavery was pervasive in a society, or that a much higher proportion of slaves (40%+) would be required to argue for a slave economy. Further, the evidence from Egypt, which suggests an uneven distribution of slaves with a higher proportion of slaves in the cities, raises the issue of the 'census society'.[40] For instance, if the total population of the Roman empire had a 3% slave element, was the empire a slave society? If Classical Athens itself has a 15% slave element, does it then qualify as a slave society? We have very little evidence, other than the census material from Egypt, that would allow us to estimate with any degree of probability or accuracy the servile population of any region in any period of antiquity.[41] Faced with these difficulties, it seems that even if we could agree that a slave society was one in which slavery was 'the basis' of society, and agree on how that base may be defined, we would be unlikely to divine from the present state of evidence the economic and demographic material that would allow us to make a plausible attempt on the question.

The critical aporia in slave studies is also reflected in discussions of ideology, which centre on the issue of slave resistance, an issue that resonates throughout most modern treatments of slavery. Slave resistance is detectable within many of our sources, and one may argue that this is a trope repeatedly (but not always) present in the representation of slaves. But the crucial question is how that resistance is interpreted.[42] One could see the absence of an obvious revolutionary ideology as significant, suggesting that although individual slaves might be unhappy with their position, there was no attempt to subvert the system itself. Similarly, micro-acts of resistance, working slowly, working badly, stealing, sabotage, were not necessarily ideological and do not represent in and of themselves an opposition to the institution of slavery.[43] Further, these reported acts do not necessarily reflect a continuous 'war' between master and slave, and we have numerous examples cited in this volume of seemingly harmonious relations between master and slave. Yet, this approach risks running into a methodological wall. If the critical question is whether there was a widespread, systemic and ideological resistance to slavery, then one also has to ask what sources we could expect to provide us with such evidence. The accounts of the Spartacus revolt, for example, are so fragmentary as to allow fundamentally differing interpretations, and the Romans are unlikely to have inquired into the ideological basis, if any, of the rebellion before crucifying the defeated slaves.[44] Nevertheless, one can argue on the basis of the repeated complaints within the literary material, the evidence of runaways, and the acts of rebellion (large and small) that resistance was systemic, manifested in different arenas, and in repeated instances.

The evidence, on which there is much agreement, can be deployed to substantiate very different historiographical models. McKeown's survey of the scholarship on ancient slavery concludes thus:

> I have tried to show ... that are often *several* plausible answers ... Too often we operate as if there were single answers. Authors need to be prepared to show their readers more of the doubts and gaps. And readers have to be prepared to accept that there will be such doubts and gaps and that they represent real difficulties, not 'bad' history.[45]

Historians do need to acknowledge the limitations on our knowledge, but if all we can say about ancient slavery is that we can only argue about it and never resolve those arguments, then the disciplinary agenda is bust. We require, it seems to me, a fundamental re-evaluation of the theoretical and methodological approaches to the subject. It seems to me that we need not just to free ourselves from the notion of a slave mode of production, but from the very notion of a slave society. If one jettisons the nineteenth-century obsession with the categorisation of societies, we can maintain a far more subtle and variegated interpretation of social behaviours.

But to do so, we need to rethink the notions of society with which much of this literature works. The theoretical distinction I offer is between societies, as distinct heuristic blocs, and social formations. Social formations are maintained through the continuous social engagement of individual actors and the dynamics of power relations in that engagement.[46] Social formations result from the application of particular technologies of domination. Actors are constrained into engagement through a technology of domination. That technology of domination may be a discourse, the application of law, an economic pressure, or violence (and one could think of other technologies of domination). Slavery as a social formation comes into being through a varied set of technologies of domination: violence, law, economic pressures, and discourses. There are various primary advantages of this approach. In the first instance, it means that we can avoid naturalising slavery or, indeed, any other social formation, since social formations are structures that are always coming into being, and must be continuously maintained through the application of power. It also allows us to think of slavery as being a non-uniform social phenomenon, coming into being through varying technologies of domination. In the second instance, it allows both for a complexity in the response of individual actors to a social formation (why would we dream that all slaves would respond in the same way to the institution of slavery?) Further, it provides for a critical focus not on the least powerful within the structures of domination, but on the most powerful.[47]

Power operating through a technology of domination brings a social formation into being, but agents will either operate against that formation or work to reinforce it. The powerful, who have an interest in maintaining certain social formations, will deploy technologies of domination to maintain a formation. A social formation may acquire supportive discourses in ontology, law, and economy that would reinforce and naturalise the social formation. Whether an individual decided to rebel against that formation or to exist in accord with that formation is largely immaterial. Thus a slave who had a friendly relationship with the master, even a loving relationship, still remained subject to the technologies of domination that might, at any moment, be asserted, and still occupied a particular and defined location within the social formation. Slave rebellion, either in macro-level or micro-level acts, may be seen as an action designed to ameliorate the slave's position within the social formation, and as such can be seen as an attempt to disrupt the structures of domination that enforced his or her slavery, but in no sense is it a requirement that a rebellious slave has an alternate ideology, or a particular utopian ideal.[48]

If we focus on the technologies of domination, we depart radically from traditional modes of analysis. For instance, Orlando Patterson's study of freedom and slavery within Western culture argues that the existence of the category of slave determined the category of free, and one could thus trace a continuity both in terms of a reception of ideas and in the homologous social forms through all iterations of Western slavery. In so doing, Patterson relies heavily on slavery being a distinct juridical status, a state of being unfree in person, and thus uses law as either a determining factor or a key signifier of the nature of the institution. This is in itself an Aristotelian or 'natural law' methodology, in which establishing the category is seen as essential to the epistemological task.[49] Understanding slavery becomes a question of defining slavery, rather than understanding the process of the coming into being of the category of slave. It is thus a philosophical rather than a social or historical analysis.

The positions held by slaves within an economic system and within an ideological structure are not obviously cross-cultural; one should thus not expect slavery to be the same in different circumstances. Particular slaves might have similar legal status in different periods, but could exist in radically different social formations and subject to very different technologies of power across periods.[50] It is that difference which would seem to be eroded in legalistic approaches, and, indeed, in socio-categorial readings. Further, the establishment of a social category (that of slave) reifies the social formation in establishing its subjective status (i.e. an individual is a slave), and obscures the objective process of domination (i.e. the act of enslavement). The reification of a social formation is in itself an act of power primarily on the ideological plane, and is, of course, continuously replicated in discourse as 'natural'.

Seeing the slave in the text works against this process of naturalisation. Page du Bois quotes Freud's visit to the Acropolis as an example of 'derealization', a suggestion that the material that is in front of us is not real because the dominance of the cultural and psychological values entwined within its reception allow the object to retain its symbolic overloading in spite of its material presence.[51] We know the labour and oppression that went into the generating of Classical culture, but the interpreters of Classical culture have consistently undertaken this process of 'derealization' so as to preserve the symbol untarnished. If we were to make the technologies of domination visible, we are reversing a tradition of evaluation of the Ancient world that stretches back to antiquity itself.[52] To see the slave is, as Fitzgerald puts it, to read against the grain, but not just the grain of Classical literature; to see the slave is to look beyond the monuments to see a different Classical world. As Peter Garnsey has so clearly demonstrated, there may among the literate free have been sympathies with slaves, and depictions of the terrible conditions under which some slaves operated,[53] but there is not a single moralist or writer from antiquity who could be easily understood to present slavery as a moral abomination.[54] It is this absence that differentiates ancient slavery from Atlantic slavery, not because slavery was any less central to society, nor because we can ameliorate the moral abomination that was slavery, but because slavery in antiquity was not a problem, whereas it was decidedly so for moderns from the seventeenth century onwards. From a methodological viewpoint, importing the 'unnaturalness' of slavery into our analyses might seem questionable, but in focusing on structures of domination we are able to 'derealize' slavery and distance our analysis both from ancient tendencies to view slavery as a normative state, and modern tendencies to emphasise the distance between ancient and modern views of society and the individual.

A focus on the representation of slavery and the process of 'reading slavery' opens up the possibilities of interpretative frameworks that are less systematic, more individual, and more flexible, and of an active engagement in the discourses. It is axiomatic that for a text to have meaning, there must be a relatively stable lexical and semiotic environment. The signs on the paper, the words in the mouth of the actor, and the images on the pottery, must be translatable into meanings in the minds of the audience. But, of course, complex cultures do not have completely stable semiotic systems. Literature is especially prone to (mis)placed readings. Fitzgerald shows how Horace especially can be (mis)read, or (mis)heard to introduce elements of lexical uncertainty and destabilise meaning. Proffitt references Bakhtin to suggest that Menander's drama employed a variety of voices and perspectives that in their very multiplicity provide counters to the dominant ideology. Although there may have been a recovery of the hegemonic ideology in the resolutions of the plays, the echoes of the alternate ideological perspectives survive and can be excavated from the text. In a similar fashion, Wrenhaven finds a radical instability in the semiotics of slavery in Greek art, in which the image of the slave switched from the ugly and misshapen, to the slave of beauty; the depiction of diminutive slaves of art generated an unreality of imagery that complicates the relationship between representation and the real.

This instability of reading creates a flexibility of interpretation that allows latent or suppressed meanings, or meanings that were hardly possible within the original readings, to find voice.[55] In the first instance, our readings (the modern readings) are at an inevitable distance from Classical readings, since we bring a post-Abolitionist mentality to the understanding of the text and inevitably and unavoidably, when we translate 'slave', it has a different lexical and semiotic value than the various Greek and Latin words that we are reading. Yet, it is those very modern intertexts that allow a critical perspective in which one can read New Comedy, Homeric epic, or Horatian verse as slave stories. These alternate readings are not, however, modern inventions: the readings must be present in the text. Within a literary form there will always be tensions and multiplicities, stories untold, and futures unlived. In fictional discourses especially (and I would count first-person Latin poetry as fictional), the deliberative unreality of the narrative allows a distancing from the socio-economic world from which the text derives. Fiction is always embedded within the mode of production of a particular social formation. Yet, the reverse of that dialectic must also apply in that fiction infects the world of reality, and is thus part of the technology of domination that brings social formations into being. Social formations may have embedded within them discourses of unreality that allow distancing from the social formation: there is thus a latent 'otherness' within fiction, even in the most realistic forms. Social formations are, then, in many instances imbued with unreality. There may in that latent otherness also be a utopianism in which all can be free, though there might just as easily be a dystopianism, in which all are slaves.[56]

As modern readings are often unstable, we cannot imagine that ancient readings were unitary, and that readers in antiquity were in a fixed relationship with 'the slave' of literary constructions. It is axiomatic that 'texts' in antiquity were produced for an elite audience, though defining the elite nature of that audience is problematic. We could conclude that most 'texts' will have been produced for consumption by the free, and, with a couple of notable exceptions, to have been produced by the free. And yet there were many slaves around these cultural products. Servile lectors eased the consumption of literature: virtually the whole of Plato's *Theaetetus*: is to be imagined being delivered by Euclides' literate slave to entertain Euclides and his friend Terpsion as they relax (142c-43c). One presumes that 'texts' were copied by slaves. Drama circulated beyond the free, heard and consumed by the unfree,[57] and by the Roman period was increasingly also acted or read by the unfree to the free.[58] Art, much of which may have been produced by slaves, passed through the hands of slaves on its way to being consumed by the masters, as Sian Lewis has reminded us.[59] Since the slaves carried the images of slaves or spoke the words of slaves, the relationship between image and bearer of image must have had a certain poignancy. We cannot, of course, know what the slaves thought of these depictions, but we can be certain, as Wrenhaven's discussion of the stylised images of ugly or diminutive images of slaves in art demonstrates, of the gap between reality and the image.[60]

This gap between reality and image means that there was a crisis of representation. We can be quite sure that what was being depicted did not 'represent' slaves. The slaves in reality, the bearers of images, were not within the images themselves, which differed radically from the norms of servile corporeality. In this crisis of representation, there is a 're-presentation' of the slave in a different form, but in that 're-presentation' there is an absence that must have been striking. One needs to ask whether the servile watchers of Menander's plays or the readers of Odysseus's homecoming revenge on the females of his household saw themselves in the texts, or re-presentations of themselves as they were obviously not. As in fictional discourses, the distance between the real and the represented demands a critical alienation.

Wrenhaven sees this representational crisis as reflecting an inherent and, indeed, structural crisis in the mode of slave-ownership. Slavery, being morally wrong, requires an exceptional explanation for its existence. The slave must be thus be understood as being somehow less than human to justify to the master his oppression, and thus the reality of the slave's humanity must be obfuscated. The explanation has considerable plausibility, establishing the justificatory logic of slavery in very much the same way as the oppression of non-whites was justified. The ugliness and the diminutive size of the slave is a 'playing of the race card' in the on-going struggle to justify the unjustifiable and Wrenhaven argues that it was in the discourses of the masters that this justification took place. The reality of the slave had no place there.

Thalmann follows a similar line, arguing that the physical representation of slaves, mostly within Classical art, points to a perhaps increasing desire to find physical differences between the servile and the free (aristocratic). Thalmann argues that although 'natural slavery' appears to be an Aristotelian invention, the ideas of slaves as by nature inferior can be found in many other representations, suggesting a tendency to 'naturalise' the position of the slave even before, or without, the theory. Thalmann continues by arguing that the discourses on slavery are enmeshed into other discourses of society, theories of race, of the body beautiful, of labour, which all contribute to the slave ideology. In an elaborate parallelism, Thalmann draws attention to labour relations as servility, pointing out that a contracted 'slave' in modern culture has at least some parallel experience of structures of domination. Although none would argue that the domination of wage labour was anything like as absolute as that in slavery, the point is more subtle: structures of domination are built into languages of power.

Such readings rely heavily on interpretations of the (in)famous passage in the *Politics* in which Aristotle may be seen to justify slavery in arguing that some are by nature (*phusis*) slaves, while others are by nature citizens. Aristotle can resolve the issue of intense inequality by arguing that by nature man is created unequal. Yet reading Aristotle in this way is problematic. The Aristotelian argument is not primarily about slavery, but about the nature of man. As Monoson argues, we can historicise Aristotle to render the argument very precisely one about the nature of the *polis* and the citizen. He is suggesting that some men have the potential to be citizens, and that this is their highest state, while others have the potential to be slaves. This is not an argument about nature (biology), but about society, and the problem arises in part since Aristotle's view appears to be that the society of the *polis* is in itself natural. Once one makes that decision, then it follows that the status divisions written through society are, in themselves, natural, and the distinctions between different political systems within the Aristotelian system become variations on the theme of the Greek *polis*. Importantly, then, we could read slavery in Aristotle as not in need of justification, though perhaps in need of explanation. As Monoson shows, this is unlikely to have been an outbreak of 'false consciousness' in which the norms of a society appear beyond analysis, but a critical decision. For Monoson, Aristotle's natural slaves reflect the requirement of citizens to have leisure: they are thus an essential element with the sociology of the Greek city. Moreover, the failure of barbarians to develop political institutions that seem to Aristotle similar to the *polis* is enough to explain his empirically-derived view that barbarians, who acquiesce in tyranny, are likely slaves.

Wrenhaven's argument is a humanist interpretation of that position, seeing in the Aristotelian position an extraordinary statement against nature in that it must have been obvious to all that slaves were equal, and the rhetoric deployed was an extreme case of a society's attempt to justify what it knew, in its human heart, to be wrong. Thalmann establishes the inferiority of slaves as part of the systematic networks of domination within language and culture and thus something so written into the Greek psyche that it would appear natural and not require justification. Slavery in this model is not a problem, and the slave is, therefore, also a work of nature. This last position seems to have much in common with Monoson's view, though it is notable that for Monoson, Aristotle appears not to need to do much (if any) work to legitimate his notion of slavery. The difference is, then, between a 'humanist' reading in which the values of humanity exist in tension with a social formation which will inevitably be recognised as unnatural, and a 'constructivist' view in which discourse normalises and naturalises particular social formations. And yet, both views would seem to face a problem in the seeming artificiality of the artistic representation of the slave, and even Aristotelian views would seem to hit a problem not with the notion of slavery, but with the person of the slave.

This separation between the theory of the social formation and the individual within the social formation is familiar to us from discussions of race, in which the racial stereotyping exists in tension with the individualism of the person assigned to the group.[61] There is thus a critical distance between the slave as represented in the text (as a social object) and the subjective being who is enslaved. I suggest that we might understand the presence of the slave in art as a 're-presentation' made possible by the invisibility of the slave as subject (i.e. the slave as individual has little or no place in most texts, and appears only as a cipher). Furthermore, instead of seeing these ancient re-presentations of slaves as raising the problematic of the slave, it seems very likely that what is being represented is the master. The servile depiction facilitates our understanding of the master. Turning the argument around slightly, the problem of reading the slave from his or her depiction is analogous to representations of the hero or the divine. As slaves are depicted as being smaller and normally uglier than mortals, so gods are depicted as larger and more beautiful. But that presentation does not justify the existence of gods. Rather it reflects the absence of the corporeal divine on a day-to-day level and a form of cosmological order which incorporates the slave, the citizen and the gods. We are thus faced with texts and images in which the slave is, for all his or her visibility, not there, as the gods are, for all their visibility, not there. Reading the art for the image of the slave becomes then not just reading against the grain of the depiction, but a focus on an absence in the image. Nevertheless, that absence must always have been under threat: the human persona of the slave threatened the ordered and hierarchical universe constructed in the discourses of power and which centre on the citizen.

Kamen's contribution nicely illustrates the problem. She assembles texts to show the 'everyday resistance of slaves', the *Realien* of master-slave power relations in Martial. In creating an agency for the slaves, Martial would seem to enable the slaves to have a personality, some freedom, some exercise of self-expression. What is notable, however, is just how limited that self-expression is, and how centred on the concerns of the master. Martial shows concerns over particular role reversals, most notably when a slave has, for one reason or another, corporeal control over the master. The barber, for instance, who marks the chin of the master, or who wielding the razor requests his freedom, offers a moment of freedom in the potential of violence. Sexuality becomes also an arena in which the slave is seen as holding some power, providing or withholding favours, or in the case of male slaves, taking the master's role and penetrating rather than being penetrated. And yet, as Kamen points out, this remains the master's game. Martial's epigrams concentrate on the sexual (and moral) status of the master, and the slaves are merely adjuncts to the master's personality, of no interest in themselves. Although there may be a role reversal in the penetrative agent, the penetrator is chosen by the master, and part of the joke depends on the size of the penises that are to be inserted into the master. The slaves remain meat, their personalities disappearing in their physicality and their agency subsumed by the master's omnipotence. In this way, even the slaves' sexual potency serves to reinforce their cultural impotence when faced with the master's power. Further, the withdrawal of sexual favours by the slave is again in the service of the master, allowing the playing of seduction and rape fantasies in which the master's power is enacted and enjoyed. The dominance over the body of the slave is never, ultimately, questioned. Even the reversals that are expressed within the attacks on 'passive' homosexuals work by representing a cultural norm that is subverted by the morally suspect and in so doing reinforces that norm.

The pattern replicates the *servitium amoris* of the Augustan elegists, which although having the potential to offer a model of masculinity which differs radically from what we perceive as normative for the Roman world, in fact reinforces those norms by offering a revolutionary reversal that preserves the categories of social expectation. Similarly, Menander's slaves have a power which is not ultimately realised, and their agency is

16

subsumed beneath the socially normative resolutions. Not only, then, do these stories exist within the mode of production of Roman and Greek social formations, but replicate and reinforce the discourses that contribute to the technology of power.

There are methodological and, indeed, philosophical and ethical problems that reading these texts present. To take Fitzgerald's point, in reporting the rendering of the slave as the minimal addition that allows the master to convince himself that he, and the world, exist, do we, in essence, merely replicate that assertion, and condemn the slaves to their (virtually) unreported lives, and lay them to rest in their (virtually) silent tombs? We are taught to avoid the anachronism, not to write our moral concerns into the cultures we study, since if we were to so do, we would be guilty of a temporal or cultural imperialism. But in a positivistic approach, we run the risk of ignoring the voice that cannot be heard. Our researches become subject to the tyranny of the archive, in which what is recorded is assumed to be all that is there. But in the case of slavery, to merely record the absence is to collude in the Classical discourse and the technologies of domination that supported slavery.

Hunnings' solution to the problem is to take the discourses as productive of norms and to argue that reality is made directly by the text. The power and authority of the text may, in part, be seen as overcoming the alienation of art and reality, of category and individual. Instead of seeing the *Odyssey* solely as a literary representation, she argues that the text is didactic and thus directly constructive of social relations. The reading of the text in later ages as normative, a type of wisdom text, means that it can be seen as establishing values that were refracted through subsequent social formations. Hunnings argues that good slaves within the *Odyssey* internalise the ideologies of slavery, acknowledge the good master and understand the paternalism within the master-slave relationship. The bad slaves, with whom Hunnings is particularly concerned, fail to adhere to these values. The issue on which their behaviour turns is sex. The slave-women's sexual agency is the height of their transgression. The giving of their bodies to the suitors is a breach of Odysseus' rights over their bodies, which Hunnings compares to a theft. Yet the property issue is only one of the elements that cause Odysseus' wrath. Perhaps as important is the issue of honour. It is honour that leads Telemachus to hang the women, and it is honour that means that the executions needed to be public. The symbolic rape (and real death) that Odysseus orders for his slave women reasserts his sexual ownership over the women. That sexual ownership is the most intimate of rights, the violating right of power that the master has over the women. It is not so much a right of property, which is reclaimed with the death of the suitors, but part of the violence with which the master asserts his power over the slaves. The punishment of the slave women turns on their neglect of the honour of the master, and of their assertion of their own will in forming sexual relations which are not

17

ratified by the powers of the house (Penelope and Eurycleia). The agency of the slave girls operates to break their bonds with the household, and they are killed in their exclusion from the household which they have betrayed. In the absence of the master, the structures of domination have broken down, and they are restored in the most violent of fashions. That restoration is necessarily communal, demonstrating the return to order and the public power of the newly restored household. Whereas the murder of the slave women would be completely irrational if they were merely property, their killing becomes rational in a reassertion of order.

Hunnings' argument brings to the fore the issue of 'social death'. The slave women are only to a limited extent socially dead. Hunnings argues that their position in the narrative is scenographic. They slip quietly through scenes and emerge as representative symbols of the corruption of the household, though it is their noisiness and their finding of a voice that initiates Odysseus' wrath. The sexual activity of the women acts as a dramatic counterpoint to the loyalty of Penelope, but in representing corruption they also point to the dangerous and liminal situation of Penelope herself, whose sexual fidelity is at stake. The women are, there-fore, props to the identity and importance of the master and mistress. They are also denied agency, and in that denial of agency there is a loss of individuality. But even if there is a loss of honour/virtue in the slave status (a man loses 50% of his 'excellence' when he is enslaved, according to Eumaeus at *Od.* 17.322-3), the slave women retain some character, history and agency. There is a 'back-story' to the slaves' lives that we are allowed to see in part. The denial of freedom is not a social death, since the slaves instead are given an identity within the household. The paternalistic possibilities of that identity are, however, rejected by the disloyal slaves. The sexual violence, the threats and actuality of death, all dramatically demonstrate that slavery is dependent on a relation-ship of extreme violence.

Rankine's contribution follows a parallel course, and also takes a his-torical-materialist line. He sees the *Odyssey* as reflecting the ideologies of slavery of the archaic period, a period before 'mass' slavery in Classical Greece. If we put this alongside Hunnings' contribution, we can see the *Odyssey* as presenting a formative stage in the ideology of Classical slavery. Whereas Hunnings relates that formative stage to the particular cultural resonances of the Homeric text, Rankine sees the ideology as coalescing around labour relations and property rights in the seventh century. This historical realism of the *Odyssey* is emphasised in seeing the person of Odysseus 'as being in danger of slavery', and, indeed, in under-going something approaching a sexual slavery in his incarceration by Calypso. The disasters that befall the hero, and his reduction to a wretched state not only at times rob him of his identity, but put him in a position in which he might be vulnerable to the application of an enslaving power. Rankine points out that Odysseus is normally able to negotiate these situations and remain as *xenos*, the guest-friend, and avoid enslavement, but Rankine argues for a slavery that is circumstantial rather than ontological: that is, he suggests, individuals are enslaved by circumstances beyond their immediate control rather than being naturally servile. In pointing this out, Rankine suggests that slave status becomes fragile, and both free and slave can be subject to change in status. Re-reading the *Odyssey* as a journey around slavery (and perhaps to freedom), we can see that slave status can be achieved, and in the circumstances of the mythical heroic age, identity remains worryingly uncertain. Sex again plays an important part in this story, with Calypso's 'ownership' of Odysseus being sexually expressed. One could read the relationship as conjugal or servile, and it is not entirely clear how we should decide between those readings. Odysseus among the Phaeacians is also a sexual tale in that, on his first appearance, it is Odysseus' sexual status that is apparent. He is not to be feared because he cannot be predatory and enslave (rape) the princess, since she is the one of power in that land, and this is in spite of the mythic exempla of raping deities. Further, the Odyssean storytelling is notable for the way in which identity is constructed in the narrative in the absence of other markers of identity (notably the story is told by an authorial persona with no identity other than that constructed in the narrative and by a man whose identity is hidden, other than to his slave nurse and his dog). In returning to the conjugal home, Odysseus needs to reassert his identity and his sexual dominance, needs to move from a position of outsider (beggar who runs the risk of being enslaved) to becoming master of the bedroom. The sins of the servile women are then also to be under-stood in this model of shifting status. In insulting Penelope and Odysseus, they assert status against them, assert a sexual freedom, but also threaten Odysseus with the physical chastisement that could be meted out to a slave; Penelope herself, with her chastity under siege, is always in a dangerous position.

Although Rankine makes extensive use of Patterson's typologies of slavery, it seems clear that Odysseus is often threatened by violence, but never with social death. One might argue that the one moment in the epic when Odysseus undergoes social death is in the cave of Polyphemus. It is this episode which forms the basis of Nikolsky's contribution, though Nikolsky looks primarily not to the Homeric text, but to the Euripidean recension of the tale in the satyr play, *Cyclops*. Nikolsky starts from the assumption that the subjugation of the satyrs to Polyphemus is a form of slavery, but then notes that Odysseus, who undergoes a similar kind of subjugation, does not respond in the same way. Instead of seeing the text directly through the lens of slavery, Nikolsky argues that we should read the text as political allegory in which the freedom of the various partici-pants as political beings is under discussion. In this reading, Polyphemus becomes the tyrant, who is threatened by the noble, aristocratic, Odys-seus, and in challenging the tyrant Odysseus enacts his freedom. The satyrs, however, who fail to act, represent a different manifestation or version of freedom. Their freedom is more licentious, more Bacchic, and this creates a very different dynamic in which the tyrant is the cannibalistic consumer of men, the nobles respond to the tyrant, and the satyrs – the masses – are somehow less than fully human, less than fully moral. Nikolsky sees in this an ambivalent reading of democracy, in which considerable doubts are expressed about the moral status of the masses, but ultimately Odysseus and the satyrs leave together, leaving the tyrant to hurl stones in vain at the departing ship. In this image, there is a democratic union that provides an optimistic vision of the city.

The Nikolsky reading is not, however, without problems. Nikolsky concludes by stating that slavery, 'ever-present in the Athenian democracy, is nevertheless effaced through metaphorical transference into the creation of free men's identity'. And this theme of 'the effacement of slavery' appears regularly in contributions to the book. Yet, partly because slavery undergoes 'metaphorical transference' into the identities of the free, slavery is continuously written into the political narratives of citizenship in disturbing ways. Nikolsky points to the liberal Russian tradition in which the emancipation of the peasantry went hand in glove with the ending of absolutism (a perspective not so very different from the historical trajectories of Western Liberalism), but in so doing points out that the status of being unfree tended to cross from slave, serf, to citizen depending on political circumstances and rhetoric. The ideological structures of slavery were thus embedded in the political ideologies of democracy, even if effaced. We are, thus, examining a homology in social discourse between the political subordination of the citizen and the absolute subordination of the free. In such a reading, we can, and probably should, read back from the political structure to the servile structure. And this is in part where we encounter problems, for the tyrant-master becomes the anthropophagous Cyclops, the tyrannicide becomes the master-killer, the over-turner of order, and citizen-satyr slave emerges in freedom in a revolutionary escape from the blinded master. As the Tsars would surely have recognised, revolution stalks the stage.

The revolutionary potential of the *Odyssey* has long been recognised since, as Adorno and Horkheimer saw, the dialectic of Western society lies within the text, if in a protean state.[62] For Adorno and Horkheimer, Odysseus' 'trick' in of adopting the non-identity of 'no one' in the cave of Polyphemus frees the hero from his history and social expectation. It enables him to deal with Polyphemus. In the conquest of the 'natural' entity, the barbarian, this assumption of a non-identity is problematic. On the one hand one could read it as an assumption of a universal identity, seeing 'no one' as a universalising everyman whose triumph secures the Western (Greek) victory over the forces of the world about to be colonised. Polyphemus is thus trapped in his identity, while Odysseus is able to create and remake his. On the other hand we could see Odysseus' denial of his own identity at that moment as a social death since he is, temporarily at least, 'talking meat'; his identity is lost in the act of being enslaved. That identity is resumed when he leaves the island and taunts the blinded Polyphemus. But it is notable that this non-identity is a trick, a way of establishing trust with the 'master', an assumption of a social death from which he will violently escape. The conquering Western individual triumphs precisely in the falsehood of a social death, but in the lie, there remains the possibility (the unachieved possibility) that Odysseus is potentially meat, and, conversely, that the slave is potentially Odysseus. The possibility that the slave will assume the position of the master (*pace* Trimalchio in Petronius' *Satyrica*) is potentially revolutionary, and threatens the social and political order.

In the several instances assembled by Rankine in which Odysseus is threatened with slavery, although there is a threat of incipient violence that could result in death, there is no ritual slaying that will take place before his enslavement, nor any expectation that enslavement is death delayed. Indeed, one might argue that the characteristics of later slave systems (the removal from home, the renaming, the loss of identity) are not features of these Odyssean enslavements. Instead, as Hunnings also shows, it is brutal and continuously reinforced violent acts of domination that maintain the circumstances of enslavement. The paternalism of the good master is secondary to the violence that is required to maintain the master's dominance, and the sexual violence, the complete bodily subjugation of the individual, is central to that violence. It is the fragility of slavery and circumstantial nature that demands the obscene application of violence, and in this foundational text, when the institutionalisation of slavery was in its infancy, that violence sustains slavery, and by implication the homologous structures of political society. Hunnings and Rankine can be read as explaining the necessity of a brutal regimen of control in order to maintain that structure of dominance, a structure of dominance that must be restored for Odysseus to return home. Although slavery itself is an ideological formation, being a slave is circumstantial, and not an ontological position.

Such a view is in some tension with 'natural slavery' interpretations or theories of 'social death' in slavery. It may be argued that Homer, as Rankine and Hunnings suggest, is at a formative stage in the Classical ideologies of slavery, that these ideologies develop over the Classical period and that the discourse on slavery became increasingly sophisticated. If we adopt such a scheme, one would see the circumstantial slavery of the Homeric texts becoming increasingly ontological in the texts, as ontological discourses are 'attracted' to the circumstantial representation of slavery, very much as I have argued that Aristotle's view of the *polis* as an ideal society attracted an ontological association to the status groups within society. Slavery thus becomes natural in the development of the discourse. Such a development would both reinforce the institution of slavery and could, in practical terms, have moved violence towards the background in the maintaining of slavery. We could thus the texts that we analyse as (broadly) constitutive of historical reality, establishing the epistemes by which society is understood. In so doing, we would be operating with a (broadly) Foucauldian model of historical reality. Yet, there remains a problem in this tension between circumstantial and ontological understandings since the Foucauldian analysis would tend towards an ontological resolution of the social formation in the discourses of the self that are generated within the epistemic universe of antiquity. But the circumstantial view would tend to resist naturalising discourses, suggesting that the slave remains an individual reduced by his or her circumstances to the servile state. The circumstantial position would not determine his or her ontological position. In this tension between circumstantial and ontological state, one finds the capacity for resistance.[63]

It is in this context that Hall's contribution becomes central. Not only is Hall's the latest text in this volume in chronological terms, but it also brings to our attention this clash between ontological and circumstantial understandings of slavery. Hall considers Artemidorus' collection of dream interpretations, an unusual text not least because it gives voice to slaves. Artemidorus seems to have been as interested in how slave dreams may be interpreted as in dreams of the free and thus reports servile dreams alongside the dreams of free people. There follows from this a whole series of implications, problems, and observations. Most striking is that there is no absolute division between free and slave in the land of dreams. In modern psychological terms, one would argue that there is a recognition of a common psyche and thus a shared humanity between the dreamers. If the slave dreamers were less than human, one would not expect their dreams to be reported, being of no interest to Artemidorus and his readers. Hall's analysis leads to two fascinating conclusions, one sociological and the other ideological. In the first instance, it seems established that slaves would consult dream interpreters, and that slaves received interpretations of their dreams. One thus needs to envisage a socio-economic situation in which a slave has sufficient cash and agency to approach a dream interpreter. Although Hall suggests that dream interpreters may have been of all social classes, there may have been a connection between dream interpreters and the socially marginal (very like magic and astrology), which would establish the art as one that crossed socio-economic boundaries. In the context of the Roman empire, one might expect dream interpretation to be a dangerously uncontrollable art. Dreams would thus be potentially unstable, a source of social worry.

A second feature becomes obvious when reading Artemidorus against Freud. As Hall points out, Freud read Artemidorus in order to give a historical depth to his dream analysis, but Freud's interpretive framework differs radically from that of Artemidorus. Freud read dreams through the lens of sexuality and the family, which were, for Freud, the key to an archaeology of the self and established the key elements of a transhistorical psyche. The culture of a society might establish a particular symbolic code, but the meaning of the code was embedded at a deeper psychic stratum that was not culturally specific. It was this master theory which differentiated Freud's reading of dreams from other de-coders, who relied on a 'known' set of symbols that could be applied in different contexts. By contrast, Artemidorus' dream interpretation is dependent on social context, and this is remarkably fine-grained. What a slave dreams depends not only on his/her servile status, but on his/her precise position within the household. In this way, we have a dreaming community, but a differentiated dreaming context. For Artemidorus, the Freudian patina is reversed. Whereas sex is the common key to humanity operating at a level beyond social convention, for Artemidorus, society is the key that determines sex and other human experiences. Sexually explicit dreams make little sense until decoded into socially specific messages.

In Artemidorus, the slave dreams, and is thus ontologically human, but the slaves' dreams are different. This is the Foucauldian critique: the interpretive framework of dreams is so different in antiquity that it does not reflect just a different discourse of dreams, but also a different discourse of the self.[64] The antiquity of the Freudian self is assaulted and dispatched and that leaves us with the psyches that are differentiated by historical context. But the Artemidoran interpretation raises yet more problems, since the subjection to social values is such that within the recognition that slaves are human is also a recognition that they are different dreamers, and thus that their semiotic framework is different from that of the free. In Foucauldian terms, there is thus a different episteme for slaves and a different psyche. Methodological problems abound, but the distinction between slavery as circumstantial and ontological starts to seem too crude. Instead, one can start to see a model in which the social structure defines the ontological state: if one is a slave circumstantially, since circumstances define one's ontological situation, then the ontology also shifts.

Yet the methodological problems raise nagging doubts. In the above, armed with the modern psychoanalytical experience of dream interpretation, I have been reading from Artemidorus' text towards the psyche of the slaves, but in so doing, it is very easy to lose sight of Hall's suggestion that dream interpretation crosses social classes (and thus conventions). If we keep a close focus on the text, we run the risk of missing the potential dangers that lurk within the dream world, and in differing interpretive systems. Although Artemidorus had direct (and indirect) access to slave dreams, we still read those dreams through the prism of Artemidorus' 'free-man' collection, a collection which may excise dreams that did not easily fit his interpretive model. Further, it seems likely that the interpretive model determined much of the editorial management of the text. Given that there is a religious and prophetic aim within the text (we are interested only in dreams that come true), then the collection is in itself not working towards an insight into the psyche of slaves, or, indeed, of their masters. In a Foucauldian reading, that might not matter since the discourse continues to have force whatever its authorial intent; one could argue that the religious interpretation was cosmological, establishing an order within the epistemological universe in exactly the same way as sociological or psychological literature of modernity seeks to uncover a fundamental order within society or the self.[65] Nevertheless, whereas Foucault's engagement with the discourses of madness or sexuality could plausibly argue for the construction of those concepts within those defined discourses, for slavery, we are looking at a discourse about something else (the master, religion, political organisation, etc.) which is being read by moderns as constructive of slavery.

Fitzgerald treats these issues from a slightly different angle. He notices the almost absent slave within the poems of Horace and Propertius. The ontological status of these slaves is in considerable doubt. Fitzgerald suggests that the Lygdamus who appears in two poems may not be the same slave, merely a presence conjured up to fulfil certain local needs of the poet. In very much the same way, the slave who accompanies Horace flicks in and out of existence, appearing as an ear, and then disappearing in the text. Fitzgerald argues that it is not the ontological status of the slave that is in question in these poems, but the status of the master. The master is dependent on the slave, but that dependency is complex. In the Propertius poem, the slave is a voice that is continuously instructed to speak, but is never allowed to speak, in spite of the fact that it is the means of communicating with the world. This voice exists in a world of reversals in which Propertius and his love, Cynthia, are subjugated to love, enslaved themselves, and in their enslavement become dependent on one of their dependants. Horace's slave again parallels Horace's position of subjugation, of being a voiceless ear in his relationship with the man who demands his company, but whereas the servile ear never speaks, Horace exacts revenge at the end of his poem. Crucially, the texts can hardly be seen to be constitutive of the position of the slave, since the slave is almost absent, but are constitutive of the position of the master, and it is the master who defines himself in relation to slavery. Further, the parallels between the poet and the slave are so drawn that the poet himself risks his ontological status, drifting in and out of silence, becoming merely an ear, losing a connection to the world.

In a Foucauldian reading, the slave would drift into invisibility if he/she were to read Horace. But there is a gap between the physicality and vocality of the slave and the reduction of the slave to an ear or to voicelessness. Further, the reversals in the texts offer a circumstantial enslavement of the free, reducing them to impotence, temporary in the case of Horace and more structural in the case of Propertius. Yet, the implications of the subjugation of the free individual in Augustan society are deeply political, suggesting that the boundary between free and slave can easily be crossed, and that the structures of domination in the public sphere are enslaving. Further, the man who subjugates Horace is himself dragged off at the end of the poem, continuing the process of slippage between slave and free. In this prospect of enslavement, the zone of freedom becomes illusory, maintained only in the interiority of the self which has limited connection, ironically through a slave, into the world. It is central to the Foucauldian method that the episteme constructed within discourses is likely to be complete, a totalising system. But Fitzgerald draws our attention to what is outside the text, what is the major addition of the human that stands alongside the minimal addition of the ear. The slave thus exists beyond the text, and further that existence beyond the text must have been obvious. In that lack of assimilation to the textual world, there is a prospect of alienation, and of difference, that operates to destabilise the epistemes generated by the free.

The consequence of this argument is that we should see slaves as a subaltern group; a group without their own historical voice; a group potentially not integrated within the hegemonic ideological systems of antiquity, and also a key sector of the labour force that produced ancient society. If we return to Hall's community of dreamers, we can postulate a different interpretation of dreams, not one which turned that dreaming community into a mirror of Artemidorus' ordered and conventional society, but one in which the shared dreams surpass the conventions of interpretations and retain a disruptive element. Hall suggests to us different interpreters of dreams (ancient and modern), who would give the slave a different voice and render those voices disruptive. We could refer to the slaves of New Comedy discussed by Proffitt, who proclaim their alternate voice, a voice that cannot be quite buried in the resolutions of the plot, and we can imagine servile viewers whose experiences resonated with the cries of the slaves rather than the rejoicings of the free. We can think of Homer's slave girls, achieving agency and being slaughtered.

The implications of this observation are, I think, profound. As in the colonial situation, the slave may operate with the mask of the master, and in accord with the ideologies of the master, but behind the mask, there is an additional humanity and resistance. In a similar way as we can read against the grain of slave texts, so one can re-read Polyphemus, with Sylvia Wynter, constructed as the monstrous other, proclaiming an injured, blinded humanity.[66] I suggest that the representation of slavery operates largely in the absence of the slave. The slave can be re-presented because the slave is largely absent from our ancient discourses, sublimated to the master. If the slave is not present in the text, then the slave exists, has ontological status, outside the epistemes of conventional discourse. The slave is the unrepresentable, and the very existence of that which is unrepresentable is a threat to the established episteme. But the slave is also a real human, with a physical and emotional existence. The boundaries of the epistemic social human then are so drawn in conventional discourse that the real humans exist in opposition to or outside that framework. These humans may be slaves, but the very fact that slaves are not within the discourse creates a fundamental tension: the slave is always largely and potentially not a slave. Furthermore, the free is always potentially a slave. The result of this is that the structures of domination that establish the social formation of slavery are, then, remarkably fragile. Being a slave is not an ontological state (since that would be a state of not being), but a circumstantial state, and this does not change from Homer through to the second century CE.

Maintaining the human in the circumstantial state of slavery depended on violence. The oft-mentioned relative absence of rebellion looks at the problem from one side, the side of the disempowered, and ignores the violence of the empowered, lulled by normative, naturalising representations of social formation (ancient and modern). It is the violence inherent within slavery remains throughout the Classical period, often latent, but never absent, that is a leitmotif of the literature and art surveyed in this volume. That brutal, violent reality shines through all our readings.

Notes

1. See Alston, Hall and McConnell (2011).

2. The first major discussion modern discussion of antique slavery was from a staunch Abolitionist, Wallon (1847). Bradley (1994) 9 suggests that drawing on the evidence of New World slavery for understanding of ancient slavery is controversial, but perhaps in this field more than any other we see an explicit adoption of a comparative perspective. For the Greek world, see the comparative perspective informs influential work from Cartledge (1985) and (1993) and more recently e.g. Katsari and Dal Lago (2008*a*) and (2008*b*), and Kleijwegt (2006). For a partial survey of the historiography, see Garlan (1988) 1-23, Finley (1980) esp. 11-66, and McKeown (2007).

3. 'Slave systems' other than the Atlantic have been used for comparison: see Kudlien (1998) and more recently Wickramasinghe (2005).

4. Such a concentration on literary and artistic material reflects a disciplinary shift in which literary historians have become more willing to engage in socio-historical critiques, and social historians have become more confident with fictional discourses.

5. Millar (1981); Hopkins (1993).

6. Konstan (1995); Hall (1989*a*), (1989*b*), (1995) and (1997).

7. See the essays by McCarthy, Johnstone, Connolly and Clark in Joshel and Murnaghan (1998).

8. Although systemic approaches underline the integral role slavery within ancient society, they can also be used to consign the slave to the margins in the study of antiquity (alongside other specified groups such as peasant farmers, shoe-makers, gladiators, the poor, and women) as a sub-group in sociological analyses, but not categorically exceptional.

9. See a summary account in Garlan (1988) 1-23, and most recent accounts in

McKeown (1999) and (2007) 52-76, though note that the most important Marxist reading of the ancient city, de Ste Croix (1981) gives relatively little attention to slavery (pp. 133-74).

10. References to this issue in Marx's own work are scattered and often somewhat contradictory. For summaries, see Lekas (1988) and Garlan (1988) 3-7. Marx's interpretation is somewhat surprisingly focused on Roman history. Texts are conveniently collected in Hobsbawm (1964).

11. See Finley (1985a) 62-94. The Marxist position seems to be that slavery confused the class struggle within antiquity, and one could argue that it is only with the enserfdom of the lower orders (itself historically questionable) that class struggle could be freed from that confusion. See Lekas (1988) 116-29; de Ste Croix (1981) 133-74 argues that slavery is a category of unfree labour and it is unfree labour that is the foundation of the Classical world. He point out (147) that it was perceived that the unity of citizens protected against slaves. For the extension of class conflict and the erosion of differences between slave and free, see 453-503. Wood and Wood (1978) also see slaves as a category of the labouring poor, a group whose presence influences the outcome of class conflict, but neither determines it nor prevents it.

12. Patterson (1991). A central argument of Finley (1980) is that the price of ancient equality was slavery, and although Finley regarded such a position as a political and moral absurdity, this was for Vogt (1975), the target for Finley's polemic, a justification for slavery.

13. Finley (1959) points out that the debate on slavery has been central to the reception of Marxism in Classical studies. In part that derives from the citation of slavery by Marx and Engels in in *The Communist Manifesto* (1848). One could read Vogt (1975) as an anti-Marxist tract and from that dynamic springs much of the analytical energy in slave studies. Nevertheless, slavery is not a significant element of mainstream Marxist theory.

14. See, for example, Bradley (1998), who argues that the rebellions of this period were not revolutionary since they were not ideological. See, contra Bradley, Urbainczyk (2008a).

15. As Finley (1959) 161 puts it, 'in the guise of a discussion of ancient slavery, there has been a desultory discussion of Marxist theory, none of it, on either side, particularly illuminating about either Marxism or slavery'.

16. Yet an order is not necessarily a better analytical tool than class, since it, too, fails to account for the manifest differences of life experience between members of the same order.

17. Wood (1981) 10 argues that the 'relationship between citizens and slaves ... is difficult to characterize as a simple class relation based on the social division of labour', on the basis that slaves worked in many different contexts and often alongside free labour. Nevertheless, the social relationship of slaves to production was different from that of their free colleagues. Maintaining the class-basis of slavery maintains the analytical and theoretical importance of slavery (see below).

18. The confusion derives in part from overly literal readings of the depiction of class struggle as driving historical change in *The Communist Manifesto* (1848), whereas there is a rather more nuanced view of the role of slavery in Roman politics in the preface to Marx's *The Eighteenth Brumaire of Louis Bonaparte* (1852) in which 'class' conflict is limited to the free population.

19. The notion of a particular consciousness within each class owes much to Lukacs. By contrast, Gramsci represents political consciousness as a function of intellectual endeavour and that individuals may, and indeed regularly do, operate

outside their class interests, while the French Marxist tradition as represented in the works of J.-P. Vernant and P. Vidal-Naquet sees a lack of class-consciousness in ancient Greece. Marx's fundamental notion of 'false consciousness', problematic though it may be, lies behind many of these debates.

20. More striking is the fundamental Weberian notion employed by Finley in which the hegemonic political conceptions employed in a society are those which will determine political actions, and it is against this argument that de Ste Croix (1981) sets himself. See Finley (1985*b*) and (1980). It would follow from Finley that notions of status would articulate political actions, though it is similarly difficult to perceive the affective actions resulting from status as it is to perceive those resulting from class and the absence of a political mobilisation of slaves is less explicable from a Weberian perspective.

21. The fundamental Marxist perception is that Man makes history by his own actions, but not in conditions of his own making. This would suggest that political acts are conditioned by class structure, but are the actions of free agents. There is thus a distinction between Marxist views of history and what is frequently categorised as 'economism'. There is an enormous bibliography on this, but important contributions include Gramsci (1971) 13-23, 191-204; Thompson (1978); Zizek (1994); Eagleton (1994), esp. 195-7; Althusser (2008); S. Hall (1978).

22. See, most notably, Carandini (1988), conveniently summarised at 327-38. Carandini (337-8) does, however, conclude that section by asserting that 'I Romani non sono Greci'. See also Giardina and Schiavone (1981), Anderson (1974), and de Ste Croix (1988); but Wickham (1984) interprets the transition in other ways.

23. The concept of the slave mode of production is popular within Italian Marxist circles, though English Marxists have been less keen on its adoption. It plays no part in de Ste Croix (1981), Haldon (1993) or Wickham (2002).

24. Finley (1968).

25. de Ste Croix (1975).

26. See, most notably, Marx's *The Eighteenth Brumaire of Louis Bonaparte* (1852). The issue of the political status of peasant actions continues to haunt Marxist thought. Hobsbawm (1969) has been much criticised for seeing (social-) bandit activity as being pre-political. For similar views, see Guha (1983).

27. Meyer (1910); Toynbee (1965).

28. In *The German Ideology* (1845-1846), Marx argues that slavery exists within tribal societies (his first stage of historical evolution), and continues to exist in the second stage (the city stage, identifiable with the *polis* and Classical antiquity). He argues that slaves were communal property, and it was this communality that obliged the Romans to maintain their state in some form of ideological unity. With the impoverishment of the peasantry in the second century BCE, the proletariat came into prominence, but never established 'independent development', remaining trapped within an ideological unity with the landowners. On Marx's reading, it becomes a matter of dispute whether one would locate the hegemonic mode within the 'peasant mode' or the 'slave mode' and the natural reading of our primary source material is that politics, as traditionally defined, was located primarily within the sphere of the *polis* and smallholders rather than the slave mode.

29. The alienation of a major part of the production of the ancient world from the hegemonic economy continues a traditional Classics focus on the elite.

30. See Konstan (1975), arguing against the 'slave mode'. Wood (1981) traces the slave mode of production back to Engels' ill-informed writings on Athens, and argues that although in certain periods Rome might have had a hegemonic slave mode, Classical Athens never did.

31. See Roth (2007) on the invisibility of female slave labour, which is analogous to the invisibility of female domestic labour in modern economic systems.

32. Salmeri (2008).

33. [Xenophon], *Constitution of the Athenians* 1.10-12.

34. The issue, of course, is very different from that in the Americas where somatic markers meant that slave status could hardly be escaped.

35. Turley (2000).

36. Dal Lago and Katsari (2008*a*), especially 3-5, rely on quantifiers such as 'large part', 'high percentage' and metaphors such as slavery being 'at the heart of economic and social life'.

37. Scheidel (2008).

38. Hopkins (1978) 99-102. This numbers game can be usefully played but the fragmentary data on which it is based renders it difficult, and there is a tendency to circularity.

39. The issue turns on estimates for the size of the free population of Italy. If that population was low, as argued by Brunt (1971), and as has been accepted since the late nineteenth century, then one must assume a high servile population, but if that population was high, as argued by Lo Cascio (1994*a*) and (1994*b*) and (2001), then a lower slave population and a mixed model of labour becomes more probable. See also Morley (2001) and Alston (2002).

40. Bagnall, Frier and Rutherford (1997) 98. There is also a considerable issue as to the representative nature of the census returns.

41. See the speculative assessments from Scheidel (1997) and (1999) and also and Andreau and Descat (2006) 65-85, who tend to high estimates for the slave population.

42. Bradley (1998) not only limits his discussion of 'rebellion' to the major outbreaks under the Roman Republic, but argues that these rebellions were not against slavery, but against these individuals being slaves. The rebellions were non-revolutionary in his view.

43. See also Vogt (1975) 40.

44. See the critique offered by Urbainczyk (2008*b*).

45. McKeown (2007) 163.

46. I am here employing a modified form of Bourdieu's *habitus* theory, or Giddens' structuration theory. See Bourdieu (1977), (1990*a*), (1990*b*) and Giddens (1984).

47. It is simply a perversion of the analytical mode that the behaviour of slaves is closely analysed for evidence of 'class struggle', when the actions of masters, the empowered within the system, tends to be ignored. The perspective adopted here means that the relative absence of a 'slave voice' within the literature is less of a problem.

48. Slave rebellion or slave flight may have been attempts to escape a particular social formation and thus represent in basic form the utopian escapism necessary for ideological revolt.

49. Patterson (1991). Fisher (2008) argues that in certain circumstances the status of slaves in fourth-century Athens was indeterminate, showing that law was not an absolute determinant of status.

50. If we see slavery as primarily a legal category, then the modern piecemeal abolitionist drive has in most respects driven slavery from the world. International law bans slavery law and no state law contravenes that ban. 'Slave' is still applied to individuals, both in popular parlance and in quasi-legal contexts and modern 'slavery' exists in diverse forms, the sex trade, child labour, indentured labour, but

the common determinant is that these forms of labour are within the social and economic twilight zones of modernity, non-legal or even criminal, in which rights of contract are suppressed by extra-legal or violent forms of oppression, but it would still seem to exist. See Bales (2005) and (2007).

51. duBois (2003) 7-11. See also Armstrong (2005).

52. One might argue that Atlantic slavery's days were numbered from the moment when the process of enslavement (the creation of the category of the slave) came to be regarded as unnatural.

53. See, perhaps most famously, Apuleius, *Metam.* 9.12 and Diodorus Siculus 5.36-8.

54. Garnsey (1996).

55. See Derrida (1988) 1-21.

56. On the utopian form of Greek drama in relation to slavery see Hall (1997*a*) 118-26. Jameson (2005) 1-9 argues that the utopian urge is politically engaging. One might argue that the dystopian tendency, which one can see in Christian and stoic writers, is politically enervating. If all men are slaves, why struggle against slavery?

57. See the evidence and arguments in Hall (2006) 196-206.

58. See Brown (2002).

59. Lewis (1998/9).

60. Compare Wiles (1988) showing that slave masks were distorted.

61. Such an observation starts to open the door to a post-colonial reading of ancient slavery.

62. Adorno and Horkheimer (1979) 43-65.

63. There is a parallel here with debates over the hegemonic ideologies of the working classes in the early twentieth century. If the working classes were convinced that their state was ontological rather than circumstantial, there would be no resistance to their circumstances.

64. Foucault (1986) 4-36.

65. There is a formidable bibliographic industry on Foucault, including at least one journal. But see especially Foucault (2001) and (1977). For a general survey of the importance of discourse, see Foucault (2002). On Foucault's psychology, see Ransom (1997) and Toews (1994).

66. Wynter (2002); see Hall (2008) 94-7.

References

Adorno, T. and Horkheimer, M. (1979) *Dialectic of Enlightenment*, tr. J. Cumming. London & New York.

Alston, R. (2002) 'The role of the military in the Roman revolution', *Aquila Legionis* 3, 7-41.

———, Hall, E. and McConnell, J. (eds) (2011) *Ancient Slavery and Abolition: From Hobbes to Hollywood*. Oxford.

Althusser, L. (2008) *On Ideology*. London & New York.

——— and Anderson, P. (1974) *Passages from Antiquity to Feudalism*. London.

Andreau, J. and Descat, R. (2006) *Esclave en Grèce et à Rome*. Paris.

Armstrong, R.H. (2005) *A Compulsion for Antiquity: Freud and the Ancient World*. Ithaca, NY & London.

Bagnall, R.S., Frier, B.W. and Rutherford, R. (1997) *The Census Register P. Oxy 984: The Reverse of Pindar's Paeans*. Brussels.

Bales, K. (2005) *Understanding Global Slavery: A Reader*. Berkeley, CA.

1. Rereading Ancient Slavery

—— (2007) *Ending Slavery: How We Free Today's Slaves*. Berkeley, CA.

Bourdieu, P. (1977) *Outline of a Theory of Practice*. Cambridge.

—— (1990a) *In Other Words: Essays towards a Reflexive Sociology*. Oxford.

—— (1990b) *The Logic of Practice*. Cambridge.

Bradley, K.R. (1994) *Slavery and Society at Rome*. Cambridge.

—— (1998) *Slavery and Rebellion in the Roman World 140 BC-70 BC*. Bloomington, IN & London

Brown, P.G.McC. (2002) 'Actors and actor-managers at Rome in the time of Plautus and Terence', in P.E. Easterling and E. Hall (eds), *Greek and Roman Actors*, 225-37. Cambridge.

Brunt, P.A. (1971) *Italian Manpower 225 BC-AD 14*. Oxford.

Carandini, A. (1988) *Schiavi in Italia: Gli strumenti pensanti dei Romani fra tarda Repubblica e medio Impero*. Rome.

Cartledge, P. (1985) 'Rebels and Sambos in Classical Greece: a comparative view', in P. Cartledge and D. Harvey (eds) *Crux: Essays Presented to G.E.M. de Ste Croix*, 16-46. Exeter.

—— (1993) 'Like a worm i' the bud', *Greece & Rome* 40, 163-80.

Dal Lago, E. and Katsari, C. (2008) 'The study of ancient and modern slave systems: setting an agenda for comparison', in E. Dal Lago and C. Katsari (eds) *Slave Systems: Ancient and Modern*, 3-31. Cambridge.

de Ste Croix, G.E.M. (1975) 'Karl Marx and the history of classical antiquity', *Arethusa* 8, 1-41.

Derrida, J. (1988) *Limited Inc*. Evanston, IL.

duBois, P. (2003) *Slaves and Other Objects*. Chicago, IL.

—— (1981) *The Class Struggle in Ancient Greek World*. London.

—— (1988) 'Slavery and other forms of unfree labour' in L.J. Archer (ed.) *Slavery and other Forms of Unfree Labour*, 19-32. London & New York.

Eagleton, T. (1994) 'Ideology and its vicissitudes in Western Marxism', in S. Zizek (ed.) *Mapping Ideology*, 179-226. London & New York.

Finley, M.I. (1959) 'Was Greek civilization based on slave labour?' *Historia* 8, 145-64, repr. in M.I. Finley (ed.), *Slavery in Classical Antiquity: Views and Controversies*, 53-72. Cambridge.

—— (1968) 'Slavery', *International Encyclopedia of the Social Sciences* XIV, 307-13. New York.

—— (1980) *Ancient Slavery and Modern Ideology*. London.

—— (1985a) *The Ancient Economy*. London.

—— (1985b) *Ancient History: Evidence and Models*. London.

Fisher, N. (2008) ' "Independent" slaves in Classical Athens and the ideology of slavery', in C. Katsari and E. Dal Lago (eds), *From Captivity to Freedom: Themes in Ancient and Modern Slavery*, 123-46. Leicester.

Foucault, M. (1977) *Discipline and Punish: The Birth of the Prison*. London.

—— (1986) *The Care of the Self* (*The History of Sexuality* III). London.

—— (2001) *Madness and Civilization: History of Insanity in the Age of Reason*. London & New York.

—— (2002) *Archaeology of Knowledge*. London & New York.

Garlan, Y. (1988) *Slavery in Ancient Greece*. Ithaca, NY & London.

Garnsey, P. (1996) *Ideas of Slavery from Aristotle to Augustine*. Cambridge.

Giardina, A. and Schiavone, A. (1981) *Società romana e produzione schiavistica*. Rome.

Giddens, A. (1984) *The Constitution of Society: An Outline of the Theory of Structuration*. Berkeley & Los Angeles, CA.

31

Gramsci, A. (1971) *Selections from Prison Notebooks* (ed. & tr. Q. Hoare and G.N. Smith). London.

Guha, R. (1983) *Elementary Aspects of Peasant Insurgency in Colonial India*. Oxford.

Haldon, J. (1993) *The State and the Tributary Mode of Production*. London.

Hall, E. (1989a) *Inventing the Barbarian*. Oxford.

—— (1989b). 'The archer scene in Aristophanes' *Thesmophoriazusae*', *Philologus* 133, 38-54. Revised version in Hall (2006) ch. 8.

—— (1995) 'The ass with double vision: politicising an ancient Greek novel', in D. Margolies and M. Joannou (eds), *Heart of a Heartless World: Essays in Cultural Resistance in Honour of Margot Heinemann*, 47-59. London.

—— (1997) 'The sociology of Athenian tragedy' in P.E. Easterling (ed.) *The Cambridge Companion to Greek Tragedy*, 93-126. Cambridge.

—— (2006) *The Theatrical Cast of Athens*. Oxford.

—— (2008) *The Return of Ulysses*. London.

Hall, S. (1978) 'The hinterland of science: ideology and the "Sociology of Knowledge"', in *On Ideology*, 9-32. London, Melbourne, Sydney, Auckland & Johannesburg.

Hobsbawm, E. (ed.) (1964) *Karl Marx, Pre-Capitalist Economic Formations*. London.

—— (1969) *Bandits*. London.

Hopkins, K. (1978) *Conquerors and Slaves*. Cambridge.

—— (1993) 'Novel evidence for Roman slavery', *Past & Present* 138, 3-27.

Jameson, F. (2005) *Archaeologies of the Future: The Desire called Utopia and other Science Fictions*. London & New York

Katsari, C. and Dal Lago, E. (eds) (2008a) *From Captivity to Freedom: Themes in Ancient and Modern Slavery*. Leicester.

Katsari, C. and Dal Lago, E. (eds) (2008b) *Slave Systems: Ancient and Modern*. Cambridge.

Kleijwegt, M. (ed.) (2006) *The Faces of Freedom: The Manumission and Emancipation of Slaves in Old World and New World Slavery*. Leiden & Boston, MA.

Konstan, D. (1975) 'Marxism and Roman slavery', *Arethusa* 8, 3-27.

—— (1995) *Greek Comedy and Ideology*. New York & Oxford.

Kudlien, F. (1998) *Sklaven-Mentalität in Spiegel antiker Wahrsagerei*. Stuttgart.

Lekas, P. (1988) *Marx on Classical Antiquity: Problems of Historical Methodology* (Sussex & New York

Lewis, S. (1998/9) 'Slaves as viewers and users of Athenian pottery', *Hephaistos* 16/17, 71-90

Lo Cascio, E. (1994a) 'La dinamica della populazione in Italia da Augusto al III secolo', *L'Italie d' Auguste à Dioclétien*, 91-125. Rome.

—— (1994b) 'The size of the Roman population: Beloch and the meaning of the Augustan census figures', *Journal of Roman Studies* 84, 23-40.

—— (2001) 'Recruitment and the size of the Roman population from the third to the first century BCE', in W. Scheidel (ed.) *Debating Roman Demography*, 111-37. Leiden, Boston & Cologne.

McKeown, N. (1999) 'Some thoughts on Marxism and Ancient Greek history', *Helios* 26, 103-28.

—— (2007) *The Invention of Ancient Slavery*. London.

Meyer, E. (1910) 'Die Sklaverei in Altertum', *Kleine Schriften*, 169-212. Halle.

Millar, F. (1981) 'The World of the Golden Ass', *Journal of Roman Studies* 71, 63-75.

Morley, N. (2001) 'The transformation of Italy, 225-28 BC', *Journal of Roman Studies* 91, 50-62.

Patterson, O. (1991) *Freedom in the Making of Western Culture*. Cambridge, MA.

Ransom, J.S. (1997) *Foucault's Discipline: The Politics of Subjectivity*. Durham, NC & London.

Roth, U. (2007) *Thinking Tools: Agricultural Slavery Between Evidence and Models*. London.

Salmeri, G. (2008) 'On the Moregine *ancilla* or slavery and prostitution at Pompei', in C. Katsari and E. Dal Lago (eds) *From Captivity to Freedom: Themes in Ancient and Modern Slavery* , 57-70. Leicester.

Scheidel, W. (1997) 'Quantifying the sources of slaves in the early Roman empire', *Journal of Roman Studies* 87, 156-69.

———— (1999) 'The slave population of Roman Italy: speculation and constraints', *Topoi* 9, 129-44.

———— (2008) 'The comparative economics of slavery in the Greco-Roman world', in E. dal Lago and C. Katsari (eds) *Slave Systems: Ancient and Modern*, 15-26. Cambridge.

Thompson, E.P. (1978) 'The poverty of theory or an orrery of errors', in E.P. Thompson, *The Poverty of Theory and other Essays*, 193-7. London.

Toews, J.E. (1994) 'Foucault and the Freudian subject: archaeology, genealogy and the historicization of psychoanalysis', in J. Goldstein (ed.) *Foucault and the Writing of History* , 116-34. Oxford & Cambridge, MA.

Toynbee, A. (1965) *Hannibal's Legacy*, vol. 2. London.

Turley, D. (2000) *Slavery*. Oxford.

Urbaincyzk, T. (2008a) *Slave Revolts in Antiquity*. Stocksfield.

———— (2008b) 'Rewriting slave rebellions', in C. Katsari and E. Dal Lago (eds) *From Captivity to Freedom: Themes in Ancient and Modern Slavery*. Leicester.

Vogt, J. (1975) *Ancient Slavery and the Ideal of Man*. Cambridge, MA.

Wallon, H.A. (1847) *Histoire d'esclavage dans l'Antiquité*. Paris.

Wickham, C. (1984) 'The other transition: from the Ancient World to Feudalism', *Past and Present* 103, 3-36.

———— (2002) *Framing the Middle Ages*. Oxford.

Wickramasinghe, C.S.M. (2005) *Slavery from Known to Unknown: A Comparative Study of Slavery in Ancient Greek* poleis *and Ancient Sri Lanka* (BAR int. series, 1463). Oxford.

Wiles, D. (1988) 'Greek theatre and the legitimation of slavery', in L.J. Archer (ed.) *Slavery and Other Forms of Unfree Labour*, 53-67. London & New York.

Wood, E. (1981) 'Marxism and Ancient Greece', *History Workshop* 11, 3-22.

———— and Wood, N. (1978) *Class Ideology and Ancient Political Theory: Socrates, Plato, and Aristotle in Social Context*. Oxford.

Wynter, S. (2002) ' "A different kind of creature": Caribbean literature, the Cyclops factor and the second poetics of the *propter nos*', in T.J. Reiss (ed.) *Sisyphus and Eldorado: Magical and Other Realisms in Caribbean Literature*, 2nd edn, 143-67. Toronto, NJ & Asmara, Eritrea.

Zizek, S. (1989) 'How did Marx invent the symptom?', in S. Zizek, *The Sublime Object of Ideology*. London. (Reprinted in S. Zizek, *Mapping Ideology*. London & New York 1994, 296-331.)

Odysseus as Slave: The Ritual of Domination and Social Death in Homeric Society

Patrice Rankine

Eumaeus, in his first protracted exchange with Odysseus in Homer's *Odyssey*, goes a long way towards conveying what it means to be a slave in Homeric society.[1] Disguised, Odysseus is a guest to Eumaeus, but he is also a beggar who could become a dependent in the same way that Eumaeus had. Emphasising that guests and beggars are sacred to Zeus (14.56-8), Eumaeus talks about his role in Odysseus' household. His labour (14.66) increased his master's holdings, yet Eumaeus' focal point, the way in which he frames his speech is not labour, *per se*, but honour and power.[2] It is not right (*themis*) to dishonour a guest, but even so, 'it is the habit of slaves always to be in fear, whenever young kings are in power' (14.59-60). Eumaeus links his master's power, and the ability to take in a beggar who could become a slave, to the gods. Odysseus has come to a place where people respect standard social practice: gods come first, kings are kind, and dependants – guests, beggars, slaves – honour their lords. That is, people in Ithaca respected these practices until Odysseus left for Troy, when he 'swore many things' to his slave Eumaeus, 'had he grown old here' (14.67). Odysseus of course has gone to Troy to fight for honour (14.70), and in his absence affairs have degenerated into chaos. Nevertheless, Eumaeus wants his guest – Odysseus as beggar – to know what's what.

The implications of the sleight of hand, so to speak, by which Odysseus is transformed here into beggar, and elsewhere into slave, as I will argue, have not been fully appreciated in Homeric scholarship. Odysseus' false stories, which reiterate the possibility (introduced in earlier books of the *Odyssey*) that he could in fact become a slave, emphasise the slipperiness of social status in Homeric society, a slipperiness that makes individuals dependent on gods and kings. And yet no one has mined the text of the poem (or the texts of the period) for evidence of the shifts in social status, aside from Odysseus' lies, whereby he might have become a slave. This is because the focus of scholarship on ancient slavery has been on ideology and iconography.[3] Regarding the former, the slave belongs to the category of 'other', barbarian, or conquered, which, from the time of the Persian Wars onward, certainly is tantamount to *non-Greek*. Even inversions such as Edith Hall discusses in connection with tragedy in *Inventing the Barbarian* (1989) depend on the construction of normative categories. Aristotle's theory of natural slavery reifies a dichotomy that we might trace to Aeschylus' *Persians* but that we impose on texts before the classical period. Despite our ideological constructs, however, slavery is at core a relationship to power and is not intrinsically linked to ethnicity or social background. Regarding iconography, Kelly Wrenhaven argues (in this volume) that Greek artists depicted slaves as other through labour, torture, and physiognomy. Yet one wonders, again, to what extent readers impose this classical iconography onto their view of the Homeric age. The result is an optical illusion that negates the possibility of seeing Greeks as slaves. That is, while the evidence of Odysseus as slave permeates the Homeric texts, the actuality is the furthest thing from the reader's mind. As Eumaeus converses with the beggar in front of him, the reader forgets that this same Odysseus *has* actually evaded slavery, through cunning (*mêtis*), at various points in the poem.

In this essay, I read the evidence of slavery as a real possibility for Odysseus. 'Odysseus as slave' is an important reading of the text because it helps to remove the *Odyssey* from ideological and iconographical prisms that distort our understanding both of Homeric society and slavery. We are also, ultimately, able to compare slavery in the Homeric context to other periods, such as modern America, where freedom and slavery depend on optical illusions of a similar sort.

A comparative, sociological approach to slavery, such as that of Orlando Patterson, is useful for challenging entrenched ideological assumptions.[4] Patterson sifts through many of the prevailing ideas about slavery to salvage its core components: the absolute domination of one person over another person, on the one hand, and on the other, the social death of the individual dominated. This approach is most compelling when we consider its counterparts. For example, Peter Garnsey offers the idea that 'a slave was property',[5] but what, exactly, is property? Is Eumaeus simply Odysseus' property?[6] Patterson sees the notion of property as one of the *post festum* ideas to which Marx points as having already 'acquired stability' by the time it is named.[7] In Homeric society, a man recognises that he has 'stuff', *ktêmata*, but there is a clear distinction between the *inanimate* goods won in war, for example, and a slave. The discussion of Eumaeus with which I opened this essay certainly points to this distinction. In the *Iliad* Achilles elevates his slave Briseis to the level of wife.[8] A slave is more than property and evokes deep emotional and ontological responses, as Page duBois (2003) suggests. For Patterson, saying a slave is property begs the question; property is a complex notion that develops over time (Greek practice, Roman law, and so forth). Slavery, moreover, is not specifically, in origin, a mode of production, although as the institution develops, it partakes in mass production (as with Athenian slavery of the fifth century BCE).

If we accept Patterson's broader, comparative approach, a component of slavery is the absolute domination of one party over another. It is 'one of the most extreme forms of the relation of domination, approaching the limits of total power from the viewpoint of the master, and total powerlessness from the viewpoint of the slave'.[9] According to Patterson, slavery as a mode of domination includes the threat of violence, a 'psychological facet of influence', which has a bearing on the slave and non-slave alike, and a 'cultural facet of authority', whereby members of the society who might not be slaveholders, nevertheless have a claim to domination. In Athens, where Solon 'outlawed debt-bondage and other forms of dependent labour affecting the free residents of Attica',[10] to be a slave was certainly to be viewed, by an entire society, as an outsider and thus to be susceptible to certain abuses. (Garnsey also sees that such outlawing is in part what led to the need to import slaves.[11])

Since to be a slave was to be so thoroughly dominated, it will be useful to question why anyone would accept this status. Put otherwise, why is Eumaeus content with his circumstances? Here Patterson offers the idea of social death as a partial answer to this question.[12] According to Patterson, the slave's status always began as 'a substitute for death, usually a violent death'.[13] Nowhere is this fact better demonstrated than in the American context, where the institution of lynching immediately replaces slaveholding when the latter was abolished.[14] Notwithstanding the potential productivity of slaves, slaveholding, equally importantly, bestowed noble status upon Southerners.[15] Even American whites who did not own slaves shared in the privileged status of whiteness.[16] Thus when slaveholding ended, white Southerners continued to exercise their domination over black bodies through such practices as lynching. Lynching, therefore, becomes part of a history of force – over bodies – that serves a similar purpose to slaveholding: namely, the illusion of fixed social categories, here black and white, noble and subservient. The rise of lynching after Abolition extends the role of slavery as a sign of a power that can lead to the death of the dominated.

In the ancient world, many of the slave's kin – her husband, her child – have already been killed in war, and only the master's will has saved the slave. 'Social death' means that the *person* of slave is kept alive within the society of his or her domination, but the social personality of the slave – his or her culture of origin, social relationships, in sum, his or her identity – is dead or vitally fragmented.[17] The slave's true identity is relegated to the realm of memory, to the past. Just as lynching showed in the American context, Eumaeus' comments about fearing the domination of young kings reveal slavery's harshness; Eumaeus is a bodily extension of even the 'kind king,' and he recognises the extent to which his life depends upon this kindness.

A few other aspects of Patterson's analysis demystify slavery in the ancient world and allow us to imagine Odysseus as a slave. In the first place, our knowledge of the ancient Mediterranean and Near East corroborates the view that slavery was not widespread during the eighth to sixth centuries BCE. Although slavery 'was a nearly universal phenomenon', slaveholding was not a mass institution.[18] Terms used for slaves, such as *urdu* in Assyrian, are used of persons as property, or even of a free person who has a superior. Given the absolute domination characteristic of slavery, why was there not a widespread movement toward freedom until the classical period? Why was slave status not only tolerable, but at times even desired? Certainly Eumaeus seems to have been fairly content before the departure of his master or the advent of the suitors. Patterson suggests that, for the most part, enslavement was a means by which an individual was enmeshed within a social network: 'To belong, to be bonded, was to be protected, by one's patron and one's gods. To be personally free was to be deprived of this vital support.'[19] To be free was to be orphaned, as Egyptian *nmh* conveys, and only the lowest members of society, such as prostitutes, were free from a patron. Although we might not consider as slaves such members of society as a child handed over to a temple for permanent care, such a person is certainly subject to the absolute domination – or the mercy – of someone more powerful. There is a clear example from 545 BCE, in Uruk, of a woman handing her two sons over to be slaves (*širku*) of the temple, during a famine.[20] The practice that we name 'slavery' in English has a breadth that transcends the European and American chattel slavery that it has come almost exclusively to designate.

Patterson's description of a Tupinamba practice gives a template for what he calls the ritual of domination and social death, and in the reading I offer here, the framework can be applied to Homer's *Odyssey*. The ritual includes role-playing, or a sort of game in which the slave becomes a mock member of the society of his or her domination.[21] The temporary preservation of life and the good treatment of the captive is in the interest of the captor because the slave, in these cases, has a religious status and a social role to play. The slave reifies the master's social (and religious) status. The preservation of life, however, is only a game because labour and property (reasons for life's preservation) are not the *telos* of slavery:

> Among the cannibalistic Tupinamba of South America we find slavery in its most primitive form. Most captives were eventually eaten, but in the many years between capture and execution the captives lived as the slaves of their captor and were usually well treated. Before they entered their captor's village the captives were stripped, dressed as Tupinamba, and decorated with feather ornaments ... They were given the weapons and other belongings of the deceased [member of the community] to be used for a time, after which they were handed over to the rightful heirs.[22]

The social death of the captive is here marked on the body and through ritual. Powerless, the captive is stripped and then 'dressed as Tupinamba'. The corporeal mark (of clothing) is part of an act, wherein the captive *becomes* a living member of the collective, but not as him- or herself;

rather, the captive is 'given the weapons' and belongings of a dead person within the community. In other words, although powerless and all but dead, the captive is kept alive for a purpose, which could be labour but is in this case sacrifice. The powerless slave takes on a kind of power. As an armed member of the community, he could enact war against outsiders, or he could feasibly turn those arms against the society that holds him captive. The power, however, is fleeting. The captive's temporary status and (impending) defeat only serve to reinforce the master's domination. The ritual reifies social roles of captor and slave, insider and outsider. Any hope of freedom is dashed, as the captive is turned over to his death and dismemberment.

Patterson offers this ritual as a model in traditional societies. Before proffering Odysseus' potential abduction in Scherie as a parallel, a few other examples should evidence the model's operability in ancient Greece. In the first instance, Diodorus Siculus reports that on Agathocles' defeat of Carthage in 310 BCE, the Greeks found 'more than twenty thousand pairs of handcuffs' (20.13), in which the Carthaginians had hoped to carry off the Greeks as slaves. Although the mass enslavement that the amount of manacles suggests is not a feature of Tupinamba slavery or of the Homeric sort, other features of Diodorus' story are indicative of the primal institution. In the process of explaining why the Carthaginians, on the occasion of losing to Agathocles, sacrificed two hundred of their own children (14.5), Diodorus gives a glimpse of slavery in Carthage. We learn that Carthaginians at some point used to sacrifice their own noble children to Cronos (Baal). Whether because of shortage or some moral compunction, sacrifice of Carthaginian children falls out of practice, and the Carthaginians began to abduct children from elsewhere. These children were nurtured among Carthaginians, brought up as if Carthaginians (similar to slaves among the Tupinamba).

Slavery as ritual domination and social death is discernible in another example from ancient Greece: the legend of Theseus' enforced journey from Athens to Crete.[23] Theseus was to be one of fourteen Athenian youth ritually sacrificed in Crete. That seven boys and seven girls were to be fed to the Minotaur, an aberration with a human body and bull's head, removes the story from the realm of history or social practice to the sphere of myth and fantasy. Nevertheless, the myth of the sacrifice of young people to the Minotaur and Theseus' subsequent slaying of the beast bears some remnant of reality. Plato's *Phaedo* traces a ritual of the fourth century BCE to the Cretan levy of Athenian youth. In the beginning of *Phaedo*, Echecrates wonders why some time passed between Socrates' condemnation and his actual death. Phaedo says that, on the day before Socrates' trial, a ship set sail from Athens to Delos. Legend had it that the ship was the same one on which Theseus and the others sailed to Crete. The legendary Athenians were of course saved, and Echecrates reports that the ship sails to Delos every year to thank Apollo: 'It is the custom among them during this period to cleanse the city and for no one to be killed publicly, before the vessel arrives in Delos and back again' (Plato, *Phaedo* 58b).

In Bacchylides' *Ode* 17, Minos, the king of Crete, is present on a ship to convey the youth from Athens. When Minos begins to act upon his lust for one of the maidens, Theseus intervenes to dissuade him from sexual violence. Although the Bacchylides fragment does not reveal why the youth are going to Crete, it conveys a great deal regarding the power dynamic and social hierarchies at play between Theseus and Minos. As a king, power and might are at Minos' disposal, yet Theseus urges the lord – *hêrôs* – to 'restrain his overweening might' (17.23). Later, Theseus warns Minos that, even before he displays the 'might of his hand' (17.45), a divine force (*daimôn*) will decide the outcome. Certainly *biê*, 'force', or domination, is the propriety of a *hêrôs*. Theseus, however, suggests that Minos might be going too far, if he rapes the young girl. The master's sexual whim is not the purpose of her captivity. Theseus, who himself is later also referred to by the honorific title *hêrôs*, asks Minos to 'check his grievous hubris' (17.40-1). Minos prays to Zeus, who as we know from Hesiod is the giver of *dikê* to kings, and Minos receives a favourable sign. At the same time, Theseus shows his bravery by jumping overboard, and he is also favoured, saved in a miraculous fashion.

The ode reveals something both of what was viewed as a normative social order, and of its disruption. Both Theseus and Minos belong to an aristocratic class. They are both a '*hêrôs*', and the gods show favour to each lord. Minos proves what we have already heard Eumaeus say: it is in accordance with *dikê* for a king to exercise power, which is why a kind king is beloved. At the same time, the gods' favour of Theseus (Apollo saves him when he jumps overboard) shows that only circumstance disrupts his position in the world (his relationship to the power, as *hêrôs*). While Minos is welcome to use *biê*, as a king, the same gods that protect him also protect Theseus.

Thus slavery is not ontological but circumstantial. The slaves in Carthage and Theseus lay bare the nature of domination in the ancient world. Anyone, even a *hêrôs*, could be dominated. Because of the play of power, the dominated individual might not even fully experience his or her social death until the final moment. That is, the captive, in many cases, is treated well for a time; the shame that he or she experiences as a result of being mocked (whether implicitly or explicitly) might be the slave's only indication that something worse is looming, as would have been the case for the Tupinamba, the slaves in Carthage, and Theseus.[24]

As I have argued throughout the first half of this paper, slavery was not a widespread institution in the Mediterranean society from which the Homeric poems emerged, but a social practice with a certain degree of instability. Although this is not the place for an exhaustive look at slavery in the Homeric texts, it is worth noting the role of slaves in the home. In the case of Menelaus and Helen in *Odyssey* 4, the hero is fresh from a triumph in war. When Telemachus arrives at Menelaus' court, a double wedding is taking place, the weddings of Menelaus' daughter, Hermione, and his son, Megapenthes 'from a slave woman' (4.12). The poet seems compelled to justify Menelaus' extra-marital offspring: 'The gods were no longer showing issue to Helen after the time when she first bore her lovely child, Hermione' (4.12-14). And there are other slave women (*dmôiai*) apart from Megapenthes' mother; servants (*amphipoloi*, 4.133) attend Helen. The inconsistency of the terminology applied to slaves – *doulê, dmôia, amphipolos* – reveals a range of functions for slaves in an aristocratic household in Homeric society.[25] Slaves serve Menelaus and Helen in various capacities, from sexual service to help around the house.

The view from Odysseus' home amplifies what we hear in Sparta. After Odysseus slays the suitors, he receives a report from Eurycleia (22.420-3):

> You have fifty slave women (*gunaikes dmôiai*) in your halls, whom we taught to do work, to comb the wool, and to endure slavery (*doulosunên*). Of these women as many as twelve stepped into shamelessness, and they honour neither me nor Penelope.

Odysseus' slaves are part of the household labour force, and Eurycleia suggests that slavery is a long-term lot to be endured. In addition to this, slaves are to uphold the honour of a household, as Eumaeus indicated. Yet it is also worth noting that 'fifty slaves' may be a number suggested primarily by the presence of an oral formula. Alcinous and Arete also have fifty slaves (7.103-7).

In these rare glimpses, slavery is moving toward becoming a stable institution (for labour), with its attendant features of the slave as part of a labour pool and as property, and also towards becoming an abstraction, 'slavery', designated by the noun *doulosunê* used by Eurycleia above.[26] Even so, the hanging of the twelve disloyal slave women recalls the master's complete domination of the slave, showing that his requirement for labour was secondary to his requirement for honour. It is important to note that Eurycleia does *not* say that the women fail to serve their function as part of a labour force (though see Hunnings, this volume). Rather, they (all of the women) have brought shame to the household, violating their rightful status and position in relation to their owner Odysseus by disrespecting those he had left behind to represent his rights as slave master.

What we see more broadly in Homeric society are intimations of the more primitive, widespread role of slavery, similar to what we have already been discussing. The Homeric hero is free in so far as he is not under any compulsion (*anangkê*) and we know that *anangkê* can come from a defeat in war or some other misfortune. Upon his arrival at Ithaca, in the first in a series of lies in which Odysseus presents himself in relation to slavery, he offers Athena a very plausible autobiography. The story reveals the nature of freedom and *anangkê* in the Homeric context. Odysseus claims to have gone so far as to kill a Cretan man named Orsilochus, Idomeneus' son, because Idomeneus wanted Odysseus to serve him (*therapeuon*, 13.262-6). Although it is a lie, Odysseus's story conveys the values of Homeric man. Odysseus' false persona kills someone to avoid becoming a dependent, and Odysseus, who is at the time surrounded by Phaeacian loot, warns his audience (Athena) about the threat of violence that results from interfering with a man of *biê* and the material symbols of that might.

Power – self-domination and the possession of property and people – as opposed to external *anangkê* is also the contrast at play when Odysseus is captive to Calypso. Athena raises the issue at the beginning of book 5:

> Father Zeus and other blessed gods who are eternal, let not any sceptered king be kind hearted and gentle, nor knowing *themis* in his mind! Let him be always difficult and cruel, since no one of the people over whom he rules remembers godlike Odysseus, although he was a gentle father. But now he is on an island and he suffers hardships in the halls of Calypso the nymph, who restrains him by *anangkê*. He is not able to go to his homeland (5. 7-15).

Here Athena conceives of homecoming in terms of power as opposed to *anangkê*. Her approach to Zeus signals a right-relationship between the ruler and the ruled, the king and his people, and gods and men in Homeric society. This is a relationship to which Eumaeus points, as we have seen. If the kindness of a ruler – or father – such as Odysseus no longer yields a right relationship within the Homeric order, then kings ought not to be kind. Odysseus's kindness, which should bring him favour in the eyes of the gods, has, Athena claims, resulted in servitude; he is held against his will. He has no power (*ou dunatai*, 5.15) – is not free – to serve his role in society. Although Calypso does not threaten Odysseus with death, his relationship to her is not one where he possesses power or authority.

These passages only begin to hint at the possibility of Odysseus as slave. Although in the Calypso passage we do not see Odysseus as completely subject to the goddess' domination, the episode is indicative of the limits of Odysseus' freedom. It has not been unusual for modern readers (such as Toni Morrison) to raise the question of Odysseus' polygamy, his *use* of Calypso, so to speak.[27] Yet under the prism of slavery, we see that to assume Odysseus is free to act as he wants with Calypso would be as inappropriate as reading the American slave woman's coitus with her master as voluntary.[28] The text implies that Odysseus, for a time, gained something from his relationship with Calypso (5.153), but he proceeds under compulsion (*anangkêi*) unwilling to fulfil the goddess' wishes. The details of Hermes' trip to release Odysseus are indicative of the restoration of the correct social order, which is a reflection of a divine one: Zeus the father has sent Hermes, under compulsion (*ouk ethelonta*, 5.99) and it is

Zeus, reports Hermes, who now bids Calypso 'to send him off as quickly as possible' (5.112). Calypso yields to a higher authority; it is not Odysseus' fate, as a surrogate on earth of Zeus, on whom devolves Zeus' authority, as a kind king, to be under such restraint.

If the Calypso passage intimates the possibility of Odysseus as slave in Homer's *Odyssey*, then Odysseus among the Phaeacians illustrates the situation compellingly. The episode, in fact, in many ways resembles the three examples of primitive slavery that we have seen: the Tupinamba, the foreign children in Carthage, and the Athenians among the Cretans. Details that have not been read in the context of ritual domination look different in light of slavery. For example, Athena offers Nausicaa's preparation for her future wedding as the reason for her to wash clothes by the river, while Nausicaa points to Alcinous' five sons, 'two married, three robust and unmarried' (6.63). Although Nausicaa picks up on Athena's theme of marriage, it could also be said that her brothers, as unmarried and strong, are also of the age to wage war and defend their city. This reality is clear from the presentation of the main occupation of the men at Alcinous' court as athletics and dance, both of which we know can 'stand in' for warfare in archaic literature during times of peace.[29] The 'beautiful clothing' (6.111) of these draft-aged men, moreover, will serve as garb for a naked Odysseus (6.228). Certainly Odysseus solicits the clothing, a need at which he hints throughout his interaction with Nausicaa (6.144, 6.179), but wearing Phaeacian clothes masks Odysseus as a (socially dead) member of that community.[30] He is similar, in this respect, to the Tupinamba captives.

Readings of the passage, including that of Thalmann, have elaborated on the play on marriage that runs throughout; Nausicaa is of marriageable age, and Odysseus is an attractive stranger.[31] Nausicaa, however, suggests another possibility when her playmates express fear regarding her flirtations with a stranger:

> Stay still, my maidens. To where are you fleeing because you've seen a man? Surely you don't at all think that he is one of our enemies? There is not any mortal man slippery [enough], nor would there be, who would come to the land of the Phaeacians bearing hostility. The gods love us. We live far away in the surging sea, at the extremes, nor does any other man among mortals mix with us (6.199-203).

Odysseus' very presence negates Nausicaa's statement. Nausicaa claims that no one ever visits this land, but Odysseus *is* present, even if on account of extreme circumstances, and if present, there is every reason why he could be a hostile enemy. The presence of slaves in Alcinous' household corroborates the inference that the community has either brought back captives from war, or the Phaeacians are in contact with traders, from whom they would have been able to buy slaves. Thus the focus on marriage obfuscates the real danger involved for Odysseus.[32]

2. Odysseus as Slave

So far we have two features of the story that parallel slavery among the Tupinamba, the Carthaginians, and the Cretans who enslaved Athenians: the potential role play of captives (here Odysseus) in foreign clothing; and, in the case of the Tupinamba and the Cretans, the suggestion of warfare and defeat as Odysseus' point-of-entry into Phaeacian society. The emphasis on Odysseus as *xenos* in Alcinous' house obscures the danger he faces. Nausicaa's formula is one that Eumaeus echoes later: 'We ought to take care of this man because all strangers and beggars are from Zeus, and even a small gift is welcome' (6.207-9). The role of *xenos*, however, belies the hostile subtext that prompts the need for Odysseus to enter the court under the cloak of darkness with which Athena protects him, for him to address Arete first rather than her apparently less hospitable husband, and for Alcinous to be chided into offering hospitality by a respected elder. Odysseus' safe reception has by no means been guaranteed, and Alcinous' slowness to welcome him 'contrasts sharply with an earlier passage – Telemachus' visit to Menelaus's house in Sparta'.[33] All apparent indicators point to Odysseus as *xenos*, but this status is unstable.

The athletics competition in book 8 contains strong intimations of potential trouble. Athletics amount to surrogate warfare, and the captors want a formidable opponent they can claim to have dominated, as they would have done in war. Domination might not be Alcinous' intention, but what of the other kings? Alcinous is one of thirteen kings who have come to scrutinise the guest. Like Odysseus, Alcinous is anxious to keep the situation from getting out of control. Though he is in his own home, Alcinous' dominance over the other kings is not absolute, and thus his *xenos* is not entirely secure. Alcinous probably needs the help of others to secure Odysseus' passage home. Thus the Phaeacians are called to his halls to 'make a trial' of Odysseus (8.23). As the interaction unfolds, we find that there are indeed many wills at play.

Alcinous' suggestion of games is aimed at distracting his guest from the song of Demodocus, which had reduced Odysseus to tears. Here again, Odysseus is not presented as powerful, but is indeed emotionally and psychologically overpowered by the narrative of Troy.[34] Alcinous' suggestion of the games is perhaps another poor diplomatic move. One contestant, Laodamas, teases Odysseus relatively mildly: 'He has been broken by many hardships. I don't think there's anything worse to confuse a man than the sea, even if he may be especially strong' (8.137-9). But Odysseus cannot ignore Eurylaus' harsher status-based taunt (8.159-64):

> Stranger, I don't think that you look like a man that is skilled in all the athletics events that abound among men, but like one who shuttles to and from on his benched ship, such as abound among men, a captain of merchant seamen, one who takes care of freight and is in charge of conveying his cargo and his greed-gotten gains. You do not look like an athlete.

Odysseus responds angrily to Eurylaus' recklessness (he says he is *atas-thalos* (8.166), a dangerous characteristic that in turn, when displayed by Odysseus, will cause the deaths of his own men), saying: 'I will make a trial of the games, because your word hurts my heart, and you have provoked me to speak' (8.185). He then hurls the discus almost inconceivably far. As the Tupinamba example shows, the fact that Odysseus is a formidable opponent is exactly what makes him a worthy captive.

What separates the narrative of Homer's *Odyssey* 8 from our other examples of enslavement narratives around the eighth century BCE is simply that we anticipate and receive a different outcome. The structure, however, follows that of our examples of enslavement: the entry of an outsider, the mock cooption of the outsider into the community, and the trial of this potential opponent, which leads to his domination. Odysseus' mastery of key interactions – which we might compare with Theseus' seduction of Ariadne in that story – is a crucial factor in his avoidance of captivity. We have already discussed Odysseus' interaction with Nausicaa, and his supplication of Arete, rather than Alcinous, secures him a safe reception at the palace. As the narrative progresses, Alcinous and Demodocus become critical to Odysseus' release. We have also noted that Alcinous' recognition of Odysseus emotional distress – his tears in response to Demodocus' song – prompts the king's attempt (albeit unsuccessful) to help him. Given the taunts that follow, we might well argue that these Phaeacians are bad hosts, but they are merely acting from an impulse to dominate a potential foe.

Odysseus, cheered by a timely visit from Athena, becomes less angry but reflects that a man in his position is in danger of doing comprehensive damage to his position (*panta kolouei*, 8.211) by issuing challenges to men who are his hosts. Fortunately, Alcinous recognises this cue to himself as Odysseus' sponsor, and he puts an end to the competition before his guest embarrasses himself. The guest's failure could lead to more than shame, as was the case of Minos' son, Androgeos, He was killed by his host Aegeus, resulting in the ritual enslavement of Athenian youth to compensate for the death. In the case of Odysseus' ambivalent position as captive/guest in Phaeacia, Alcinous shifts the focus from domination back to *xenia*, but his words point to the possibility of another outcome.

The return of Demodocus marks an important shift in the narrative. Although there are no *direct* words between Odysseus and Demodocus, the bard's choice of topics for his next song is telling: an incident in which a powerful god, Ares, is dominated and embarrassed. The topic of Demodocus' tale is, at first blush, odd. Hilary Mackie has argued that in the *Odyssey*, as opposed to the *Iliad*, songs of bards tend toward recent events. In the *Odyssey*, Phemius and Demodocus both sing about events at Troy, as if demonstrating their ability to stay up-to-date with heroic exploits. Even speakers like Menelaus and Odysseus tell tales about their recent journey homewards. Mackie suggests that 'perhaps the Phaiakians are –

by Odyssean standards – even a little behind the times'.[35] Yet one way of explaining Demodocus' choice of theme is to acknowledge that the motives of mockery of the captive, ritual honour, and domination are present both in the *muthos* and in Odysseus' circumstance. Within our framework, Demodocus' story is clever in drawing attention, through an unexpected *muthos*, to the situation at hand: the capture and domination of an otherwise powerful warrior. Odysseus' chief rival, Euryalus, has already been compared to Ares (8.115), as Braswell reminds us.[36] Demodocus' tale is the story of Ares' affair with Aphrodite, and how Hephaestus, with the help of Helios, traps the adulterers. What are the tactics and values that Odysseus might take from Hepahestus in order to conquer *his* Ares? To borrow Braswell's language, how does Odysseus's intellectual superiority, similar to Hephastus', defeat Euryalus' might?

The language of domination and dependency that distinguishes slavery from guest-friendship is clearly echoed in the *muthos*. Hephaestus devises traps full of trickery (8. 281). The dominant party 'forges bonds that are unbreakable and unable to be loosened, in order that they might remain there firmly' (8.274-5). Hephaestus puts chains 'all around the bedposts in a circle' (8.277-8). Demodocus' emphasis is not on the act of adultery *per se* but rather on the binding; *xenia* has certainly gone wrong. When Ares and Aphrodite lay in bed, 'the crafty bonds of cunning Hephaestus fell, and in no way were they able to stir their limbs nor to raise them up. And then in fact they knew that they could no longer escape' (296-9). Within the *muthos*, the outcome is clear: the ostensibly weaker party, Hephaestus, wins by cunning.

The story suggests that, for Odysseus, neither freedom nor captivity is already determined. Although Demodocus presents the celebration of the cunning of Hephaestus to Odysseus, the trap and the mockery that Ares faces in the story in fact offers a closer parallel to Odysseus' present situation. Like Ares, Odysseus is trapped. As Brown argues, the laughter of the gods, which parallels the behaviour of Odysseus' hosts, brings shame to the object of scorn.[37] Gods, holders of might, gather to see Ares trapped, while the goddesses hold back out of shame. Yet although Odysseus is threatened, in this event it turns out that *Euryalus* is Ares. Odysseus' foe will suffer defeat at the hands of a weaker but more cunning opponent.

Recognising his vulnerability and the trap in which he finds himself, Odysseus takes immediate action. Wasting no more time, he bathes and says his goodbyes, as if he has already gained passage home. Odysseus then asks Demodocus to sing about Troy. Harrison rightly calls attention to Odysseus' unusual actions here: 'In a display of quite unparalleled rudeness the hero proceeds to assume control of the proceedings, first presenting Demodocus with a choice piece of pork from the table of his host (474f.), and then himself nominating the theme to be treated by the bard in his next song (492f.).'[38] Harrison surely has a point in arguing that

Odysseus has set Demodocus up in order to mislead him purposely. Odysseus, not Demodocus, will tell the most captivating story and win his freedom.

The possibility of Odysseus as slave – the ever-present possibility that he will be enslaved – returns us to the folkloric core of Homeric narrative, the reality from which the poet draws when portraying his character in action in a specific environment. Something, some mastery of social options, however, separates the individual, heroic, folkloric character from his or her context. Part of Odysseus' heroism, in a modern sense of the word, that which separates him from any other hero in his own poem (and that which also distinguishes Theseus in Bacchylides) is a dignity independent of social class, as Thalmann showed in *The Swineherd and the Bow*: determination, resolve never to fail, or never to be *entirely* dominated. This is one sense in which Odysseus is *polymetis*, resourceful; he always finds a way.

Odysseus' Cretan stories, told later in the narrative during his interactions with Eumaeus, reify the hints of the real possibility throughout the text – the possibility I have sought to demonstrate here – of Odysseus as slave. These stories, along with the details of Eumaeus' life, reveal a specific Homeric *Weltanschauung*: the world is cruel, full of obstacles to individual freedom, and in such a world human values – in terms of kind treatment, hospitality, trust – do matter. And yet such a system of dependency can also create a social optics whereby relations of dependency, slavery, and power appear natural. The constructed order of things takes on the reality of an ontology, which is reinforced culturally through iconography and ideology. Odysseus as slave undoes this ontology.

A North American parallel should serve in conclusion. In his narrative, Frederick Douglass introduces us to the institution of slavery (and the rules of domination) through a 'terrible spectacle' of behaviours, interactions, and rituals of violence. The 'terrible spectacle' renders slavery a near-permanent – real, immutable, inborn – status for the dominated. Douglass tells us, or shows us, how his master humiliated his Aunt Hester, stripping her 'her from neck to waist, leaving her neck, shoulders, and back, entirely naked'. Douglass would observe the 'warm, red blood (amid heart-rending shrieks from her, and horrid oaths from him)', which 'came dripping to the floor'.[39] Douglass's focus is always optical: 'I was so terrified and horror-stricken *at the sight*, that I hid myself in a closet, and dared not venture out till long after the bloody transaction was over.'[40] The spectacle shows Douglass, who is a boy at the time, what his value is in nineteenth-century American society. Seeing violence against his aunt not only teaches Douglass his social role as slave, but his master thus also reifies his own value as dominant.

The spectacle of domination, which opposes individual character, is so convincing in North America that it takes an equally enchanting vision to undo it. If observing domination and degradation iterates and reiterates roles in American society during slavery, then imagine the spectacle of the

Negro, the non-human, thing-being slave, mounting an argument for his freedom, publically. In 1845, William Lloyd Garrison wrote the following about watching Douglass at an anti-slavery convention four years earlier, in 1841:

> I shall never forget his first speech at the convention – the extraordinary emotion it excited in my own mind – the powerful impression it created upon a crowded auditory, completely taken by surprise – the applause which followed from the beginning to the end of his felicitous remarks. I think I never hated slavery so intensely as at that moment; certainly, my perception of the enormous outrage which is inflicted by it, on the godlike nature of its victims, was rendered far more clear than ever. There stood one, in physical proportion and stature commanding and exact – in intellect richly endowed – in natural eloquence a prodigy – in soul manifestly 'created but a little lower than the angels' – yet a slave, ay, a fugitive slave, – trembling for his safety, hardly daring to believe that on the American soil, a single white person could be found who would befriend him at all hazards, for the love of God and humanity![41]

The grounds on which the Negro was enslaved were its inhumanity, its soullessness, its proximity to beasts of burden. Violence and enforced ignorance transformed social circumstances into ontological truth. If this is the case, if slavery was akin to an optical illusion, then the reality of a Frederick Douglass – an educated, eloquent, extraordinary Negro – pledges to undo the magic trick or to restructure ontology. Douglass is to Garrison a religious apparition, an epiphany that produces a miraculous transformation of society.

It would not be extreme to say that the Abolitionist serves for Douglass a similar role as does Alcinous for Odysseus. Each agent becomes the vehicle that helps to transport the slave to freedom. Odysseus' heroism, then, is similar to what we see in Douglass. We find that the origins of freedom lie in inner force and intellect that counter domination and social death. The sleight of hand that Odysseus performs is no different from the way in which Douglass crafts freedom for himself. Odysseus as slave, therefore, shows us how to be free.[42]

Notes

1. For a discussion of the hierarchical structure of Homeric society and Eumaeus' role in it, see Thalmann (1992), especially 84-100. See also Donlan (1980) and Rose (1992) 92-140. In general, it is worth noting that throughout this essay, 'Homeric society' and 'Homeric culture' refer not to an actual historic culture, but rather to the layers of culture from perhaps as early as Mycenaean times to the eighth or seventh century BCE which are fused and represented in the Homeric texts. This approach is similar to that of Thalmann (1998) and Redfield (1994).

2. In Odysseus' Cretan story to Eumaeus, Odysseus claims that, in Egypt, some of his men are killed, and others are taken alive, and *forced* to work (14.272). Tellingly, in this passage, the problem of working (*ergazesthai*) has to do more with

dishonour than industry. The 'false' Odysseus, as a son of a Cretan lord by a concubine, is conscious of his status alongside his noble brothers. He makes it clear that he prefers sailing to field labour (*ergon,* 14.222), but the issue again is honour.

3. See e.g. Cartledge (1993), Garnsey (1996), and even to some extent Thalmann (1998).

4. Patterson (1982) and (1991). See further the discussion of Alston in Chapter. 1 above, pp. 19-22.

5. Garnsey (1996) 1.

6. Although this is not the place for a full discussion, Page duBois's notion of the slave as object/thing is somewhat more subtle than that of Garnsey (1996); duBois (2003) 6 sees 'that being human is not an absolute condition but rather a gradual one, on a sliding scale on which some humans approach the status of things, of objects'.

7. Patterson (1982) 17-27.

8. Redfield (1993) proffers this as an actual option, but elaborated the theme even further in a presentation for the National Endowment for the Humanities Summer Institute at Grambling State University, 2007. I am indebted to Redfield for the general approach that I offer here.

9. Patterson (1982) 1.

10. Garnsey (1996) 4.

11. Slaves are gained as a result of 'military strength, or the capacity to capture slaves as booty from other, weakened communities (and any defeated enemy population might in principle be enslaved)' (Garnsey [1996] 3). Throughout the Mediterranean world, one might also come into slavery at the hands of pirates or merchants.

12. An aspect of slavery for which Patterson might not fully account, because of his binary opposition of 'slavery' and 'freedom', is resistance. Resistance extends the space, so to speak, between *alive* and *dead*. For Patterson, 'freedom' might well be the primary purpose of resistance, but *during* enslavement, modes of resistance including storytelling and rituals do combat the master's intention of having the slave as an extension of himself, a symbol of his domination. Robert Farris Thompson's *Flash of the Spirit* (1984) is one example of an attempt to account for such resistance.

13. Patterson (1982) 5.

14. On lynching, see Patterson (1999).

15. duBois (2003) sees this, as does Nadel (1988) in his analysis of Ralph Ellison's *Invisible Man* (1952) and the representation of Southern culture in that novel.

16. On whiteness as a social status, see Allen (1994) and Roediger (1998).

17. A weakness of the idea of social death is that it does not allow for the retention or 'memory' of social practices, the remnants of the society from which the slave is taken (see also Hall's chapter below, pp. 204-6). In places like Brazil in the modern world, these fragments, pieced together along with practices adapted from the new culture, lead to new cultural formations. See Thompson (1984) and Merrell (2005).

18. Patterson (1991) xv; see also 33, where he takes on, though not entirely convincingly (since this instance would be the exception to his rule), the question of Israelite presences in Egypt as an instance of mass slavery.

19. Patterson (1991) 36.

20. Boardman (1970) 254.

21. Games, and even to some extent game theory, are useful ways of talking about these types of social interactions, where power and domination take on a ritualistic dimension, each party knowing and 'playing' – or not playing – his or her expected role. See, for example, Herzfeld (1985) and Dugatkin (1996).

22. Patterson (1982) 52.

23. Artistic representations of the event to which Phaedo refers existed as early as 650 BCE, according to Gantz (1993) 262, and both Bacchylides (17) and Sappho (fr. 206) refer to the 'seven boys and seven girls' (see Servius on *Aeneid* 6.21). For a general discussion of the Theseus myth, see Walker (1995).

24. Although war is the primary mode of captivity, we see in the case of the Carthaginians that slaves could also be bought from traders or pirates. See, for example, Redfield (2003) 179.

25. For a systematic look at the language of slavery in Homer's *Odyssey*, see Thalmann (1998). Thanks to Barbara Graziosi for providing the scholia here.

26. Thalmann (1998) 17-19, though see Fitzgerald's chapter in this volume.

27. See Taylor-Guthrie (1994) 26.

28. As in, for example, Jacobs (1987 [1861]) and Douglass (2001 [1845]).

29. See Sansone (1998) on athletics and Hall (2010) on dance.

30. Another permutation of the theme of clothing comes in Odysseus' story, told to Eumaeus, that he was shipwrecked among the Thesprotians on his trip from Egypt. (He is of course telling falsehoods, but the central issues of narrative expectation and convention remain.) He is given aristocratic garb: 'They dressed me in the cloak and tunic' (14.320). When the Thesprotians, independent of the king Pheidon, sell him into slavery (his *doulion êmar*, 14.340), the aristocratic clothes are the first to go: 'They took the cloak and tunic from me, and they threw another ugly rag on me and tunic, this one ratty, which you yourself can see with your own eyes' (14.341-3).

31. Thalmann (1991) 153-70; see also, for example, Gross (1976).

32. Thalmann, in his reading of Bellerophon's death sentence because of Anteia in *Iliad* 6, reminds us of the link between marriage and death in Homeric narrative. Bellerophon's successful evasion of death secures him the king's daughter, but failure would have meant continued servitude, or death (Thalmann: 144-6, 157). G. Rose (1969) and Gross (1976) emphasise that the encounter with the Phaeacians is not friendly but one fraught with perils for Odysseus.

33. G. Rose (1969) 395.

34. If Mackie (1997) is correct that characters in the *Odyssey* master their grief by telling their own story, then Odysseus's narrative dominance does not occur until book 9.

35. Mackie (1997) 81.

36. Braswell (1982).

37. In sum, 'mockery can serve as a mechanism of popular justice' (Brown [1989] 291), as is the case of the mockery of the adulterer here.

38. Harrison (1971) 378.

39. Douglass (2001 [1845]) 16.

40. Douglass (2001 [1845]) 16-17, my italics.

41. Douglass (2001 [1845]) 3-4.

42. Thanks to Barbara Graziosi for calling my attention, too late to incorporate the information into the main narrative of this chapter, to *Iliad* 4.385-400, where Agamemnon, chastising Diomedes, tells the story of the latter's father Tydeus, who escaped possible enslavement and similar challenges.

References

Allen, T.W. (1994) *The Invention of the White Race*. New York.

Braswell, B.K. (1982) 'Two supplementary notes on Pindar', *Philologus* 126, 310-13.

Brown, C.G. (1989) 'Ares, Aphrodite, and the laughter of the gods', *Phoenix* 43, 283-93.

Cartledge, P. (1993) *The Greeks: A Portrait of Self and Others*. Oxford.

Donlan, W. (1980) *The Aristocratic Ideal in Ancient Greece: Attitudes of Superiority from Homer to the End of the Fifth Century BC*. Lawrence, KS.

Douglass, F. (2001 [1845]) *Narrative of the Life of Frederick Douglass, an American Slave. Written by Himself*, ed. J.W. Blassingame, J.R. McKivigan and P.P. Hinks. New Haven, CT & London.

duBois, P. (2003) *Slaves and Other Objects*. Chicago, IL & London.

Dugatkin, L.A. (1996) *Cooperation among Animals: An Evolutionary Perspective*. New York and Oxford.

Ellison, R.W. (1952) *Invisible Man*. New York.

Gantz, T. (1993) *Early Greek Myth: A Guide to Literary and Artistic Sources*. Baltimore, MD.

Garnsey, P. (1996) *Ideas of Slavery from Aristotle to Augustine*. Cambridge.

Gross, N.P. (1976) 'Nausicaa: a feminine threat', *Classical World* 69, 311-17.

Hall, E. (1989) *Inventing the Barbarian: Greek Self-Definition through Tragedy*. Oxford.

———— (2010) ' "Heroes of the dance floor": the missing exemplary male dancer in ancient sources', in F. Macintosh (ed.) *The Ancient Dancer in the Modern World*. Oxford.

Harrison, E.L. (1971) 'Odysseus and Demodocus: Homer, *Odyssey* VIII. 492 f.', *Hermes* 99, 378-9.

Herzfeld, M. (1985) *The Poetics of Manhood: Contest and Identity in a Cretan Mountain Village*. Princeton, NJ.

Jacobs, H. (1987 [1861]) *Incidents in the Life of a Slave Girl: Written by Herself*, ed. L. Maria Child; edited with an introduction by J.F. Yellin. Cambridge, MA.

Mackie, H. (1997) 'Song and storytelling: an Odyssean perspective', *Transactions of the American Philological Association* 127, 77-96.

Merrell, F. (2005) *Capoeira and Candomblé: Conformity and Resistance in Brazil*. Princeton, NJ & London.

Nadel, A. (1988) *Invisible Criticism: Ralph Ellison and the American Canon*. Iowa City.

Patterson, O. (1982) *Slavery and Social Death: A Comparative Study*. Cambridge, MA.

———— (1991) *Freedom in the Making of Western Culture*. London.

———— (1999) *Rituals in Blood: Consequences of Slavery in Two American Centuries*. New York.

Redfield, J.M. (1994) *Nature and Culture in the Iliad: The Tragedy of Hector*. Durham, NC & London

———— (2003) *The Locrian Maidens: Love and Death in Greek Italy*. Princeton, NJ.

Roediger, D.R. (1998) *Black on White: Black Writers on What it Means to be White*. New York.

Rose, G. (1969) 'The unfriendly Phaeacians', *Transactions of the American Philological Association* 100, 387-406.

Rose, P. (1992) *Sons of the Gods, Children of Earth: Ideology and Literary Form in Ancient Greece*. Ithaca, NY.

Sansone, D. (1998) *Greek Athletics and the Genesis of Sport*. Berkeley, CA.

Taylor-Guthrie, D. (1994) *Conversations with Toni Morrison*. Jackson, MS.

Thalmann, W.G. (1992) *The Odyssey: An Epic of Return*. Boston, MA.

———— (1998) *The Swineherd and the Bow*. Ithaca, NY.

Thompson, R.F. (1984) *Flash of the Spirit: African and Afro-American Art and Philosophy*. New York.

Walker, H.J. (1995) *Theseus and Athens*. New York.

The Paradigms of Execution: Managing Slave Death from Homer to Virginia

Leanne Hunnings

Eulogists of Homer declare that he has been the educator of Hellas, and that he is beneficial in education and the administration of human affairs, and that we should study him repeatedly and regulate our whole lives according to what he says. (Plato, *Republic* 10.606d)

In this chapter, I attempt to extend the analysis of the manner in which discourses surrounding the institution of slavery operated in antiquity, and suggest that they may have informed slave-owners' behaviour, by focusing on Homer's representation of slaves within the *Odyssey*. I argue that the representation of slaves within this epic poem offers a series of literary exempla which serve to define, consolidate and perpetuate the institution of slavery. As a correlative to this, I posit the view that the execution of the twelve slave girls in book 22 represents the culmination of a work imbued throughout with prescriptive elements concerned with the management of slaves. Moreover, due to the *Odyssey*'s widespread reception and powerful influence both within the ancient world and beyond, I argue that this harsh instance and episode of slave execution is a crucial part of a vital imaginative exercise which has resonances beyond the world of myth and fiction.

My approach is influenced by historical materialist theory: such a theory rejects the idea of art as a metaphysical or purely aesthetic entity, believing it, rather, to be inextricably rooted within the cultural circumstances of the moment of its production, creating and reproducing the social, political and religious ideas of the day. This theory does not deny the contribution of the author, and does not seek to challenge concepts of artistic value or authorial brilliance, but takes issue with concepts of the artist which assume that he or she has somehow transcended the ideological and cultural practices of his or her own historical period. By this definition, art cannot either challenge or innovate without at first, implicitly at least, addressing the current context. Moreover, no work of art materialises in a separate bubble from social reality since the tools required to create art are inextricably rooted in social institutions. Thus the text is a cultural reaction, interpretation and articulation of the foundations of the social context or contexts in which it was produced. As such, this work has the potential to reveal much about the ideologies and philosophical currencies of its time.[1] With this in mind, I believe that fictional texts from the ancient world which deal with slaves and slavery, such as the *Odyssey*, if their ideological layers are unpeeled, can expose owning-class interests and attitudes.

This is an approach broadly speaking shared by William G. Thalmann, summarised thus in his seminal *The Swineherd and the Bow*:

> The depiction in the *Odyssey* of people low in the hierarchy and of their relations with their superiors cannot automatically be taken as faithful reflections of actual dependents and their social relations in the eighth century BCE ... Any picture we can derive ... is inevitably simplified and otherwise distorted in the process of representation. But that very distortion is of great interest ... For the fact of this distortion and its dynamics in the texts can give us a sense of ... the partially enchanted picture of that society which those in control of public discourse wished to convey in order to secure general assent to its actually unequal structures ...[2]

Thalmann thus inverts the 'historical' problem constituted by both the paucity of our knowledge regarding the chronological period which produced the *Odyssey* and the overwhelming owning-class bias manifested in textual evidence. He achieves this by focusing on the representation of the lowly characters within the epic in its own right, as a 'historical, social and literary' phenomenon. I aim in this chapter to engage with the text in a similar manner, and also hope to augment his study of the perpetuation of owning-class ideology by considering the overall exemplarity of the treatment of slavery within the *Odyssey*. This exemplary quality we can even call its 'didacticism', to adopt the ancient Greeks' own concept that poets were teachers, *didaskaloi*, which reaches its classic articulation in Aristophanes' *Frogs*.[3] I see certain aspects regarding the representation of slaves within the epic not only as fulfilling an ideological aim of maintaining and enhancing owning-class control but, moreover, as the active materialisation of an underlying social discourse which functioned to exert a direct influence on action and behaviour regarding the treatment of slaves.

This project is equivalent to arguing that the *Odyssey* can be read as perhaps our earliest version of an archaic work imaginatively anticipating – and therefore informing – the 'slave handbook' genre. Its ancient precursors can be found in works such as Xenophon's *Oeconomicus* and later in the treatises entitled *On Agriculture* (*De re rustica*) by Cato and Varro. However, the slave handbook as a specific genre is most strongly evidenced in antebellum American plantation slavery, where tropes and ideas about negro slaves and their large-scale management appeared in agricultural journals aimed at maximising the profit of slave-produced goods, although they were not always without concern for the humanitarian welfare of the slaves. For most, however, discussions about the provision of good food and shelter had more immediate resonances for the efficiency with which the negroes would work, rather than for altruistic concerns about their welfare.

Slave handbooks deal with a wide variety of aspects regarding the maintenance of slaves, including provision of food, shelter, discipline, working hours, working conditions, as well as more generic racially configured statements concerning the 'typical' personality traits of negroes and how this would affect their productivity. There is also a sense that plantation-owners were engaged in a pseudo-scientific dialogue regarding the nature of the negro, and the best environment within which to nurture this particular race. It appears that plantation-owners were engaging in social experimentation in an active manner, reinforced by the circulation of prize-winning and commissioned essays on the subject.[4] I do not of course wish to argue that the *Odyssey* engages in this 'handbook' style in the same idiom and discursive manner as these written articles or texts. However, I find in the genre a useful model within which to structure and read the apparently cursory comments regarding slaves in Homer as well as the more developed polarising rhetoric and comparative treatment of 'loyal' and 'disloyal' slaves. Thus I suggest that these individual episodes, taken together, articulate one possible way – indeed the 'proper' way – to exert owning-class authority with respect to slavery in a practical, 'hands-on' manner.

Hesiod's *Works and Days* of course also displays some of this functional didactic quality; while Osborne is quite correct in pointing out that 'one cannot learn how to farm from Hesiod',[5] Hesiod the narrator constructs himself as a figure imparting knowledge to Perses, repeatedly using imperatives (e.g. 9, 214). In a study of what didacticism actually means in the case of Hesiod, Heath distinguishes three categories of didacticism – instrumental, formal and final – and argues that Hesiod's didacticism is of a 'formal' and not necessarily of a 'final' type. That is to say, he thinks that the authorial voice of *Works and Days* does indeed present itself as 'purporting to be intended to instruct', but he queries whether we can say with absolute certainty that the final outcome of the poem is that it does indeed 'instruct'.[6] While Hesiod's *Works and Days* is *explicit* that it is formally didactic, since it sets the author up as a figure imparting knowledge, Homer's *Odyssey* is not explicitly a didactic poem. However, I intend to demonstrate in the rest of this chapter that it may have had a socially didactic function in 'finality' with specific respect to the institution of slavery. Whether an element of teaching was intentional or not, seeing the *Odyssey* as prescriptive is perfectly plausible, especially given the great cultural authority exerted by the Homeric poems. This is valid both for the classical period and beyond, after the poems had been written down,[7] and in the archaic period when knowledge could be imparted to a preliterate society through oral poetry. That the epic poets were teachers is of course widely acknowledged across ancient literature, and memorably realised in the competition between different genres of hexameter poetry in the 'Hesiodic' poem *The Contest of Homer and Hesiod*.

First, then, I will consider any possible material in the *Odyssey* which is evidence of thought processes addressed to the question of how to 'manage slaves' – any explicit prescriptions, episodes or descriptions which seem to provide a clear model regarding an aspect of the relationship between slave-owner and slave, or the experiences of either. These help to build the interpretative framework for our understanding of the figuration of slavery within the epic, and the ideology it promulgates explicitly in its text, so widely circulated in the ancient Greek world. These comments can be arranged within a four-part taxonomy: first, those dealing with the practicalities of the slave existence; secondly, those addressing the necessity for servile acclimatisation; thirdly, discussions of methods of rewarding slaves; finally, the use of instrumental violence against slaves. On this last question, I focus in particular on the fate of the twelve slave-girls in book 22.

When it comes to the practicalities of subsistence, Cato outlines precisely the necessary provisions for agricultural slaves (*On Agriculture* 56):

> Rations for the hands [*qui opus facient*]: Four modii of wheat in winter, and in summer four and a half for the field hands. For the overseer, the housekeeper, the foreman, and the shepherd [*vilico, vilicae, epistatae, opilioni*] three should be provided. The chain-gang [*conpediti*] should have a ration of four pounds of bread through the winter, increasing to five when they begin to work the vines, and dropping back to four when the figs ripen.

While the *Odyssey* contains no exact parallel to these precise food quantities, it does address the issue of the allocation of adequate slave provisions in lines spoken by Odysseus as a beggar to his slave, the swineherd Eumaeus, in order to assure him that his life as a slave has not been so bad, after all:

> Yet Zeus after all has brought you good, side by side with evil. After much distress you came to the house of a kindly master, and by his care you have food and drink enough; your way of life is a good way of life. (15.488-91)

The prescriptive force of the statement that Eumaeus has received sufficient food and drink is here enhanced by the proverbial tone of the line about Zeus' ultimate role in allocating good and bad elements within the life of a man.[8] The comment of the disguised Odysseus does not engage with the details of the slave diet, of course, in the same manner as this anonymous contribution to a debate on the proper method of slave management between two Virginia planters published in the *Farmer's Register* in 1837:

> But corn meal bread, with little or no meat, and no vegetable diet, is extremely hard fare. I believe that there are extremely few masters who starve their slaves to actual suffering; in fact, I am unacquainted with

any such. But, I have no doubt that the slow motion, and thin expression of countenance, of many slaves, are owing to a want of sufficiency of nourishing food.[9]

Yet Odysseus' remark still has paradigmatic worth, since it provides a classification of the deeds of a 'good master'; he is kind and provides adequate food. His dutiful provision of food and drink is reciprocally rewarded in the loyalty of a good slave, exemplified by Eumaeus. Such a concept of directly relational interplay between loyalty and provisions is similarly articulated in the nineteenth-century recommendation published by the Virginia planter, who while recommending firm discipline cautions that it be exercised with moderation:

> It is not intended by this remark to justify harsh and reproachful language on all occasions, from the master. His authority should be exercised in a firm, but mild manner ... I never saw any degree of courtesy shown to a negro, (that was kept under good subjection,) but was returned with usury.[10]

Before he had realised the beggar was Odysseus, Eumaeus had lent him his own cloak, remarking that there are no extra ones to spare: 'Here there are not many cloaks and tunics to change into; it is one man, one cloak' (14.513-14). As Thalmann notes, Eumaeus does in fact have an extra cloak and 'in other ways, too, whatever may be true of other *dmôes*, he seems to have enough and a bit more besides'.[11] But it seems from these statements regarding the basic essentials of a slave's life – food and clothing – that the epic presents it as a kindly master's duty, and indeed in his best interests, to provide sufficient resources to maintain his slaves' bodily wellbeing, but that this need not be at all superfluous to basic need.

One of the topics discussed in handbooks on slave management is the necessity – and difficulty – of acclimatising slaves to their status and role. In Varro's *On Agriculture* the character Scrofa discusses the matter thus (1.17):

> Slaves should be neither cowed nor high-spirited (*Mancipia esse oportere neque formidulosa neque animosa* ...). They ought to have men over them who ... are dependable and older than the hands whom I have mentioned; for they will be more respectful to these men than to men who are younger.

Implicit within this pronouncement is the conviction that there is an optimum psychological state in which slaves should be maintained. Centuries earlier, a passage spoken by Eurycleia in the *Odyssey* articulates the similar principle:

> My child, I will tell you the plain truth. You have fifty slave women here whom we have trained in their proper duties – to card wool and to bear servitude. (22.420-3)

Eurycleia is an older slave who has nursed two generations of men in Laertes' family, both Odysseus and Telemachus. As an older, authoritative slave she offers a parallel with the older agricultural slaves in Varro's text. Eurycleia specifically emphasises a psychological process through which the slaves whom she oversees learn to endure and tolerate their slave status.[12] This line suggests that entry into slavery necessitates a concurrent educational engagement, and within this it is possible to learn coping mechanisms to deal with being in a state of servitude. Unfortunately Eurycleia does not expand upon this, and the modern audience is left ignorant of the mechanics behind the ancient process by which slavery was made 'endurable'. An audience contemporary with Homer's epic might well have been able to ascertain the methods behind this through familiarity with the processes undertaken within their own society. Nevertheless, Eurycleia supplies a signal that no one is immediately reconciled to slavery, and that there is a process of acclimatisation which one must undergo psychologically in order to become a 'good' slave. A slave who finds his or her slavery difficult to endure will constantly question an owner's right to impose rules and orders, and will struggle and chafe against bondage. The exemplary good slave, then, must be one who learns passive acceptance and how to internalise slavery psychologically in a state of social death.

My other example of the statement in the *Odyssey* of the requirement for slavery to be psychologically internalised is voiced by Eumaeus, when speaking about Odysseus' dog Argus:

> This dog's owner has died far away. ... Now his situation is hard, because his master has died away from his homeland, and the women do not look after him. Slaves never work properly when their master is not there to govern them, for far-thundering Zeus removes half a man's excellence (*aretê*) when the day of slavery takes him down. (17.312-23)

Eumaeus has internalised owning-class ideology. He uses condemnatory language of the neglectful women and condemns men who do not do their work 'properly'. He is the paradigm of a slave who has successfully acclimatised to his subordinate roles and duties, and now measures his own actions and those of other slaves against a yardstick of appropriate servile behaviour created by owning-class ideology. The other male slaves have lost the compulsion under which they laboured before, due to the ongoing absence of their master Odysseus. But Eumaeus himself startlingly attributes this refusal to work properly to the inherent loss of half a man's excellence when the day of slavery envelopes him, constructing it as an inevitable occurrence with the change in status, and not something which any individual can control in any way. He does not exclude himself from this statement explicitly, but through his condemnation of the behaviour of the other slaves he elevates himself beyond them, concomitantly exhibiting the 'unconditional submission ... upon which slavery should be placed'.[13]

This episode highlights the *stasis* which potentially may result from the absence of the male householder, thus setting up the structure for the demonstration in the next books of how this corruption within the *oikos* is revealed through the behaviour and interactions of the lowest class in the Homeric world. From a didactic point of view, then, the epic could be interpreted as emphasising the need for constant vigilance by the owner, in a similar manner to the negative paradigms of ill-run and unsuperintended households of women and slaves offered by Greek tragedy.[14] Eumaeus' words also underline the importance of care to ensure that due attention is given to the 'breaking' down of the slave in order that he or she become acclimatised to their servile condition, on a permanent and sustainable level.

The epic implicitly recommends rewarding those slaves for whom owning-class ideology remains internalized, such as Eumaeus and Philoitios. Patterson writes of the significance of the interplay of punishment/reward within the slave holder/slave relationship, adding a perspective ostensibly absent from this epic:

> However firm their belief in their ideological definition of the slave relation, slaveholders simply could not deny the stark fact that their slaves served under duress: a combination of punishments and rewards was essential. While it was true that the whip struck not just the body of the slave but his soul, slaveholders everywhere knew that incentives were better than punishments to promote efficient service. Treating the slave well was one kind of inducement, though it also supported the slaveholder in a variety of ways. The well-looked-after slave redounded to the generosity and honor of his holder, emphasised the slave's apparent 'dependence,' and gave credence to the paternalism that the parasite craved. For precisely these reasons the slave, even while accepting and allowing himself to be spurred by these incentives, also resented them.[15]

In his *Oeconomicus* Xenophon mentions rewards that could be offered as 'good behaviour' incentives slaves could hope for, none of which include manumission. They pertain to improvements in the slave's current living conditions, and might consist of a share in the profits of the *oikos* (9.11-13, 12.9-15), good clothing (13.10), abundant food (13.9), 'for you will do much with them by filling their bellies with the food they hanker after', and permission to reproduce by having children (9.5). At the concluding passages of the recovery of order in the *oikos*, Odysseus rewards Eumaeus and Philoitios in similar terms, emphasising the *Odyssey*'s engagement with a reward system:

> ... if the god subdues the proud suitors beneath my hands, I will find wives for you both and give you possessions and well-built houses near my own;

and from henceforward in my eyes you two shall be comrades and brothers of Telemachus. (21.213-16)

It is not clear whether Odysseus is offering manumission at this point, though Thalmann argues he is not.[16] What is apparent is that Odysseus has absolute authority over these slaves and can choose to free them if he so wishes. The lesson to be learned from this passage is that it is important to offer rewards to slaves from whom one expects continuing obedience even in difficult circumstances. The system of rewards reveals an underlying paternalism in the owner/slave relationship within the epic, perhaps even reflecting a benevolent model of slavery to which contemporary slave-owners might have subscribed.

Despite these discursive engagements with the importance of rewarding slaves, the management activity in which the *Odyssey* engages most heavily and most strikingly is the disciplining of slaves in moments of crisis in which slave conditioning appears to break down. In these instances Odysseus does not hesitate to employ physical violence to reaffirm his owning-class authority. The Homeric approach to violence towards slaves in the *Odyssey* is strongly suggestive of a didactic presentation. Exemplary episodes demonstrate both how to maintain the status quo and, in the event of a failure of owning-class authority, how to bring about a recovery of authority.

Almost without exception, slavery, transculturally speaking, is an enforced state of servitude, and physical violence, both threatened and actualised, is imperative as a form of control to its survival. Patterson is so convinced of its foremost significance in the experience of slaves that it has become a crucial element in his definition of what it is to be a slave: 'Slavery is the permanent, violent domination of natally alienated and generally dishonoured persons.'[17] This immanent connection between slaves and violence is manifested in the epic even against those essentially presented as 'loyal' slaves;[18] Eumaeus and Eurycleia are both threatened with assault. Odysseus' threat of potential violence is accompanied with a physical demonstration of his ownership and his bodily power over Eurycleia in the recognition scene when she bathes him and recognises his scar from the boar's tusk, in the process nearly giving away his identity to Penelope:

> 'My own dear child, you are Odysseus beyond a doubt, yet I did not know you for my master till I passed my hands all over you.' As she spoke these words she turned her eyes to Penelope, eager to show her that there her own husband was, but the queen failed to meet her glance or pay heed at all, because Athene had turned her thoughts elsewhere. But Odysseus felt for his nurse's throat, clutched it with his right hand while he pulled her towards him with his left, then whispered: 'Nurse, are you bent on my destruction? You reared me once at your own breast, and now after many griefs and trials I have come back in the twentieth year to my own country.

Since you have seen the truth and the god has revealed it to your mind – say not a word; make sure that no one else in these halls comes to know. If not, I will tell you what will come to pass. If the god delivers the suitors into my hands, I will not spare you, nurse of mine though you are, when I kill other maidservants in these halls.' (19.474-90)

In this astonishing scene, a god's intervention is necessitated by the ability of a faithful old woman swiftly to recognise the man she looked after in his childhood, even twenty years after last seeing him. The resourceful Odysseus underestimated his own slave, thus jeopardising his plan which relied on delaying his revelation to Penelope. It is unsurprising, then, that he responds in a somewhat vehement and fierce manner to Eurycleia. First, he physically demonstrates his power over her by taking her by the throat, but also threatens her with the same execution he is already planning for the 'disloyal' slave-girls. In the fraught context of the inherently contradictory institution of slavery, Eurycleia's life-long loyalty to Odysseus counts for nothing. She is reassigned instantly to her inferior status and made aware of his total power over her, which extends to his right and ability to kill her.

The violence with which these 'good' slaves are threatened actualises the words spoken by Odysseus-as-beggar to Melantho in book 19; that a slave's owners may feel anger and come to hate him or her (19.83-4). The fragility of the position of even a favoured slave is evident. Ultimately within the epic it is the 'bad' slaves who are punished, and the 'good' slaves are rewarded for their loyalty. However, it is the susceptibility to threats of violence which unites all the slaves – either 'good' or 'bad' – and strongly hints at the potential for favour to be lost or to be won almost arbitrarily. Violence is perhaps the principal way by which this fluctuating interplay is manifested, by perpetuating a situation within the epic in which 'no one is safe'. The *Odyssey* appears to be promoting such an ideological framework as an essential condition of slave management. As Patterson's transhistorical research illustrates, vulnerability to 'violent domination' is an essential component of a slave's identity. If a privileged slave begins to view him or herself as exempt from the physical consequences of misdemeanour, he or she begins to view themselves as possessing a degree of security which is essentially 'unslavelike'.

The most poignant and most socially instructive display of violence against slaves within the *Odyssey* is however perpetrated against those who are considered to have transgressed incontrovertibly. The climax to the punishments meted out in the epic is the mass execution of the twelve 'disloyal' slave-girls whom Eurycleia identifies in book 22:

'... Of these there are twelve in all who have trodden the path of shamelessness, heeding neither me nor the queen herself. As for Telemachus, he had only begun to grow towards manhood, and his mother would not let him assume command over these women.' (22.423-7)

The girls' disdain for the authority of Eurycleia and Penelope (Telemachus is here exempted on the ground of his youth) is coupled with the sexual transgressions constituted by their liaisons with the suitors. As Odysseus' property, the right of sexual access to them belonged to him. By bestowing sexual favours on the suitors, therefore, they were effectively stealing from Odysseus what was rightfully his. They were also acting as free agents, meeting either the desires of the suitors or their own desires and rejecting their personal and sexual subordination. They have not absorbed owning-class ideology sufficiently to remain 'socially dead'. If we read the episode as exemplary for the members of the slaveholding society – whether slave or free – who listened to it in ancient Greece, the slave girls become models for the undesirable slave, in particular the undesirable *female* slave, as a poetic and cultural construct. This construct enables the epic both to demonstrate critically what warning signs might be discernible in a slave who has 'gone bad' – that is, one who has not been successfully and permanently acclimatised fully to subservience – and also to present paradigms for dealing with the transgressive slave.

The punishment as ordered by Odysseus operates on more than one level. It has an immediate consequence of transgression for that individual transgressive slave (or, in this instance, for the twelve slaves). But, more importantly for the steady maintenance of the institution, it provides a visual and psychological reminder to *every slave* within the household. Given the continuing impact throughout antiquity of the *Odyssey*, it is imperative to establish exactly what were considered to be the girls' crimes and what reasons make their punishment, even execution, justified.

The slave-girls play a noticeably small role throughout much of the epic; they perform a quiet almost scenographic role in the background of the main action and are not given the attention that would reveal individual characteristics: they are mostly not named. However, one slave-girl, Melantho, is afforded more attention than all the others, and, while she is not explicitly listed among those executed, her behaviour strongly suggests that she is one of the twelve. Melantho can be seen as representative of the other deviant slave-girls.

The first extensive encounter with Melantho occurs in book 18, where crucial aspects of her life and conduct are revealed. The exchange between Melantho and the beggar-Odysseus here provides us with a window on the major ways in which she has overstepped her social boundaries as a slave:

> At these words of his the serving-maids laughed, and glanced at one another. One of them mocked him insultingly. This was the lovely-cheeked Melantho. Dolius was her father, but Penelope had brought her up, cherishing her like her own daughter and giving her toys for her delight. Yet despite all this the girl's heart was without compassion for Penelope, and she was mistress and bedfellow to Eurymachus. She it was who insulted Odysseus now: 'Miserable stranger, you must have had your wits battered out of you if you will not go to the forge to sleep, or to some other meeting-place for idlers – if instead of

that you stay on to chatter here. Have you quite forgotten yourself because you worsted the vagrant Irus? Take care, or a better man than Irus may challenge you, batter your skull with sturdy fists and send you out from the palace here streaming blood all over.' (18.320-33)

At the most basic level, Melantho expresses a sense of individual identity, independence and even autonomy altogether separate from her owner's. This in itself is a critical transgression by a slave. Docility in slaves is nurtured by propagating the sort of unquestioning obedience and loyalty found in Eurycleia and Eumaeus. A slave exhibiting the sort of freedom of expression and autonomous thought, as Melantho does here, threatens to undermine the authority of an owning class.

There are three primary dimensions to Melantho's overstepping of the line of acceptable behaviour. The one given most prominence is her treatment of Odysseus as beggar. That her abuse contravenes the manner in which her owners would wish a guest to be treated is confirmed elsewhere: Penelope is aghast to hear of the treatment of the beggar-guest by Antinous, who throws a footstool at him (17.492-4); she expresses her disgust to her slaves, and later also scolds Melantho for her treatment of the beggar-guest (19.91-5).[19] Moreover, by a dangerous inversion of underlying statuses, Melantho is directly abusing her own true master. There is a fault of non-recognition of the master here.

A second dimension to Melantho's transgressive behaviour is her ingratitude to Penelope, who, it is remarked, took her into her own home like a daughter, and lavished gifts upon her. For a direct contrast to this ingratitude, we have Eumaeus' comments about his master:

'He himself has perished in some such place, and for those who loved him nothing is left henceforth but grief – for me more than anyone, because never now shall I meet with a master as kind as he was, go where I may – no, not if I returned to my own father's and mother's house, to the birthplace where they brought me up; not even for them do I grieve so much, happy though I should be to set eyes on them in my home again. But for lost Odysseus my longing is overpowering.' (14.137-44)

Eumaeus later recalls that he was brought up by Anticleia as a member of her own household alongside with her daughter Ktimene, than whom he was 'only a little less favoured' (15.365). The parallelism between the lives of Melantho and Eumaeus is underlined. Both are slaves, and are both favoured enough to be brought up in personal contact with the mistress within the household and apparently treated well. But where Eumaeus' vocalisation of the loss of his master Odysseus betrays the close familial link he has made as a slave placed in a new household, Melantho has responded less favourably to the establishment of the new fictive kinship ties, of which Patterson speaks of when considering the familial integration of slaves:

> On the surface the relationship appears to be a straightforward adoption. All over the world we find the master being addressed as 'father' and the slave as 'son' or 'daughter' … It would be a great mistake, however, to confuse these fictive kin ties with the claims and obligations of real kinship or with those involving genuine adoption … In order to avoid confusion it is best that we distinguish between two kinds of fictive kinship, what I shall call adoptive and, following Meyer Fortes, 'quasi-filial.' Fictive kin ties that are adoptive involve genuine assimilation by the adopted person of all the claims, privileges, powers, and obligations of the status he or she has been ascribed. Fictive kin ties that are quasi-filial are essentially expressive: they use the language of kinship as a means of expressing an authority relation between master and slave, and a state of loyalty to the kinsmen of the master.[20]

An owner might believe such a filial relationship to be 'true', unaware that the relationship is founded on quasi-filial restrictions which foster and bolster the liminal position of the slave within society. For such owners, then, Melantho's behaviour might seem puzzling. Penelope has taken this unknown girl into her own household, treated her as if she were a daughter, and tried to ease the pain of her slavery by giving her gifts. Now, however, on the eve of Odysseus' return, Melantho is demonstrating something distinctly like 'familial' ingratitude, in contrast to other slaves treated the same way, such as Eumaeus, who express their love and praise for their (possibly dead) master, above and beyond even their own original family. It sends out a confused and problematic signal to a society of slave-owners; despite the care with which one might nurture a slave, they might still easily turn out bad. Similar observations are made much later by Xenophon, leading him to underline the imperative of owning-class vigilance:

> To put it shortly, I don't think I have discovered a bad master with good slaves: I have, however, come across a good master with bad slaves – but they suffered for it! If you want to make men fit to take charge, you must supervise their work and examine it, and be ready to reward work well carried through, and not shrink from punishing carelessness as it deserves. (*Oeconomicus* 12)

Yet it is probably the third dimension to Melantho's misdemeanours that truly casts her as a 'bad' slave: she is sexually active, indeed the sexual partner of the prominent suitor Eurymachus (18.325).[21] Fulkerson has argued that what is really at stake here is not slave management, but a displaced debate about Penelope's sexual fidelity.[22] There is some truth in the claim that both 'bad slaves' – Melanthius as well as Melantho – provide a structural basis on which to assess, comparatively, Penelope's own behaviour.[23] But Melantho's sexual behaviour needs to be considered separately if only for the simple reason that she is a slave when Penelope is not, and therefore she operates quite as much as a foil to the virtuous slaves Eumaeus and Eurycleia as to her owner's wife.

3. The Paradigms of Execution

As early as the first book of the poem, the audience is made aware that slaves, especially young female slaves, are the sexual possessions of their master. When Eurycleia is first introduced, we are told that Laertes never had sexual intercourse with her:

> A faithful servant lighted his way with burning torches – Eurycleia, daughter of Ops, Peisenor's son. Laertes had bought her long ago as a girl, giving twenty oxen's worth of goods for her; in the household he paid her no less regard than he did his wife, but he never lay with her in love, lest the queen should be indignant with him. (1.427-33)

The reason for Laertes' sexual reticence, which is almost comically presented, nevertheless cannot conceal the presumption that as a slave, Eurycleia could be subject to sexual intercourse with her master, as was his right as owner and her duty as property. Perhaps the greatest transgression of Melantho and the other slave-girls is their sexual autonomy; they had no right to chose with whom they would sleep.[24] Odysseus' rights of ownership over Melantho meant that Odysseus owned all of her body, including very specifically her vagina. Thus only he had right of control in deciding who had access to her sexually. In displaying even *apparent* sexual autonomy, the slave-girls had severely slighted the honour of the one man who did have the right to sleep with them; their master Odysseus, irrespective of whether or not he then chose to exercise that right.

That above all it is the sexual behaviour of the slave-girls which plays on Odysseus' mind is made apparent long before he drops his disguise and embarks on revenge at the beginning of book 22. While he lies sleeping outside the hall, plotting how he would exact retribution from the suitors,

> … women began to come out from the great hall – those who for some time past had been the mistresses of the suitors – laughing and making merry with one another. Anger swelled up in him, and for a while he asked himself if he should leap out then and there and deal death to each of them, or if he should let them lie with the haughty suitors this one last time. His heart within him growled with anger. (20.5-13)

It takes a palpable psychological effort for Odysseus to gain control over his emotions and to refrain from killing the girls there and then, unaided, before he is truly prepared; it takes the intervention of Athene truly to master this onslaught of emotion. Since these sexual relationships, and the girls' apparently cheerful acquiescence in them, represent for Odysseus the pinnacle of their misdemeanours, far worse than their ingratitude or disrespect for the laws of *xenia*, it becomes easier to interpret the initial method of execution ordered by Odysseus towards the end of book 22. He instructs Telemachos, Eumaeus and Philoitios to take the woman out into the courtyard 'and strike them with your long sharp swords till you have taken the life from them …' (22.437-43). In psychoanalytical terms, it is difficult not to see in Odysseus' request a metaphorical rape; the Odyssean sword (wielded on his behalf), under this reading, becomes a metaphor for Odysseus' own physical penetration of the women, reinstating his ownership of them one final time. They would die having learnt that they are the property, bodily and sexually, of their omnipotent master.

Yet the death by sword-stroke recommended by Odysseus is not the actually form of execution suffered by the slave-girls. Telemachus exercises his own autonomy in choosing to hang the slave-girls and, articulates his motivations for this:

> Then Telemachus addressed his helpers: 'Never let it be said that sluts like these had a clean death from me. They have heaped up outrage on me and my mother; they have been the suitors' concubines.' So he spoke, and stretched a ship's cable between a tall pillar and the round-house, fastening it high up so that no woman's feet could touch the ground. Just as long-winged thrushes or just as doves, on their way to roost, strike against a snare set in a thicket and find their death in what should have been their sleeping-place, so with their heads in a single line the women's necks were all caught and noosed, to make them die the most piteous death. For a little while their feet kept writhing, but not for long. (22.465-72)

It has been suggested that Telemachus' use of hanging symbolically serves to close the slave-girls' genitals, an interpretation which draws upon the close association of mouth and genitals in Greek medical texts.[25] But a problem with this line of argument is that the execution closes not the girls' mouths but rather their throats. Moreover, according to Telemachus' system of prioritisation here, the slave-girls' sexual transgressions apparently cede first place in importance to their insulting behaviour towards himself and his mother. For him, then, perhaps the sexualised, penetrative death mooted by Odysseus is not one which he conceives as fitting because he does not perceive their greatest misdemeanours to have been sexual. His own desire, as a youth who has struggled to be taken seriously throughout the poem, may be that the girls are once and for all reminded of their subservient position in the social hierarchy and his superior authority over them as an aristocratic male and the son of their owner. In tragedy, hanging seems more widely associated with young women than older ones, and with women rather than men.[26] Dying by the sword could perhaps be seen as more dignified, 'masculine' and even honourable, certainly less humiliating than Telemachus' idea of a mass hanging on a makeshift collective noose.

Although the slave-girls are actually hanged, it is noticeable that Telemachus and the other men follow Odysseus' orders that the twelve girls be taken outside the house, to be executed in a place which he specifies as lying between the round-house and the courtyard. There is therefore an obvious publicity about the executions; they take place outside the walls and roof of the household, far from the female domestic quarters in the external, public male sphere. There is a symbolic exclusion of the women from the household which prefigures their deaths, but also a public demonstration of Odysseus's recovery of status and honour. The slave bodies dangling outside the house would also surely be heard by the *Odyssey's* audience as a warning to others. This is reminiscent of a public execution, based on narratives of historically attested incidents, to be found in the first two stanzas of *Ala*, a poem by the Guyanan Grace Nichols in her collection about slavery, *I is a Long Memoried Woman* (1983):

> Face up
> They hold her naked body
> To the ground
> Arms and legs spread-eagle
> Each tie with rope to stake
>
> Then they coat her in sweet
> Molasses and call us out
> To see ... the rebel woman.[27]

The poem recounts the torture and execution of a slave woman who killed her own child to send 'the little new-born soul winging its way back to Africa – free', a different transgression from that of the slave-girls in the *Odyssey*. However, there is ideological kinship between the two episodes, essentially based in their public nature. In Nichols' poem, the other women are called out, as often happened in reality, to see the torture of the 'rebel woman'; this was a powerfully assertive act by an owner intending to reclaim and reiterate his authority. It is the unspoken aftermath of the execution of the slave-girls in the *Odyssey* which is potent here; even if the *physical* reminder of their bodies left hanging is not something on which the epic narrative dwells, their executions remain as a powerfully public, psychological reminder to everyone who ever read or attended a performance of the climax of the *Odyssey*.

Thus the scene leading up to and including the execution of the slave-girls articulates several vital 'rules' governing slavery. First, female slaves are sexual property, and that they have no right to chose their sexual partners, particularly when those sexual partners themselves do not support the correct authorities within the household. Secondly, it is crucial for slaves who have begun to feel themselves on a level with the free to be reminded in an unequivocal manner that they are subservient and must submit to their masters' authority. Thirdly, the epic demonstrates the public recovery of honour by the slave-owning family and shows how this recovery can be demonstrated by a punishment which acts as a warning to other potentially rebellious slaves. And so execution is a critical tool, even if only occasionally used, in the general maintenance of the institution of slavery. It is no surprise that as a slave-owner Odysseus wishes to exact a punishment for the perceived misdemeanours of his household slaves, even though he uses what to a modern audience may seem to be extreme violence. Owner/slave violence serves to reiterate the 'rightful' polarity between the two parties, to forcibly remind the slave that he or she is subservient, subject to the whims and domination of the master, and that perceived transgressions will be answerable physically. Death is at the extreme end of the spectrum of this violence.

I have tried to suggest that the *Odyssey* imaginatively anticipates the slave handbook genre by flagging up the ways in which its narrative illustrates, albeit with the extremism characteristic of myth and heroic narrative, the 'best practice' of slave management. Due to the paucity of evidence for the society that actually produced the Homeric poems, I cannot prove that this epic had explicit ramifications for the lives of slaves within that historical context, though I hope to have demonstrated that it plausibly may have done. I would now like to conclude by outlining the more demonstrable ways in which the *Odyssey*'s adumbration of the concerns of the slave handbook may, at the very least within the poem's direct reception, have influenced the treatment of slaves both within antiquity and beyond.

The epigraph quoted at the beginning of this chapter is Socrates' statement in Plato's *Republic* that many people regard Homer as an educator and regulator of the correct way to live. Although Socrates himself felt that Homeric poetry needed to be excluded from the ideal state, his comment emphasises the extent of Homeric influence within classical Greece and adds weight to my claim that Homeric treatment of slavery might well have had potent influence in the real-life activities of the owning classes. But there is of course much more extensive engagement with Homeric treatment of slavery elsewhere, even within the Platonic corpus. In his *Laws*, for example, Plato puts an allusion to the much-quoted comment on the deleterious effects of slavery, delivered by Eumaeus in the *Odyssey* (see above, p. 56), into the mouth of 'The Athenian' lawgiver. He frames the quotation as a statement that is representative of a view held by a substantial number of people. In contrast to slave-owners who advocate leniency towards slaves, they believe all slaves are essentially unsound as humans, that no sensible man should ever trust a slave at all, and their opinion is shared by 'our wisest poet, too'. For he (i.e. Homer) declared that (*Laws* 6.776e4-6.777a7),

> 'Far-thundering Zeus removes half a man's capacity (*aretê*) when the day of slavery takes him down.' Thus each party adopts a different attitude of mind: the one places no trust at all in the slave class, but, treating them like brute beasts, with goads and whips they make the slave souls not merely thrice but fifty times enslaved; whereas the other party acts in precisely the opposite way.[28]

When Plato is characterising the view that slaves are inferior in every way, he therefore immediately thinks of this passage in the *Odyssey* as evidence that supports the opinion. This discussion is part of his own consideration of how slaves are to be involved and treated within his own ideally regulated state. Taken together with reference to the Messenian slave revolts and other slave disturbances, Plato uses this information in order to infer two principles upon which slavery should be founded. First, slaves should not all come from the same country or speak the same tongue, and secondly, owners should refrain from treating them badly (*Laws* 6.777d3-7).

For Plato, then, the Homeric phrase sums up an ideological stance held by some members of slave-owning society and provides a launch-pad from which to engage with his own ideas about slave management and its role in his society. To have the phrase articulated by Homer in such a way is provocative to Plato, and encapsulates for him one view on slaves which is counterbalanced by its opposite. The appropriation of this Homeric phrase by Plato, then, is strongly indicative of at least a subconscious debate on Homer's views on slavery, conducted between the slave-owning Greeks brought up and informed by Homer.

The influence of Homer, however, spread far beyond the ancient Mediterranean worlds. For the southern slave-owning landholder of antebellum American slavery, the Classics offered a revered point of reference for the human condition.[29] A Classical education distinguished southern gentlemen, who collectively held a belief in the intrinsic value of classical culture, with George Grote's *A History of Greece* lauded by the *Southern Quarterly Review* as being 'essential to every library', and the University of Virginia insistent upon competence in Virgil, Horace, Xenophon and Homer as a condition of entry.[30] Thomas Jefferson, a slave-owner, and one with extensive intellectual influence, went so far as to claim that 'American farmers ... are the only farmers who can read Homer'.[31] In an entry in the diary of William Byrd, a large-scale Virginian plantation-owner in the early eighteenth century, he recorded that he 'rose at 6 o'clock and read a chapter in Hebrew and 200 verses in Homer's *Odyssey*'.[32] It seems likely, then, that within such an educational milieu, the treatment of the slaves in the *Odyssey* may have had resonances for slave-owning farmers and, moreover, may have impacted upon their own discourses regarding the maintenance of 'real' slaves.

One further example of the responses to Eumaeus' notorious statement seems to me to confirm the intellectual impact of Homer's epic on the theorising of antebellum slavery. It is taken from a work written by Jefferson himself, his unpleasantly racist treatise of 1787 entitled 'Administration of Justice and Description of the Laws. Notes on the State of Virginia'. In this he uses the famous line of Eumaeus, but in a new way fitting his own cultural context, which actually serves to distinguish ancient slaves from the contemporary slaves he alleges are by nature much inferior:

That a change in the relations in which a man is placed should change his ideas of moral right or wrong, is neither new, nor peculiar to the colour of the blacks. Homer tells us it was so 2600 years ago.

> Jove fix'd it certain, that whatever day
> Makes man a slave, takes half his worth away.

But the slaves of which Homer speaks were whites ... I advance it ... as a suspicion only, that the blacks, whether originally a distinct race, or made distinct by time and circumstances, are inferior to the whites in the endowments both of body and mind.[33]

In conclusion, the narrative of the *Odyssey* includes various tropes about slavery which can be plausibly read as evidence that one function the text served was to provide prescriptive *exempla* for ancient slave-owners. In particular, it offered paradigms useful to the household manager in his handling of slaves, paradigms which constituted ideological justifications for attempts to keep a slave in the ideal condition of social death. The *Odyssey* underlines the vital role in the training of slaves that psychological acclimatisation to such low status must play, and the importance of the relentless threat of violence in maintaining adequate levels of subservience and unquestioning obedience. It illustrates the decay and destruction which can meet a household in the absence of a master figure, and the troubles which disobedient or independently minded slaves can create for a household as they attempt social resurrection. It emphasises to any slaves who may be listening that loyalty will be rewarded. Conversely, it demonstrates that disloyalty will be severely punished, and champions slave execution as a solution, thus providing an intense, unforgettable mythical example of the implementation of master-class ideology. Such an exemplum would surely have helped to keep ancient slaves in check through the poetic enactment of mass execution as a punishment for an attempt at social resurrection. The *Odyssey* may not make mention of the exact sorts of foodstuffs that a slave should be provided with, nor the manner within which they should be housed, but it provides bountiful evidence, within the realm of fiction, of the ideological imperatives underpinning the institution of coerced and unfree labour. It is an ideology which might well have played an important role in the mechanics of the institution within the reality of the epic's audiences, from the earliest archaic times, through the Greek and Roman worlds, up to antebellum American plantation organisation.

Notes

1. For cultural materialism see further Sinfield and Dollimore (1985), Eagleton (1996) 198, Williams (1981), Wolff (1981). For cultural materialism in classical scholarship see Lape (2004).

2. Thalmann (1998) 15.

3. See further Dover (1993) especially 16. On Homeric didacticism in general see especially Aristophanes' *Frogs* 1035.

4. See further Breeden (1980) *passim*.

5. Osborne (2006) 144.

6. Heath (1985) 253-5.

7. See Hall (2008), especially 7-10.

8. See Heubeck et al. (1990), 262.

9. Anon. (1837*a*) 32-3, reproduced in Breedon (1980) 63.

10. Anon (1837*a*) 32-3, reproduced in Breeden (1980) 63.

11. Thalmann (1998) 58

12. See further Heubeck et al. (1992) 293. The meaning of the phrase 'how to endure their own slavery' (*kai doulosunên anechesthai*) has been disputed by scholars (see also above, Rankine, p. 40), most notably Beringer (1960), who argues that the Greek has a specific meaning of sexual bondage or concubinage. This would make the overall phrase more specifically related to the female slaves' sexual servicing of their owners (rather than, for example, the suitors).

13. Anon. (1837*a*) 32-3, reproduced in Breeden (1980) 63.

14. See Hall (2010) ch. 3.

15. Patterson (1982) 339. Strikingly, even Dolios, who has lost two children in the course of Odysseus' slaughter of the suitors, is nothing less than courteous and apparently affectionate in his reconciliation with Odysseus in book 24.

16. Thalmann (1998) 90.

17. Patterson (1982) 13.

18. Violence is, of course, perpetrated against other characters in the *Odyssey*, such as the suitors and the beggar Iros, and indeed Odysseus when he is in his beggar's disguise. However, Odysseus must make amends and atone for the deaths of the suitors in a way which he would never be expected to for his own slaves. Iros' and beggar-Odysseus' positions are somewhat more akin to the position of the slaves, but the violence is not condoned by the 'good' characters of the epic; rather, it is enacted by the socially transgressive suitors and slave-girl Melantho.

19. From our perspective, it becomes clear that Melantho is 'hedging her bets': with Odysseus absent she can no longer be sure who her owner is. From a purely opportunistic and realist perspective, then, Melantho might well assume that it would be provident to associate herself with the suitors since Odysseus' absence had become so prolonged.

20. Patterson (1982) 63.

21. That sexual promiscuity in a slave is a treacherous thing is foreshadowed in Eumaeus' discussion of his enslavement to the disguised Odysseus. Eumaeus tells how his Phoenician nursemaid was sexually lured by pirates and ran away from his father's house, taking him with her (15.417ff.). She is also punished in the epic for these transgressions, thrown overboard the ship they were travelling on after being struck down by Artemis. This episode provides a pre-emptive disciplinary model with ideological ramifications for the sexually active slave-girls.

22. Fulkerson (2002) 347.

23. For the presentation of Penelope's fidelity in the epic see further Zeitlin (1996).

24. The poem, of course, presents the fault as theirs, ignoring entirely the possibility that the suitors had coerced or pressurised these powerless members of the community. The vulnerability of the slave girls to sexual pressure and rape was brought out, refreshingly, in Margaret Atwood's novel *The Penelopiad* (2005). See further Hall (2008) 125-6.

25. Fulkerson (2002) 343.
26. Loraux (1987); Hall (2010) 82-4.
27. Nichols (1990) 23.
28. For the role of slaves in Plato's *Laws*, see further Stalley (1983) 106-11.
29. Fox-Genovese & Genovese (2005) 249; see also the essays by Monoson, Lupher and Vandiver, Malamud and McConnell in Alston, Hall and McConnell (2011).
30. Fox-Genovese & Genovese (2005) 250.
31. Fox-Genovese & Genovese (2005) 252.
32. Croom Beatty (1943) 229-30.
33. Jefferson (1787) 154-5.

References

Alston, R., Hall, E. and McConnell, J. (eds) (2011) *Ancient Slavery and Abolition: From Hobbes to Hollywood*. Oxford.

Atwood, M. (2005) *The Penelopiad*. Edinburgh.

Anon. (1837) 'Management of Slaves, &c.', *The Farmers' Register: A Monthly Publication Devoted to the Improvement of the Practice, and Support of the Interests of Agriculture* 5 (May 1) 32-3.

Balot, R. (2001) 'The Swineherd and the Bow: Representations of Class in the *Odyssey* by William G Thalmann', review in *Classical Philology* 96, 82-6.

Beringer, W. (1960) 'Die ursprüngliche Bedeutung von *doulosunên anekesthai* in *Odyssee* xxii 423', *Athenaeum* 38, 65-97.

Breeden, J. (ed.) (1980) *Advice Amongst Masters: The Ideal in Slave Management in the Old South*. Westport, CT & London.

Croom Beatty, R. (1943) 'Review of Louis B Wright & Marion Tinling's *The Secret Diary of William Byrd of Westover, 1709-1712*', *Modern Language Notes*, 58, 229-30.

Davies, M. (1994) 'Odyssey 22.474-7: murder or mutilation?', *Classical Quarterly* 44, 534-6.

Dover, K. (1993, ed.) *Aristophanes Frogs*. Oxford.

Eagleton, T. (1996) *Literary Theory: An Introduction*, 2nd edn. Oxford.

Fitzgerald, W. (2000) *Slavery and the Roman Literary Imagination*. Cambridge.

Fox-Genovese, E. and Genovese, E.D. (2005) *The Mind of the Master Class: History and Faith in the Southern Slaveholders' Worldview*. New York.

Fulkerson, L. (2002) 'Epic ways of killing a woman: gender and transgression in *Odyssey* 22.465-72', *Classical Journal* 97, 335-50.

Hall, E. (2008) *The Return of Ulysses: A Cultural History of Homer's Odyssey*. London.

—— (2010) *Greek Tragedy: Suffering under the Sun*. Oxford.

Heath, M. (1993) 'Hesiod's didactic poetry', *Classical Quarterly* 35, 245-63.

Heubeck, A., West, S. and Hainsworth, J.B. (1991) *A Commentary on Homer's Odyssey*, vol. 1. Oxford.

Heubeck, A. and Hoekstra, A. (1990) *A Commentary on Homer's Odyssey*, vol. 2. Oxford.

Heubeck, A., Russo, J. and Fernández-Galiano, M. (1992) *A Commentary on Homer's Odyssey*, vol. 3. Oxford.

Hooper, W.D. (tr.) (1934) *On Agriculture: Marcus Porcius Cato & Marcus Terentius Varro*, revised by H. Boyd Ash, Loeb Classical Library. Cambridge, MA.

3. The Paradigms of Execution

Lape, S. (2004). *Reproducing Athens: Menander's Comedy, Democratic Culture, and the Hellenistic City*. Princeton, NJ & Oxford

Marchant, E.C. (tr.) (1923) *Xenophon: Memorabilia and Oeconomicus*, Loeb Classical Library. Cambridge, MA.

Newton, R. (1998) 'Odysseus and Melanthius', *Greek, Roman & Byzantine Studies* 38, 1-18

Nichols, G. (1990) *I is a Long Memoried Woman*. London.

Olson, S.D. (1992) 'Servant's suggestions in Homer's *Odyssey*', *Classical Journal* 87, 219-27.

Osborne, R. (2006) *Greece in the Making 1200-479 BC*. London & New York

Patterson, O. (1982) *Slavery and Social Death: A Comparative Study*. Cambridge, MA & London

Shewring, W. (tr.) (1998) *Homer, the* Odyssey, with an introduction by G.S. Kirk. Oxford & New York.

Sinfield, A. and Dollimore, J. (eds) (1985) *Political Shakespeare: New Essays in Cultural Materialism*. Manchester.

Stalley, R.E. (1983). *An Introduction to Plato's Laws*. Oxford.

Thalmann, W.G. (1998) *The Swineherd and the Bow: Representations of Class in the* Odyssey. Ithaca, NY & London

Williams, R. (1981) *Culture*. Glasgow.

Wolff, J. (1981) *The Social Production of Art*. Houndmills, Basingstoke & London.

Zeitlin, F.I. (1996) *Playing the Other: Gender and Society in Classical Greek Literature*. Chicago, IL.

Some Ancient Greek Images of Slavery

William G. Thalmann

On 3 June 1996, the *Los Angeles Times* ran an article under the headline, FOR $35 AN HOUR HE'S ALL YOURS (IT'S NOT WHAT YOU THINK). The article told of a Spanish art historian in New York named Paco Cao and his enterprise, Paco Cao Rent A Body. For a fee, the customer got the right to do with him whatever he or she wished, as long as it did not involve violence or sex. So, for example, a woman who loved to make scenes in public but who had been deprived of a suitable victim by her divorce stood him on a Greenwich Village street corner and yelled insults at him for an hour. At Easter a church hired him to re-enact the crucifixion, and he was a somewhat similar prop in the window display of a local S&M store. This sort of thing, however, was the basic level in a sliding scale of services and fees. For $35 an hour you could get him as a completely passive prop. For $70, he would perform tasks as ordered and 'engage in active and dynamic conversation with the customer'. The deluxe service went at $150 an hour: at that price he offered 'total mind function'. He could substitute for you, for example, at a business meeting or a social gathering.

Although there is no sign in the article that he was aware of it, Paco Cao's performance of rental property vividly re-enacts fundamental elements of the conceptualisation and practice of slavery, in ancient Greece and Rome as well as in other societies. His entry level of service, as an inert prop, evokes the very basis of slavery, the notion, and very often the treatment, of the slave as a thing – a subject on which Page duBois has recently written eloquently in regard to Greek culture[1] – or as an animal. We might think also of the way elite Romans could use masses of slaves as a public display of wealth in a performance of social identity. What you could get at the next level – work and conversation – is Aristotle's *ktêma empsuchon* ('animate property', *Pol.* 1.1253b). As a piece of property, the slave was an instrument for performing work (at *Nicomachean Ethics* 8.1161b Aristotle also calls him an 'animate instrument'), necessary because tools cannot move themselves, says Aristotle. As *animate* property the slave could converse with the master. When he calls a slave an animate instrument in the *Nicomachean Ethics*, Aristotle says that one can be friends with the slave in the latter's capacity as human being, though not in his capacity as slave. He probably would not allow for *dynamic* conversation, since in his view the natural slave has only enough reason to be able to follow orders. But we might think of the slaves in Greek and Roman comedy, whose witty language often exposes the pretensions of the master and who are specialists at clever plotting, but whose threatened autonomy is more or less contained by play's end. The high-end service, involving 'total mind function', goes beyond what Aristotle would have granted the natural slave, but that mind function is clearly not autonomous. It is entirely subjugated to the customer and merely allows Paco Cao to perform services that go beyond labour and take the form of activities that the customer would otherwise be expected to engage in but might find tiresome. But this form of service corresponds to Aristotle's notion that ownership of a slave means that the slave stands in relation to the master as a part to the whole (Aristotle, *Pol.* 1.1254a), though in a way that Aristotle would not have accepted. It more closely recalls Seneca's anecdote about a wealthy freedman who wished to make himself appear cultured by reciting poetry at dinner parties but was hampered by a bad memory. So he bought educated slaves and had one memorise Homer, another Hesiod, and so on, on the theory that what his slaves knew, he knew too (*Epistles* 27.5-8). Finally, the coy disclaimer in the headline of the article, in its assumption of what the phrase 'he's all yours' will immediately suggest to the reader, points through its denial to the way relations of domination of all sorts, whether slavery or economic, class, or gender asymmetry, have often been expressed as sexual domination.

A legal term for 'rental' or 'sale'. at least in the United States, is 'alienation', making a piece of property another's. That is what slavery does with human property. It seeks to estrange the slave from his or her self by means of a possession so complete and so overwhelming that the slave is transformed from a subject to an object, loses all personhood and social being. Or so it is in theory, and to some extent in practice, although the reality in any slave society is much more messy: some slaves did resist, and in so doing they asserted a self beyond the reach of domination. In parallel fashion, Paco Cao was dramatising his understanding of the alienating effect of wage labour. As he expressed it, in contemporary western states 'everybody is rented in a sense. Everybody is paid for work. We think we are free, but that is not a real truth.' There is, to be sure, an important distinction between slavery and the lesson of his performance art. He was pointing to a disguised effect of economic relations. Ancient slavery was a more personal relation, economic in the root sense of 'having to do with household management'. It was not, in principle, disguised, despite forms of discourse that might seek to soften its actual brutality. Still, there are continuities, which – at least to one who approaches it with ancient slavery in mind – Paco Cao's performance brings to the surface.

These continuities point to one reason why it might be appropriate to recall slavery – in the present case ancient slavery – even as in this volume we commemorate the Abolition of the British slave trade. Not only does the example of Paco Cao reveal uncomfortable parallels between slavery and modern economic structures. We are not done with slavery itself. For one thing, it still exists, and in fact it is flourishing. Kevin Bales has estimated that there are twenty-seven million slaves in the world today, and that number is growing with modernisation and the development of the global economy.[2] Thus 'there are more slaves alive today than all the people stolen from Africa in the time of the transatlantic slave trade'.[3] Not surprisingly, human trafficking is flourishing alongside slavery. Although the forms of slavery have changed since ancient times and since the nineteenth century in the American South, in tandem with developments in economic formations, its basic character remains the same.[4]

But there are other considerations as well. We in the United States have been living with the after-effects of slavery for many generations. Many people, including some African-Americans, think that we should put slavery behind us, consign it to the past and, as they say, 'move on'. But it is, of course, futile to deny history and self-defeating to ignore the lessons that it can teach. An undisguised form of exploitation from the past might make us aware of the nature of less overt economic relations in the midst of which we are living and which may be all the harder to discern for that very reason, Paco Cao's performance art notwithstanding. There also is much to be learned from attention to ways of thinking about slavery in the ancient world that tended to justify and maintain slavery by constructing slaves as inherently inferior or as perfectly accepting of their lot in life. They illustrate, and again make more visible, widely accepted and often unspoken attitudes that today justify economic and other forms of inequality even in the absence of the actual practice of slavery.

Ideas about slavery had powerful effects in practice. Why is it, after all, that the world's two most prominent democracies, Athens and the United States originally, were slave societies? How could this incongruity persist so stubbornly? In the case of Athens, why did Plato and Aristotle so readily accept within the family the form of power that they considered an aberration in the *polis* as they theorised it – namely, tyrannical or despotic power, the kind they saw as exercised over slaves? More generally, how do otherwise decent men and women, fully equipped with the capacity for humane feelings, participate in so cruel and dehumanising a system as slavery? There are doubtless complex economic and cultural reasons, and even psychological ones; it has been suggested, for example, that in antiquity owning slaves might reinforce a person's feelings of self-worth as well as his social standing. But I want to suggest that in sustaining and perpetuating slavery a system of representation of slaves and slavery played an important role. For the master, it created a conceptual world in which slavery seemed right and natural, or at least necessary. The effect on slaves is harder to know. Certainly there was slave resistance in Greece and Rome, short of slave revolts (which were rare), ranging from breaking tools and pilfering food to running away. But we should not underestimate the power of a dominant discourse about them, either in supplementing and even replacing coercion in exacting submission from the slave or in making slavery appear to the master harmonious with the way the world is. Given this power, changes can occur only under the influence of an equally powerful system of thought. In the British case, evangelical Christianity helped bring about the Abolition of the slave trade and then of slavery itself; and as David Brion Davis has suggested, it may eventually have been abetted by an ideology of wage labour as a new economic form emerged in the wake of the Industrial Revolution.[5] In the ancient world, by contrast, no such rival ideologies seriously challenged – much less dislodged – the ideology of slavery.

As it can be pieced together from various kinds of texts (literary, philosophical, legal, and so on), Greek and Roman concepts of slavery, expressing a slave-owner's point of view, can be summarised in three propositions:

1. The slave is an object, or something that combines the characteristics of humans and things – Aristotle's 'some kind of animate property'.

2. The slave is an inferior or defective human being, lacking reason according to Aristotle (partly anticipated by Plato), but also morally defective, given to stealing and running away, and easily corruptible. Therefore the slave must be kept forcibly in subjection.

These first two propositions are compatible and more or less congruent; they naturalise slavery. But they are incompatible with the third:

3. Slaves can be loyal, capable of affection for the master and his family and of self-sacrifice in their behalf. They can be moral agents. This view is reassuring to the master (slaves are 'just like us' and not to be feared) and offers the slave a positive model of behaviour that involves acceptance of his or her status. It sacrifices naturalising slavery for an equally powerful idealisation (or sentimentalisation).

I want to argue that Greek visual representations of slaves often expressed the same complex of ideas. For illustration, I have chosen a sample of images that is anything but a systematic or complete survey but that will best make my points: mainly fifth-century Athenian vase paintings, with a few additional Hellenistic figurines.[6] My emphasis will be on how these images were informed by and conveyed dominant ideas about slaves, and my assumption will be that the primary consumers of these images were free and implicated in the slave-owning system. But of course any form of representation is open to various readings, which are importantly influenced by the reader's or viewer's own economic and social position. So I shall also, where appropriate, raise the question of the slave as viewer of vases, and whether, and to what extent, the images offered her or him a different 'subject position' from which to affirm an independent self. Images, like verbal texts, vary in their degree of 'openness'. Some of the following paintings do seem to offer slaves a position as viewers; with others it is hard to see such opportunities. And not all of the relatively 'open' images offer an uncomplicated site from which to resist domination.[7]

A dwarf guides a dog on a pelike from shortly after the middle of the fifth century by the Dwarf Painter (Fig. 4.1). As Véronique Dasen observes in her book on dwarfs in Egypt and Greece, this is a very accurately rendered case of achondroplasia: a normal trunk with disproportionately short arms and legs, a large head, depressed nasal bridge, prominent jaw, and prominent abdomen.[8] The painter has added to his ugliness by giving him very thick lips. Such closely observed detail suggests an interest in physical differences from the culturally accepted norm. But the dwarf's image appears less ideologically neutral once we view him in relation to the obviously aristocratic youth who is leading him and the dog. The dwarf is an adult, as his moustache and goatee show, in contrast to the age (adolescence?) of the youth. His stunted figure is set off by the youth's height. The two figures are complete opposites in shape of head and facial features. The dwarf's nudity (but for the *chlamys* draped over his left shoulder) emphasises his disproportionate body, whereas the youth is fully covered by drapery, but that is gathered tightly around him in a way that emphasises his buttocks and the elegant length of his right leg (that the legs of both figures are in the same position relative to each other encourages this comparison). The swivelling of the dwarf's torso, which is thus almost frontal, makes his body seem twisted, whereas the youth is in profile and striding forward, his whole body moving in harmony.[9] The faces are pointed in opposite directions. The dwarf, of course, helps to define the youth's budding elite qualities, his *kalokagathia*, and so class can be read on the body.[10] But the youth also helps define the dwarf's ugliness and therefore his almost certainly non-elite status.[11]

But is he a slave?[12] There are other depictions of dwarves in Greek art, and it is hard to be sure of their status. Dwarfism in itself does not define a slave – although as we shall see slaves are regularly depicted as shorter than their masters. But in this case, because his task – taking charge of the dog – is menial, there is a good chance that he is a slave. If he is, then his association with the dog as well as the contrast with the youth might suggest that he is less than fully human and thus would reflect the common assimilation of slaves to animals. To speculate further, if he is a slave the way that he is twisted and half-turned backward might also reflect the recalcitrance of a slave. Or so a slave-owner might be predisposed to view the image by the common view of slaves as morally inferior. He or she might feel the pleasure of prejudices gratified and might enjoy the slave's ugliness, not only as a curiosity but also because it, along with the striding youth, naturalised differences in status. But a slave seeing the vase might find in the dwarf's physical attitude, along with the dog's bared teeth, a welcome token of resistance. Here, then, is an image that seems open to differing responses, but this can be insidious. Identifying with the dwarf would mean accepting the host society's view of slaves, expressed

Fig. 4.1. Attic red-figure pelike depicting a dwarf, c. 440 BCE. Photograph ©
2010 Museum of Fine Arts, Boston.

here on the body, as humanly inferior. So if the image offers a foothold for slave autonomy, it does so far from straightforwardly. And how would a Eumaeus, who accepts the slave's loss of *aretê*, have responded to this image (*Odyssey* 17.322-3)?[13]

A hierarchy made visible on the body is prominent also in the famous picture of a bronze-caster's workshop that runs around the outside of a kylix decorated by the Foundry Painter around 490-480 BCE (Fig. 4.2). The scene can be read from the extreme left of side A under one handle to the extreme right of side B, where the other handle, with a blank area beneath it, demarcates end from beginning. A nude workman with a cap on his head squats on a stool beside a furnace, while a boy who is working the bellows peeps out from behind the chimney and, to the viewer's right, a nude youth stands in a relaxed pose. Farther to the right, another workman, standing bent at the waist and draped around the hips, attaches the right arm and hand to a bronze statue of a nude athlete that is now more or less supine but that will eventually stand upright on a base, poised for action. The head, still unattached, lies between the workman's feet. The statue's body, extending under the handle with the feet projecting into side B, links the two sides of the cup. On side B, two clothed and bearded men in relaxed poses watch from either side while two workmen – one again nude but for a workman's cap and squatting on a stool, the other upright and draped around the hips – put the finishing touches on a statue of a nude warrior with helmet, shield, and spear striding to the viewer's right. Thus the scene, taken as a whole, 'provides a summary of the major workshop procedures involved in the production of bronze statuary ... from the melting of the bronze alloy to the joining of one statue to the final coldworking of another one'.[14] Despite the continuity, however, the scenes on the two sides of the cup are relatively self-contained (it would, after all, be impossible to see both sides at once). Compositionally, they invert each other. On side A, two vignettes of labour flank a central standing onlooker, whereas on side B two spectators frame and draw the eye to a central group of workers and their product.

Further discussion of the scene is complicated by uncertainties about identifying the figures. I am going to read the vase as an exploration of different relations to work as defined by status, although other interpretations are possible. There is clearly a relationship between the two squatting figures on different sides of the vase: both are nude, both wear caps, and both are in a position that signifies labour and low status, one frontal and the other in profile with his buttocks thrust out. The other two workmen are also related to one another in that they stand, are draped around the hips with torso bare to facilitate work, and do not wear caps. The workmen on side B are distinctly shorter and in smaller scale than the two onlookers, and they are positively dwarfed by the even larger statue on which they are working. Size alone indicates that they are of lower status than the onlookers, who are, reciprocally, marked as of high

Fig. 4.2. Red-figure kylix showing scenes in a foundry, c. 490-480 BCE. *Above* left: workers at the oven; right: man working on a statue whose head is missing. *Below* two men working on a statue of a warrior. Antikensammlung, Staatliche Museen, Berlin.

status. The difference in status is reinforced by further contrasts: between work and leisure, between the squatting and upright postures, and between the workmen's complete or partial nudity and the onlookers' fully draped bodies.

Who these observers are is uncertain. Mattusch proposes that they are the sculptor and founder of the statue of the warrior.[15] Ridgway, who mentions a suggestion by Homer Thompson that they are the owners of the workshop, thinks that they could be 'visitors interested in the artistic production, or simply in the company of the masters, as Sokrates is reputed to have been.'[16] It is quite plausible that they are visitors, perhaps the men who commissioned the statue, which is clearly intended as a dedication,[17] and who are checking on its progress.[18] A clue to their status may be given by the oil flask and strigil that hang on the wall next to each man. If we think of these implements as having a purely signifying function within the picture rather than as reflecting some improbable circumstance in which oil flasks and strigils would hang on the wall of a foundry, they tell us that these are elite men accustomed to hanging around the gymnasium who are here as visitors and possibly patrons, not participants in the labour of production.[19] As such, they would fittingly frame the scene of work on the statue and draw our attention to it, as though we are invited to watch through their eyes and perhaps share their perspective on the work that is being performed.

As we have seen in connection with the Dwarf Painter's vase, and as we shall see again, the figures in this scene have to be read in relation to one another. Just as 'class' is a relational concept, the social identity of each figure (or its lack in the case of slaves) is best understood through the system of correspondences and contrasts that is created in the picture. I believe that Side A sets up the same contrast between craftsmen and the elite, but the contrast works somewhat differently. Here we have a similar pair of workmen to those on side B, but they go about different tasks and are separated by the standing youth. This figure, instead of helping to frame the scene, is placed prominently at the centre, and he is more an object of the viewer's sight than a means of directing it to the work being done. In fact, he may not be looking at anything at all, but may just be standing self-absorbed and self-sufficient. Who is he? A workman or a visiting athlete, suggests Ridgway.[20] An athlete seems quite possible. If a naked visitor seems unrealistic, so do completely nude craftsmen. But the youth's symbolic significance seems to override considerations of verisimilitude. He has the muscular and well developed body of an athlete, and his pose, with one hand on hip, resembles that of the two onlookers on side B; this suggests that he is of higher status than the labourers. In fact, he should be seen in conjunction with the statue that is being pieced together to his left (our right). Together, the two figures are a study in the athletic male body, one straining in, or just before, action (the statue), the other in repose. The placing of such a study in a foundry scene may have something to do with the statue as representation,[21] but there is, at the same time, a striking contrast between the youth and the workman towards whom he is turned.[22] If, on side B, the opposition between leisured men and labourers works partly through the contrast between clothed and (partially or

80

completely) unclothed figures, here it works through an extreme difference in posture of the nude body. The athlete's body is upright, as Aristotle says the body of free men should be;[23] the labourer's body is doubled over, folded in two. So, if the youth in conjunction with the statue embodies the athletic masculine ideal, the squatting labourer and the youth together define that ideal with reference to its inverse and define workers through the same contrast.

It seems to me likely that the two squatting workers are slaves. There are several markers of this status.[24] The most prominent one is, of course, their posture itself. Himmelmann illustrates vase paintings and figurines from the early fifth century BCE down into the Hellenistic period in which slaves squat or sit on the ground.[25] A dramatic parallel to our figures, which Himmelmann does not discuss, is offered by a black steatite statuette of the Alexandrian period found in Corinth that represents an African.[26] He is nude, his knees are drawn up to his chin, and his ankles are chained together; he is clearly a slave, or a captive soon to be a slave. In the second place, there is the decidedly unhandsome face of the squatting worker on side B of the cup. The caps that both figures wear appear on slaves in other vases, although free workmen can wear them as well. Finally, nudity can also mark the slave, especially in contrast to clothed non-slaves, in vase painting. The situation on this vase is complicated, of course, since nudity is the shared feature used to contrast the squatting workmen with the athletic youth and statue on side A and the statue of the warrior on side B. In Greek art, nudity means different things in different contexts;[27] but here it might well contrast idealised types of elite males and non-idealised slaves. None of these features in itself is conclusive; all can also be associated with free workers.[28] Taken together on this vase, however, they seem to point to servile status. But again figures in these paintings need to be considered in relation to one another, and another important consideration here, it seems to me, is the systematic contrasts between these squatting workmen and the ones who stand.

The two workers on side B are also distinguished from each other, not only in posture and degree of nudity but also in facial features. The face of the squatting worker is ugly, whereas that of the standing worker is indistinguishable from the faces of the two probably elite observers. Thus it is worth taking seriously Himmelmann's suggestion that the squatting workers are slaves and the standing ones are free but lowly craftsmen or *banausoi*.[29] If that is the case, and if I am right about the onlookers, the vase represents three statuses involving two distinctions that were conceptually very important in Greek society: first, the distinction between slave and free citizen, which separated even humble labourers who controlled their own bodies from those who did not; and second, that between those who had to work and those who did not.[30] The latter distinction lumps together slave and free labourer in opposition to the elite.[31] The slave works by coercion and the *banausos* out of economic necessity; both are smaller than the elite men on side B. The difference between leisure and work is marked on side A by the fact that the idle 'athlete' is supporting himself with a mallet, which is a larger version of the tool used by the workman on the right to attach parts of the statue together. On Side B it is marked by the contrast between the workers and the onlookers. Equally remarkable, however, is the difference between these diminutive workers and the more-than-life-sized statue of the heroically nude warrior, between his warlike pose, with spear, and their work with tools. The lowly are outside the heroic/aristocratic ideal but work in service to it – literally as well as symbolically, if the statue is intended for dedication and aristocratic display, and the visitors are the men who commissioned it. The scene thus reflects the aristocratic attitude to labour, as well as the definition of the free citizen of whatever class by reference to slaves.

Not all slaves are physically marked as such, of course, except (often) by their smallness. For example, the slave who massages his master's foot in the *palaistra* on a late-archaic calyx crater attributed to Euphronius[32] is physiognomically indistinguishable from the athletes; but his task, his demeaning posture, and his smaller stature mark him as a slave. So probably does his name, which is inscribed above him: Tranion.[33] He is a *pais* ('child,' a term often applied to slaves of any age), and he embodies, despite his well-developed physique, the notion of the slave as socially and culturally less than an adult male, no matter what his age.[34] The athlete has his hand on the slave's head and is using him to balance himself – using him, therefore, as a prop, an object. The slave (a girl with cropped hair or a boy?) who stands between two women on a red-figure pelike attributed to the Syriskos Painter[35] is likewise dramatically smaller than the other two figures but otherwise indistinguishable from a free person.

Another side of slave labour – work in the country – may be represented by a vintage scene on an amphora of about 540 BCE (Fig. 4.3). The full-sized man collecting bunches of grapes may be an overseer or the owner of the vineyard. The smaller figures in the tree picking grapes, with their prominent genitals, are definitely humble and are probably slaves. This scene is closely comparable to a picture of Dionysus in the vineyard on an only slightly later amphora by the Priam Painter (*c.* 520), where satyrs do the work of gathering the grapes (Fig. 4.4). A complementary scene on a krater from about 460 by the Orchard Painter shows the treading of grapes.[36] A bearded man wearing a cap who stoops at his work has a foil in the beardless and somewhat taller youth to his right and must be a slave. An amphora also decorated by the Orchard Painter shows a closely similar scene, but here again, instead of humans, satyrs do the work.[37] Satyrs, as slaves of Dionysus, are interchangeable with slaves, and slaves once again are felt as only marginally human, if at all. As Himmelmann notes, Silenos as well as slaves can be depicted in the frontal squatting position we saw earlier.[38]

Fig. 4.3. Attic black-figure amphora depicting a grape harvest, sixth century BCE. Louvre, Paris.

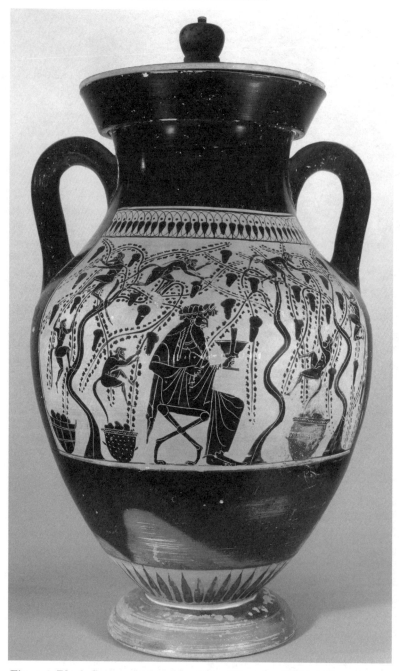

Fig. 4.4. Black-figure amphora depicting Dionysus under grape vines, fifth century BCE. Museo Nazionale di Villa Giulia, Rome.

Fig. 4.5. Red-figure pelike depicting women at a fountain, *c*. 470-460 BCE. Louvre, Paris.

To turn to women slaves with their domestic functions,[39] a hydria from around 470, attributed to the Aegisthus painter, shows three water carriers who are identifiable as slaves, partly because of their short-cropped hair, which is characteristic of slave women in Attic iconography (Fig. 4.5). Their tattoos also mark them as slaves and as barbarians, probably Thracians,[40] among whom, according to Herodotus (5.6), tattoos were a sign of high birth, whereas not to be tattooed was to be base-born. This is one vase that shows slaves without a contrasting free figure and therefore as the sole focus of attention. This picture emphasises, in and for itself, the 'otherness' of slave and barbarian that is the implication of Herodotus' statement about Thracian tattoos (and of course for a male viewer the slaves' gender and feminine task would add a further dimension of difference); but it is an 'otherness' that is at once stressed and tamed by these women's menial work. They are filling and carrying hydrias just like the one on which they are depicted. The vase itself, as an implement of labour, is thus a tangible symbol of the relation between master and slave.

If a slave-woman in fact used this hydria to fetch water from a fountain, she saw herself in this picture, and whether she was a Thracian or not she saw herself typified as 'other'. But she also saw her labour made an object of interest, and she saw depicted her contribution to the household.[41] She could see value in her work. That would be important for her, but we should be clear about the implications. To take pride in coerced labour might be a way of rising above her status, but it could equally confirm her subjection by making it appear something positive.

85

Another Thracian appears as a mourner at a tomb in a white-ground lekythos of the third quarter of the fifth century attributed to the Phiale Painter.[42] Her tattoos are most clearly visible on her arms, but they are indicated by lines on her face and neck as well. Her figure is balanced by that of the woman standing to the left of the tomb, and once again we have elaborate contrasts between slave and free: in the colours of their clothing, in the free woman's upright posture as opposed to the kneeling slave, in their hair (the slave's is short, as opposed to the other woman's long, luxuriant, and carefully arranged hair), and in their demeanour: the free woman's restraint contrasts with the intensity of the slave's mourning, a suggestion perhaps of the difference between Greek and barbarian. If Oakley is correct to suggest that the free woman is the occupant of the tomb and the Thracian is her nurse,[43] then this picture is a moving example of affection between slave and owner, and at the same time a visual instance of the representation of slavery as benign through the figure of the loyal slave.

Another nurse appears on a lekythos attributed to the Timokrates Painter from around 460 BCE,[44] but instead of affection we see something else. The slave, contrasted with her mistress by her smallness, her short hair, her black dress, and her frontal position, holds a child on her shoulders who is eagerly reaching out to his mother. All the emotional weight of the scene is in the relation between mother and child, which is poignant because the mother is surely the person being mourned. The slave is merely a prop, and she looks impassively out at us in utter contrast to the feelings at play in the scene that we witness but she does not. Except for her practical use, she is not there as far as the participants in the scene are concerned. This is a striking representation of the slave as instrument.

And yet her gaze outward from the scene and from the lekythos challenges the viewer – any viewer, that is, who is not disposed, as the Greeks so often were, to take a slave's presence for granted.[45] What is she thinking, this clearly unwilling and indifferent adjunct to her owner's expression of maternal love? What would she say if she had a voice? A slave seeing this image might well see in that stare psychological resistance and identify with it. This is one vase, I think, that unambiguously offers a slave viewer a position that is an independent assertion of selfhood.

There could hardly be a starker expression of the difference between slave and free in Greek family life. By contrast, the mistress and slave are exchanging looks on a lekythos of 470-460 BCE attributed to the Nikon Painter.[46] The mistress seems to be smiling; and so there seems to be an affectionate relationship between the two. But the girl's servility is expressed in the usual ways, her small stature and her short hair. In addition, she is 'obviously laboring'[47] to hold up the heavy chest she carries. As her legs (in profile) carry her away from her mistress, she twists her torso and neck to look back at her in a pose like that of the dwarf on the Boston pelike. This is clearly not the way an elite person holds his or her body on vases. On this lekythos, in fact, as on the Boston vase, there is a marked contrast with the more graceful bodily attitude of the owner, who is fully in profile.

Another female slave mourner appears on a lekythos of around 440 attributed to the Sabouroff or the Bosanquet Painter (Fig. 4.6). Her servile status is indicated by the footstool that she carries on her head (slaves carry implements on their heads on other vases as well) and once again by her short hair. She seems to be exchanging looks across the tomb with another woman, who holds a lekythos and seems to be another mourner. The first woman is in profile, whereas the second woman's body is in a frontal position while her head is turned to look at the other woman. Thus, although there is no contrast in colour of clothing (both women wear white dresses), the facial features – specifically the noses and lips – of the two profile heads differ markedly. The second figure is Greek, whereas the iconographically marked slave is African – or more precisely, as Snowden

Fig. 4.6. White-ground lekythos depicting a female slave mourner at a tomb, *c.* 440 BCE. Antikensammlung, Staatliche Museen, Berlin.

says, mulatto.[48] Africans were a familiar enough sight in the Greek world,[49] but this vase may be evidence of a tendency that grew over time to identify slaves with non-Greeks. In the fourth century, Aristotle cites a view among Greeks that the natural slave was a barbarian, and his own arguments tend in the same direction (*Pol.* 1.1255a, 1252b).[50] Not that all Africans in fifth-century Athens were necessarily slaves: rather, it became more and more the assumption, and to a large extent (though not exclusively) the practice, that slaves were barbarians.[51]

A janiform aryballos of the late sixth century, now in the Louvre, consists of the conjoined heads of an African male and a Greek woman, both carefully observed and portrayed with dignity (Fig. 4.7). The contrasts between their features, however, are dramatic – for example, between the noses: the African's broad and flat, the woman's slender and delicate. These janiform vases, often contrasting Africans and Greeks, became more common in the fifth century; they were mould-made and presumably mass-produced. This example shows that at least by the late archaic period the physiognomical differences between Greek and African were a matter of interest. In fact, this and similar vases offer a dramatic demonstration of the dynamics of reciprocal definition between Greek and non-Greek. It has been suggested that the African is a slave and the woman a prostitute.[52] In that case – to pursue for a moment what is only a speculative possibility – we could say that we have two categories of subjected and exploited humans, as barbarian and male and as Greek and female. This representation would have particular point in that an oil flask such as this one would have been carried and used by an elite male at the gymnasium and would have reinforced his own self-definition.

There are, however, no good reasons for these identifications as slave and prostitute, and they are not especially likely. But the juxtaposition of the aryballos with the picture of the mulatto slave-woman on the lekythos discussed above suggests that around or shortly after the mid-fifth century, in the case of Africans (as well as Persians and Thracians), the discourses of slavery and of ethnicity had begun to overlap and become implicated with each other.

This intertwining can be observed especially well in some striking statuettes of slaves in the Hellenistic period. A bronze statuette of a standing nude African male, from Chalon-sur-Saône and now in Paris but probably manufactured in Alexandria, is particularly impressive.[53] Although Snowden considers the pose 'graceful',[54] to me it seems painfully contorted, because his weight is almost equally distributed between his legs, in sharp contrast to the much more relaxed attitude that contrapposto would have suggested. As a result, his right hip is thrust far out, and not through any natural movement – there is no gentle bending here, as Snowden would have it. This figure is usually interpreted as a musician, partly because of the similarity of his posture with that of a stone figure now in Athens, on whose left shoulder is a remnant of what was clearly a

Fig. 4.7. Janiform aryballos in the form of two heads, *c.* 520-510 BCE. Louvre, Paris.

musical instrument.[55] Michèle Daumas, however, has made a strong argument (mainly from the position of the hands) that the bronze figure cannot be playing an instrument but must be lifting a very heavy object, perhaps an elephant's tusk.[56] Again, then, as on the Foundry Painter's pelike, we have a slave (or at the very least a slavish person) whose body is contorted by the demands of difficult labour, but this bronze figure is truly straining with the effort in a way that recalls the notorious lines of the *Theognidea* (535-6): 'never is a slave's head upright / But always aslant, and he holds his neck crookedly.' It belongs among a range of Hellenistic figurines of African slaves. The closest parallel is probably a bronze statuette from the

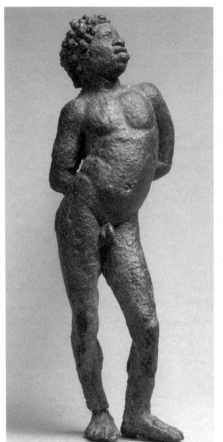

Fig. 4.8. Hellenistic bronze statuette of an African youth with his hands tied behind his back, second-first century BCE. Louvre, Paris.

Fayum and now in the Louvre (Fig. 4.8), which depicts an African also standing with his right hip sharply extruded, his right foot behind his left with both knees slightly bent, his weight again more or less evenly distributed between his legs, his torso bent in an almost improbable arc, and his hands tied behind his back (if this pose does not look painful, I invite the reader to try to imitate it while keeping his or her weight balanced on both legs). The bound hands show that this figure is a slave or a captive destined to be sold into slavery.

Do such representations convey a sympathy for the slave's plight that is lacking in earlier periods?[57] That is how we are tempted to interpret them, and how other such realistic Hellenistic portrayals of non-elite characters have been interpreted. But we should try to put ourselves into the mentality of a member of a slave society, to whom slavery was a part of the self-evident and unquestioned order of the world. Would such a person have given the human suffering caused by slavery a second thought? Or would representations like these have nurtured a new awareness?

We, at least, should want to give slavery more than a second thought. There are all sorts of reasons why studying the representations of slavery in the ancient world is useful today. It gives us a dramatic demonstration of the power of representation to confirm irrational prejudices and to overpower rational thinking. We can also gain an understanding of discourses that systematically seek to justify practices whereby some people exploit and victimise others. We in Europe and America abolished slavery, but many of those other practices are still with us: forms of economic relations that put many into the power of the few, as in Paco Cao's understanding that 'everybody is rented in a sense' by virtue of having to sell his or her labour. Ancient representations of slavery have many similarities with discourses surrounding imperialism, racism, and economic exploitation, discourses of self and other that construct the other as inferior. And as in antiquity, those discourses have consequences in the real world.[58]

Notes

1. duBois (2003).

2. Bales (2005). On how he arrived at that figure, see 87-111. On the economic conditions that are fostering slavery, see 88: 'The economic processes of modernisation and globalisation have pushed significant numbers of people in the developing world into social, economic, and political vulnerability.' Because of the rise in supply, 'slaves are now less expensive than at any point in recorded history'.

3. Bales (2004) 9.

4. Bales (2005) 68 speaks of 'an irreducible core of three aspects: the complete control of one person by another, the appropriation of labor power, and the enforcement of these conditions by threats or acts of violence'.

5. Davis (2006) 231-49.

6. Some of these images are illustrated in the excellent papers in Cohen (2000). The authors of those papers have some suggestive things to say about them but are not primarily interested in how slaves are represented; I think there is more to say. I have also been greatly helped by Nikolaus Himmelmann's 1971 survey of images of slaves in Greek art. He does not discuss particular images in much detail, so that it seems possible to add to his remarks as well. A search of the Beazley Archive with the term 'slave' turned up almost nothing; it is necessary to use as search-terms euphemisms such as 'servant' or 'maid' – a vivid example of classical scholars' discomfort with or indifference to ancient slavery, on which see duBois (2003) 6-29.

7. Lewis (1998-99) discusses the implications of slaves as viewers of Athenian vases. As will emerge, I think the subject is trickier than she suggests; and unfortunately I cannot see that her use of the term 'subversive' is justified. But as she well argues, slaves must have seen these images.

8. Dasen (1993) 172; for the features of achondroplasia, see ibid. 14.

9. The contrast in types of bodily movement between free and unfree is well discussed by Joss [Wrenhaven] (2006) 57-9.

10. The dwarf thus represents, according to Weiler (2002), 'inverted *kaloka-gathia*' See also Joss [Wrenhaven] (2006) 53-62. For evidence that there was a taste in antiquity for slaves with physical deformities and that the growth of slave children was deliberately stunted, see Weiler (2002) 23-4.

11. Dasen (1993) 166 points out that dwarves constitute an exception to Athenian vase painters' aversion to depicting physical deformity or mutilation, and concludes, 'this suggests that dwarfism was not seen as an irreducible monstrosity, to be hidden, but as an acceptable physical anomaly which could be shown on drinking vessels'. However that may be, the important point here is the contrast with the elite youth.

12. See Padgett (2000), 47-8: 'Everything about the dwarf – size, nakedness, deformity, subordinate position – emphasises his social inferiority. In fact, he is almost certainly a slave, whose foreign origin, physical deformity, and status as property make him the ultimate Other.'

13. For a very different reading of the vase see Dasen (1993) 227. She suggests that he has turned to talk to the youth who carries a walking stick on the other side of the vase, that he is exchanging a look with this youth in a sign of 'reciprocal status', and that the four figures are walking in procession, perhaps to the gymnasium. But it is unlikely that both sides of the vase formed a continuous scene because of the palmettes under the handles (contrast the Foundry Painter's cup, discussed below). But the two separate scenes can be related. Together, they form a study in *kalokagathia*: on one side in and for itself (the solitary walking youth), on the other in a mutually defining relation with the dwarf.

14. Mattusch (1980) 442.

15. Mattusch (1980) 440-1.

16. Ridgway (1977) 291-2 n. 11.

17. Cf. Mattusch (1980) 444 where she comments that the statue represents 'a standard type of dedicatory figure following specific stylistic conventions'.

18. Their attitudes of involvement with the work are as consistent with this possibility as they are with their identification as connected in some capacity with the production of the statue: the 'thoughtful concentration' of the figure on the right and the other's open mouth and restraining gesture (for these descriptions see Mattusch [1980] 441) – the attitudes of kibitzers.

19. On this equipment and on iconographic parallels to visitors in workshops, see Himmelmann (1994) 36-7.

20. Ridgeway (1977) 291-2 n. 11. Mattusch (1980) 436 seems to favour work-man, as does Himmelmann (1994) 7. The scene on a black-figure oinochoe of the second half of the sixth century (London, British Museum 1846.6-29.5) might argue for worker rather than athlete. On the viewer's left a workman squatting on a stool holds a piece of metal in a furnace with a pair of tongs. To the right of the furnace another male figure stands holding the end of the shaft of a mallet whose head rests on the ground; he must be another workman, who is waiting for the metal to be heated. But he is not leaning on the mallet, and he does not look particularly relaxed. By contrast, the idleness of the standing youth on the Foundry Painter's cup is emphasised, and so the parallel does not give much support for identifying him as a worker.

21. Neer (2002) 77-85 has suggested in other respects as well that the scenes on this vase (including the one in the tondo) are concerned with representation and 'the subversion of image-making itself' (84). It should be clear that, in seeking to identify the status of various human figures on the vase I am not making the assumption, which he rightly questions, that the painting reproduces reality; I am

interested in the transposition of reality in a representation of people and their relations that is informed by certain ideas about slave and free. I am speaking of a different kind of representation from the one he finds in his fascinating reading of the cup – one that is not self-reflexive but is concerned with real social relations. But I think that these scenes lend themselves to both kinds of interpretation.

22. There is also an interesting contrast between the youth and the workman who is assembling the statue. Both have one knee bent, and their other legs, which are more or less straight, overlap at the ankles and form opposing limbs of a V. But one is in a posture of work, with the body bent at the waist, the other in an attitude of rest.

23. *Pol.* 1.1254b; they *should* be upright, but nature does not always contrive that they are. But representation does not always have to concern itself with the way things actually are.

24. These are summarised, but without committing herself, by Pipili (2000) 155-7. See also Chadzidimitriou (2005) 136, who says that it is 'highly probable' that such features as a frontal squatting pose mark slaves, although for the most part she emphasises the difficulty of distinguishing slaves from free workers.

25. Himmelmann (1971) 34-8. The slave squatting beside the furnace may also have suggested the ritual of incorporation in which newly acquired slaves crouched by the hearth; see Joss (2006) 54. Lewis (1998-1999) 83 doubts that squatting is a marker of a slave, for reasons I do not find convincing.

26. Boston, Museum of Fine Arts 03803 – this parallel is also mentioned by Joss [Wrenhaven](2006) 54. The chronological gap between this figurine and the Foundry Painter's cup is insignificant because, as the examples shown by Himmelmann (1971) suggest, an iconographic convention evidently persisted from the classical to the Hellenistic periods.

27. A point emphasised to me by Anthony Edwards, whose comments have helped me sort out the questions here. On nudity of *banausoi* as distinct from that of heroes or athletes, see Himmelmann (1994) 37-9.

28. See Himmelmann (1994) 23-48.

29. Himmelmann (1971) 37-8. In Himmelmann (1994) 7-8, he does not make this distinction, whether because of a change of mind or a shift in subject (from slavery to realism) is unclear.

30. For the latter contrast, cf. Himmelmann (1971) 38.

31. Cf. Joss (2006) 54 on 'slavishness' as the trait shared by free manual workers and slaves, with reference to this cup.

32. Berlin, Staatliche Museen – Preussischer Kulturbesitz 2180. The other side of the vase also has two slaves who are depicted as miniature athletes.

33. See Himmelmann (1971) 27-8.

34. See Golden (1985).

35. Berlin, Antikensammlung 4496.

36. Ferrara, Museo Nazionale T 254 C VP.

37. Bologna, Museo Civico 241. Both pairs of vases are illustrated in Bérard et al. (1989) 134-5 (Figs 182-3 and 185-6). The discussion in the text is concerned with satyrs and ignores the analogy suggested by the images between slaves (or rustic labourers) and satyrs. The two vases by the Orchard Painter are discussed by Pipili (2000) 166-7, who makes a somewhat different point from mine.

38. Himmelmann (1971) 35.

39. Lewis (2002) 79-81, 138-41 gives an excellent discussion of the difficulties of distinguishing slaves from free women in domestic scenes on Attic vases and of possible reasons. She points out that as time went on slaves and their mistresses

became less distinguishable in these images and attributes this to a tendency to idealise domestic life. I will discuss vases on which the distinction seems clearly marked, but it should be borne in mind that painters could, and often did, choose otherwise.

40. Zimmermann (1980) esp. 194-6; Oakley (2000) 242; Tsiafakis (2000) 373-4.

41. On such cases, see Lewis (1998-99) 89-90. It goes too far, however, to say the 'the slave sees a heroised version of him or herself'.

42. National Museum of Athens. Inv. no. 11844. See also, below, Fig. 5.4.

43. Oakley (2000) 243; (2004) 164. For other examples of mourning tattooed nurses, see Zimmermann (1980) 192-4.

44. National Museum of Athens inv. no. 12771, viewable online at http://nam. culture.gr/portal/page/portal/deam/virtual_exhibitions/EAMV/EAMA12771.

45. Contrast Oakley (2000) 234: 'This wonderfully touching scene is one of the most moving glimpses of domestic life that has come down to us from Classical antiquity.' I would not disagree with this statement; it is a fair response to the scene between mother and child. It is, however, seriously incomplete. Although Oakley does describe the slave and notes that her 'dejected expression' shows that her part in the scene 'is work for her' (233), he makes nothing of the point, and his final assessment of the scene leaves her out.

46. Brussels, Musées Royaux d'Art et d'Histoire A 1019.

47. Oakley (2004) 46.

48. Snowden (1976) 166.

49. See Snowden (1970) 186-8, and note especially his comment (186) that 'a large, doubtlessly the largest, portion of the Ethiopians in Greece and Italy arrived as prisoners of war or as slaves'.

50. For a recent discussion see Millett (2007) 194-5.

51. See Hall (1989) 164-5, 193-4, and especially 196-7. Our written sources are mainly concerned with such peoples as Thracians and Persians when it comes to slavery and ethnicity, but Africans would naturally also be included in the same way of thinking.

52. Cohen (2006) 268.

53. Cabinet des médailles de la Bibliothèque nationale de France, Paris, France, accession no. 1009, viewable online at http://commons.wikimedia.org/wiki/File:Nubian_playing_CdM_1009.jpg.

54. Snowden (1976) 199: 'The artist chose a graceful pose for his subject[,] bending the body gently at the waist, and making effective use of the hands; and by careful attention to detail he created a sensitive face that ranks among the best in Hellenistic art.'

55. Athens, National Archaeological Museum 15170.

56. Daumas (1993). She also shows that the figurine is ancient and does not date from the Renaissance, as some have thought, and she argues on the basis of comparison with other Hellenistic depictions of mulattoes that it was probably made in Egypt during the Hellenistic period, most likely the second century BCE.

57. See, for example, the discussions in Pollitt (1986) 141-7 and Zanker (2004) 152-67.

58. It is a pleasure to thank Edith Hall for organising the conference at which this paper was originally given and for her superb editing of this volume. I would also like to thank her, her colleagues, and her students for their generous hospitality during the days of the conference. A version of this paper was also delivered at a conference on slavery at the University of California at Irvine in April 2008. I would like to thank the participants at that conference for lively discussion, and

particularly Anthony Edwards (respondent for the paper), Thomas Scanlon, Page duBois, and Noel Lenski. Finally, I thank Phillip Horky and Susan Thalmann for comments on the written version, and the latter for essential help in getting books and images.

References

Bales, K. (2004) *Disposable People: New Slavery in the Global Economy*, rev. edn. Berkeley, Los Angeles, CA & London,

———— (2005) *Understanding Global Slavery: A Reader*. Berkeley, Los Angeles, CA & London,

Bérard, C. et al. (1989) *A City of Images: Iconography and Society in Ancient Greece*. Princeton, NJ.

Chadzidimitriou, A. (2005) 'Distinguishing features in the rendering of craftsmen, professionals and slaves in archaic and classical vase painting', *Esclavage antique: Actes du XXVIIIe colloque international du Groupement International de Recherche sur l'Esclavage Antique*, 131-45. Bern.

Cohen, B. (ed.) (2000) *Not the Classical Ideal: Athens and the Construction of the Other in Greek Art*. Leiden, Boston & Cologne.

———— (2006) *The Colors of Clay: Special Techniques in Athenian Vases*. Los Angeles, CA.

Dasen, V. 1993. *Dwarfs in Ancient Egypt and Greece*, Oxford Monographs on Classical Archaeology. Oxford.

Daumas, M. (1993) 'Le nègre Caylus est-il vraiment un faux?', *Revue des études anciennes* 95, 191-206.

Davis, D.B. (2006) *Inhuman Bondage: The Rise and Fall of Slavery in the New World*. New York.

duBois, P. (2003) *Slaves and Other Objects*. Chicago, IL & London.

Golden, M. (1985) '*Pais*, "child" and "slave" ', *Antiquité classique* 54, 91-104.

Hall, E. (1989) *Inventing the Barbarian: Greek Self-Definition through Tragedy*. Oxford.

Himmelmann, N. (1971) *Archäologisches zum Problem der griechischen Sklaverei*. Mainz

———— (1994) *Realistische Themen in der griechischen Kunst der archäischen und klassischen Zeit*, Jahrbuch des deutschen Archäologischen Instituts Ergän- zungsheft 28. Berlin & New York.

Joss [Wrenhaven], K. (2006) 'Re-Constructing the Slave: An Examination of Slave Representation in the Greek Polis', PhD dissertation, University of St Andrews.

Lewis, S. (1998-99) 'Slaves as viewers and users of Athenian pottery', *Hephaestus* 16/17, 71-90.

———— (2002) *The Athenian Woman: An Iconographic Handbook*. London & New York

Mattusch, C. (1980) 'The Berlin Foundry Cup: the casting of Greek bronze statuary in the early fifth century BC', *American Journal of Archaeology* 84, 435-44.

Millett, P. (2007) 'Aristotle and slavery in Athens,' *Greece & Rome* 54, 178-209.

Neer, R.T. (2002) *Style and Politics in Athenian Vase Painting: The Craft of Democracy, ca. 530-460 BCE*. Cambridge.

Oakley, J.H. (2000) 'Some "other" members of the Athenian household: maids and their mistresses in fifth-century Athenian art', in Cohen (ed.) 227-47.

———— (2004) *Picturing Death in Classical Athens: The Evidence of the White Lekythoi*. Cambridge.

Padgett, J.M. (2000) 'The stable hands of Dionysus: satyrs and donkeys as Symbols of social marginalization in Attic vase painting', in Cohen (ed.) 43-70.

Pipili, M. (2000) 'Wearing an other hat: workmen in town and country', in Cohen (ed.) 153-79.

Pollitt, J.J. (1986) *Art in the Hellenistic Age*. Cambridge.

Ridgway, Brunilde Sismondo (1977) *The Archaic Style in Greek Sculpture*. Princeton, NJ

Snowden, F.M., Jr. (1970) *Blacks in Antiquity: Ethiopians in the Greco-Roman Experience*. Cambridge, MA.

——— (1976) 'Iconographical evidence on the black population in Greco-Roman antiquity', in J. Vercoutter, J. Leclant, F.M. Snowden, Jr. and J. Desanges, *The Image of the Black in Western Art*, vol. I: *From the Pharaohs to the Fall of the Roman Empire*, 133-245. Cambridge, MA & London

Tsiafakis, D. (2000) 'The allure and repulsion of Thracians in the art of Classical Athens', in Cohen (ed.) 364-89.

Weiler, Ingomar (2002) 'Inverted *Kalokagathia*', in T. Wiedemann and J. Gardner (eds) *Representing the Body of the Slave*, 11-28. London & Portland, OR.

Zanker, G. (2004) *Modes of Viewing in Hellenistic Poetry and Thought*. Madison, WI.

Zimmermann, K. (1980) 'Tätowierte Thrakerinnen auf griechischen Vasenbildern', *Jahrbuch des Deutschen Archäologischen Instituts* 95, 163-96.

Greek Representations of the Slave Body: A Conflict of Ideas?

Kelly L. Wrenhaven

Even a cursory look at Greek art makes it clear that the Greeks were infatuated with the human body. As Andrew Stewart writes, Greek art reflects 'an obsession with physical beauty, integrity, dynamism and power'.[1] Stewart's combination of corporal and moral virtues is well chosen, since the Greeks rarely conceived of them separately – a beautiful outer self was seen as an expression of a beautiful inner self. This idea is illustrated by the elite ideal of *kalokagathia*, a composite term referring to the virtue of being both beautiful and good.[2] In some respects, there was little difference between the terms, since the Greek adjective meaning 'beautiful', *kalos*, was not restricted to physical beauty, but, like *agathos*, could also be used to describe moral beauty, in particular nobility.[3] Yet the Greeks were not only concerned with the ideal but had a comparably strong interest in the non-ideal. By contrasting the two, they could better understand, modify and justify their own oppositional identity, thereby constructing for themselves a 'collective self-understanding'.[4] While examples of the idealised body in Greek art and literature are abundant, there is also a relatively high number of representations of figures typically considered non-ideal, such as dwarfs, hunchbacks and monsters, as well as barbarians and slaves.[5]

The ideal and the non-ideal are, of course, ideological constructions, each relying on the other for definition. However, although it might be true that 'we are now well past the stage of taking Greek art as a simple mirror of Greek life', the influence of ideology on representations of slaves in particular is often minimised in an attempt to determine what slaves actually looked like, how they acted and how they spoke.[6] As Nick Fisher acknowledges in his examination of classical Greek slavery, our sources often 'presuppose stereotypes and conventions, rather than social realities'.[7] While the sources must reflect or reproduce reality to a certain extent, they provide more information about how the Greeks perceived slaves than they do about actual slaves. Representations are not mirrors of reality but the products of choice – writers and artists chose what to convey, how to convey it and, not least, what to leave out.

As the institution of slavery developed and the idea of civic identity took shape, it became increasingly important to identify distinctions between free and slave.[8] In response the Greeks evolved a slave ideology, which I understand as a series of ideas developed by slave-owners to gain advantage over their slaves and to justify the slave-owners' power and authority. This ideology came to be appropriated by other groups, notably by less leisured free persons who, although they might not themselves own slaves, nevertheless identified with ideas about slaves perpetuated by elite slave owners.[9] As Orlando Patterson writes, for slavery to be possible, the master requires both the recognition and the support of the free members of his community 'for his assumption of sovereign power over another person'.[10] This 'assumption of sovereign power' relies upon the perceived inferiority of the slave, which is an essential element both to the success and to the justification of the institution within any given slave-holding society. In line with this, the Greeks frequently depicted slaves as fundamentally lazy, ugly, and debased creatures worthy only of submission and the whip. However, for slavery to be justified, relatively speaking, slaves should be useful. Though less frequently, they were also sometimes depicted in comparatively positive ways, as loyal and industrious servants, caring affectionately for their masters and working busily as 'bees in a hive'.[11] Slaves might even be idealised in Greek art and look little, if at all, different from Greek youths. The representations therefore express a contradiction necessary to the institution – slaves should have the negative qualities that justify their enslavement but they should also have qualities that make them desirable as slaves.

My aim here is to explore the seemingly contradictory nature of slave representation through an examination of the ways in which written and iconographic sources depict the slave's body. Aside from considerations of space, the primary reason for restricting my discussion to the body is because this is the most important location for ideas about slaves, who were, to all intents and purposes, 'living articles of property' or 'animate tools' (Aristotle, *Pol.* 1.1253b32-3, 1254a8-9).[12] By the Hellenistic period, the Greek word for 'body', *sôma*, had become a metonym for 'slave'.[13] It will be argued that ostensibly negative and positive representations should not be viewed as in conflict, but as different sides of the same coin – both are products of the ideology of slavery and are reflective of the qualities that masters desired in their slaves. The following will therefore challenge the view advanced by humanists such as Joseph Vogt that representations of good and 'faithful' slaves indicate a recognition of their humanity. Vogt, who saw drama as directly reflecting social conditions, interprets 'good' dramatic slaves as reflective of the reality that such slaves must have existed, 'for otherwise', he argues, 'society could not have survived'.[14]

Although there is some evidence of a degree of dialogue regarding the justification of slavery, this appears to have been restricted to a small group of intellectuals and, judging by the available evidence, did not reflect popular opinion.[15] The idea that the Greeks had a desire to depict the humanity of slaves in its own right is anachronistic and largely incompatible for slave-holding societies, where such ideas can pose a serious challenge to the *status quo* and might even be dangerous. To borrow Patterson's words once again, 'In our anachronistic arrogance we tend to read the history of ideas backward.'[16] The idea that slavery is fundamentally unnatural and intolerable in a civilised society is a much more recent concept. The abolition of slavery in the greater part of the modern world is, in part, the result of industrialisation – most human societies now have the 'luxury' to dispense with slavery (although this has not eradicated the problem).[17] The Greek evidence, on the contrary, points to a consistent effort to suppress any representation of slaves' humanity by restricting their represented characteristics, whether derogatory or laudatory, to those which justify and naturalise the institution. To put it simply, 'masters had a need to despise the people they oppressed'.[18] While the following will not deny that representations can reflect a historical reality, it will argue that it was not their purpose to do so.[19] It should be stressed, however, that by attempting to suppress the slave's humanity, the Greeks were, paradoxically, recognising it.

Manual labour and physiognomy

The slave's usefulness as a labourer is a suitable place to begin because it is one of the most important factors in how the slave's body and character were represented. The primary function of slaves was to provide physical service, and so, not surprisingly, written and iconographic sources tend to depict slaves occupied at various tasks.[20] Evidence for the types of tasks they performed illustrates the panoptic range of slave-labour in ancient Greece. Save for politics and some religious duties, slave-labour permeated every area of work, both private and public. Although in practice it was possible for some slaves to hold positions requiring a degree of intellectual capacity, the majority of depictions show slaves occupied at physical tasks, which might or might not reflect a historical reality.[21] Even if a slave is not depicted working, however, he or she might still be considered subject to the physical and mental degradation of labour. To this end, a consideration of Greek views of manual labour and its effect upon the body and the mind is important to the interpretation of slave representation.

The predominantly negative view of manual labour expressed by written sources is surely a consequence of their bias in favour of elite views and lifestyle – it was, after all, the members of the elite who had the education and leisure to produce literature, so it is their views that colour the majority of the sources. Philosophy and oratory in particular draw a clear distinction between the way in which slaves and the leisured free should use their bodies. While physical labour and the strength derived from it were considered the province of slaves, it was thought that free persons should focus primarily upon exercising their minds. Isocrates, in his exposition for the youth Demonicus, explicitly instructs him only to undertake 'exercise appropriate' (*tois summetrois ponois*) to his physical health, as brute strength was considered the mark of a slave (1.12, 14). In line with the Greeks' apparent inclination to measure the ideal by its opposite, however, there was the contrasting idea that sedentary work can ruin the body by making it weak. Crafts in particular required long hours of crouched or stooped work in doors, in dark, dusty, and sometimes noxious and dangerous conditions.[22] Perhaps for these reasons, Plato, Xenophon, and Aristotle considered that *banausic* (mechanical or base) labour produces people who are unable to practise excellence because labour, they maintain, produces people who are inferior in body and soul (Aristotle, *Pol.* 1.1278a22-3, Plato, *Statesman* 289c4-d1, Xenophon, *Oeconomicus* 4.2).

Perhaps as a result of the connection the Greeks made between body and soul – a pseudo-science called *physiognomonika* – the often derogatory representation of the character of slaves is likely related to the idea that their bodies were used for what were considered menial tasks. Aristotle's claim in the *Politics* that 'it is impossible for those living a menial or banausic life to practise excellence' (3.1278a22-3) is in line with Plato's claim in the *Republic* that labourers 'have strength of body sufficient for toil' but are lacking in intellectual capacity (2.371d-e). Both Plato and Aristotle notably exclude craftsmen from the governance of their ideal *poleis*. Likewise, Xenophon's Socrates represents what appears to have been the conventional elite perception of labourers when he states that craftsmen, because of their sedentary, indoor work, have bodies that become 'soft ... and this is accompanied by a considerable weakening of the mind' (*Oeconomicus* 4.2). It is noteworthy that our primarily elite sources generally make little or no distinction between free and slave labourers, since elites do not appear to have seen any significant social distinction between people who performed the same type of work. Although strong distinctions are made between the wealthy and the poor, the line between slave and free workers is rather more indistinct – it is therefore not surprising that in the political treatises of Plato and Aristotle labourers as a group were excluded from statesmanship.

The repetitive and potentially physically damaging types of activities required of slaves (whether crafts or some other type of physical work) differ considerably from the body-enhancing, outdoor activities of the elite, such as wrestling and gymnastics, or the mind-enhancing activities of politics and philosophy. Aristotle's implication in the *Politics* that the slave's body should be strong and stooped for performing 'necessary service', while freemen should have 'upright bodies (*ta ortha*) useful for a life of citizenship' (1.1254b29-31), illustrates the idea that slave and free bodies should be different – although, as Aristotle famously admits, no doubt from empirical observation, nature often produces bodies unsuitable for their purposes (1.1254b32-4). Here he expresses a conflict between ideology and reality, one that his presentation of natural slavery never really comes to terms with. However, as Paul Millett has argued, Aristotle, in line with 'Greek habits of thought ... persevered in imputing appropriate physical attributes to slaves'.[23] Aristotle is in agreement with other Greek writers and artists, who tended to associate certain characteristics with slaves, regardless of their practical experience of them. In a slave-holding society, and in particular to the elite strata which conceivably owned most of the slaves, justifying slavery through a powerful, if untenable, naturalising ideology was more important than realistic and individualistic representation.

The slave in action

The perceived lack of excellence connected with slaves could be expressed by depicting them looking and behaving in particular ways. For instance, a Greek audience would readily see a stark visual contrast between the slave character of comedy and that of the handsome young gentleman (the *kaloskagathos*) – comic slaves typically wore an 'ugly' mask, which was characterised by a snub nose, distorted eyes/brows, and an exceedingly wide mouth (Fig. 5.1). The masks, or more accurately headpieces, might also include red hair, which was typically attributed to slaves and, in this context, expressed the character's 'barbarism' and all the connotations which that term implied (discussed below).[24] These types of headpiece, however, might also be worn by other base characters (for instance, the lecherous man), so it is perhaps more accurate to contend that the 'ugly mask' is more indicative of slavishness in terms of psychological characteristics than slavery as a specific legal status.

Slave characters might also be identified by their body language.[25] Comedy frequently characterises slaves as prodigal eaters, drinkers, and gossipers, characteristics which draw a contrast with the cardinal elite virtue, self-control (*sôphrosynê*). In addition to expressing non-ideal facial features, the wide-mouthed slave mask was probably meant to represent the slave character's penchant for gossip, and perhaps also over-eating and drinking.[26] In what were probably stock slave roles, the audience of Aristophanes' *Wasps* is immediately presented with two slaves who are so drunk they can hardly stay awake, and similarly in *Knights* with two slaves gossiping about the goings-on in their master's household.

Slave characters also provided much of the physical action on stage, either running to keep up with relentless requests, or simply running in fear (by the Roman period, the running slave had become a stock character type, the *servus currens*). Outside of obvious advantages to the comic

101

Fig. 5.1. Terracotta representation of a comic slave mask;
Attic, second century BCE. National Archaeological Museum,
Athens, Greece.

genre, the running slave was a potent illustration of the idea that slaves
were not in control of themselves but were controlled, rather like puppets
pulled along by strings. In contrast, this type of frenzied behaviour was
certainly not one of the virtues of the elite *kaloskagathos*. In fact, Demosthenes associates the virtue of *kalokagathia* with a demeanour that is
'peaceable, hesitant, and slow' (25.24).[27] However, the slow walk of the elite
was also subject to Aristophanic parody, as seen in *Wasps* when Bdely-
cleon tries to teach his father Philocleon to walk 'with the delicate
(*trupheros*) gait of the rich' (1169).[28]

Aristophanes was clearly well aware of stereotypes and even plays upon
the conventional ideas of slave and master when in *Frogs* he has the slave
Xanthias switch roles with his master Dionysus during their journey
through the Underworld – Xanthias briefly impersonates not only a master but a god and, later, a hero (Heracles). Aristophanes' portrayal of
Xanthias during the first part of the play was clearly intended as a foil for
Dionysus, highlighting in humorous detail Dionysus' slavish shortcom-

ings, namely his cowardice and lack of authority over his slave – at one point Dionysus even lets Xanthias ride his horse. By the middle of the play, however, master/god and slave assume their conventional, and expected, roles. Before Xanthias' part diminishes in the second half of the play, one of Pluton's slaves even congratulates him for acting 'really slave-like' (*doulikon*) when he talks behind his master's back (743).[29]

Much of the behaviour that typifies slave characters in Greek comedy, then, can be connected with the idea that slaves were inferior and lacked control of themselves. The line between reality and ideology eventually blurred, and slaves came to be perceived as innately unable to control themselves. Aristotle reinforces this by arguing (infamously) that slaves only participate in reason, they do not possess it (*Pol.* 1254b23-5). This statement seems to imply that slaves, like other animals, have sufficient reason to perform their duties but that is all. Xenophon's Ischomachus, for instance, equates slaves with puppies and colts, each of whom, he argues, require the same type of training through the balancing of punishments and rewards (*Oec.* 13.6-12).

'Always in want of a whipping'

The slave's body is often illustrated as subject not only to manual labour, but also to physical and sexual violence, and even judicial use. As Page duBois argues, 'the abuse of slaves forms part of the landscape' of Greek literature.[30] In practice, violence and slavery are intimately linked.[31] While some violence was doubtless the result of irrational 'fits of rage' on the part of the master, most was deemed pragmatically justified and can be attributed to the need to control slaves.[32] Ilias Arnaoutoglou in his discussion of slaves in Greek inscriptions points out that the offences slaves were most often accused of and punished for 'are connected with the social position, role and expectations of slaves'.[33]

What is of interest to the present discussion, however, is the idea that violence reinforces the slave's perceived innate inferiority (both real, in legal and social terms, and ideological). While a master might use anything at hand to beat his slave, in written sources it is the whip that appears most often as the instrument of choice. Herodotus, in his story of the Scythian slaves, considers the whip so much a part of slavery that even the slaves' sons, who were half free, found themselves unable to resist submission to it (4.1-4). Greek literature furnishes a number of references to the flogging of slaves, where they are often accused of laziness, insolence and excessive behaviour. The term *mastigias*, or 'whip-fodder', was used as a metonym for 'slave' and is found in Old and New Comedy (Aristophanes, *Lysistrata* 1240, *Knights* 1228, *Frogs* 501; Menander, *Perikeiromene* 134) as well as in Plato's *Gorgias* (524c).[34] The association between whipping and slaves is not restricted to antiquity but is also prominent in later historical contexts of slavery – Patterson notably finds that 'there is no known slaveholding society where the whip was not considered an indispensable instrument'.[35] While there are countless ways to inflict physical pain, the whip has been the instrument of choice doubtless because, more than any other implement of control, it is symbolic of the slave's animal-like subjection to the master.[36] The dehumanisation of the slave is further illustrated by the very vocabulary the Greeks developed for slavery. One of the more derogatory words for 'slave' is *andrapodon*, or 'man-footed thing', a term which evokes the Greek word for cattle, *tetrapodon* ('four-footed thing').

While the whip was clearly used as a means of control and degradation, epigraphy provides further evidence for the idea that slaves were 'always in want of a whipping'. The law, as a 'conjoint expression of power and ideology' also reflects an ideology of slavery.[37] One of the more famous examples is the Athenian 'law of the coin-testers', proposed by Nicophon in 375/4 BCE. The inscription states that slave testers and retailers 'who do not act in accordance with the law' should receive 'fifty lashes of the whip' – free offenders, on the other hand, were fined the same number of drachmas.[38] In line with the literary sources, epigraphic evidence from other parts of Greece suggests that flogging was 'the standard penalty' for slaves.[39] Slaves could evidently be flogged for a variety of offences, largely connected with their failure (whether real or perceived) to fulfil certain expectations. A later example, the 'law of the Mysteries', from the Peloponnesian city of Adania, details some of the things slaves could be punished for, including stealing, cutting down trees in the sanctuary, and tampering with the water supply (92/1 BCE; *IG* 5[1] 1390).[40] It is noteworthy that these types of inscriptions represent yet another paradox intrinsic to slavery. Because they often include details of punishment, they attest to a strong distrust of slaves and the expectation that they answer offences with their bodies, while at the same time they also indicate that slaves were put in positions of trust.

The touchstone

A connection between the perceived untrustworthy nature of slaves and corporal violence is further attested by Athens' court speeches. One of the more striking (and contentious) features of forensic oratory is the existence of slave evidential torture, which the Greeks called *basanos*.[41] Torture was apparently the only circumstance under which slave testimony was permitted in court, although it appears to have been rarely used, probably due largely to slave-owners' concerns about damage to their property. By contrast, corporal violence was not usually permitted against free persons because, as Demosthenes reasons, they could protect themselves (22.55). Torture, much like whipping, made a powerful physical distinction between slaves and free people, the latter being, as Finley put it, 'human beings who are not property'.[42]

While there were surely pragmatic reasons for presuming that slaves might be reluctant to tell the truth (notably out of fear of their masters), the word used for the evidential torture of slaves provides some insight into how slaves were perceived in ideological terms. *Basanos* refers to a touchstone that can indicate the purity of gold.[43] In the predemocratic period, this term was used in poetry to assess human character.[44] Theognis, for instance, employs the term *basanos* to denote a test a man might undergo to demonstrate whether he is a 'true comrade' (415-18). In the democratic period of Athens, *basanos* retained its general meaning of a 'test' (see e.g. Plato, *Laws* 12.957d4), yet when used with reference to a person, the term was almost always restricted to slaves.[45] Therefore, while *basanos* continued to be employed as a means to identify status and worth, by the fifth century it appears to have represented a distinction between (Athenian) citizens and slaves.

The forensic speeches suggest that torture was deemed necessary because slaves were considered to be instinctively untrustworthy. Antiphon, for instance, argues that 'the testimony of slaves in general is untrustworthy – otherwise we would not torture them' (2.7). The existence of *basanos* and its frequent mention in the forensic speeches, whether it was practised regularly or not, illustrates the idea that truth was considered to belong to free persons, not slaves.[46] Not least, it is also a powerful affirmation that slaves were considered to be physical rather than intellectual beings and so must be reached through the body rather than through the mind.

Slaves in art: the relationship between height and status

The lowly status and correspondingly base character of slaves expressed by the written sources was sometimes illustrated in art by depicting them as smaller than free persons. Small slaves are often mistaken for children; John Oakley in his study of 'Death and the child' repeatedly refers to small slaves in painting and sepulchral reliefs as 'boys' and 'girls'.[47] Although size could, of course, indicate age, it was also used to signify status, in much the same way that Greek iconography and statuary often depicts gods as taller than mortals. This is in line with the literature, where size can be equated to status. For instance, the gods in Homer are, in their natural form, much larger than human beings, while heroes are generally conceived as being larger than regular mortals. Small size could also be used to show vulnerability and weakness, as it is, for example, on a plate by Paseas, which shows the tiny figure of the naked, pitiful war-captive Cassandra flanked by Ajax and a statue of Athena towering over her.[48]

The use of size to illustrate status (or lack of it) is also found outside of the mythic context. For instance, one late fourth-century stone (Fig. 5.2; 310 BCE) depicts a deceased girl named Demainete, and a female who probably represents a family slave. Slaves were often shown in grave

105

Fig. 5.2. Grave naiskos of a girl named Demainete and
a female slave holding a bird; Attic, *c.* 310 BCE. J. Paul
Getty Museum, Los Angeles, CA.

reliefs to illustrate family wealth and, as in this image, are usually
depicted carrying something for their masters or mistresses. Here the girl
towers almost comically over the slave who is looking up at her. This might
be compared to a similar relief which shows a boy, Deinias of Oê, standing
with his hand resting on the head of what appears to be a miniature
paidagôgos – the adult male figure is fully formed but unnaturally small.[49]
These images clearly do not represent a physical reality, but rather the
low status and vulnerability of slaves, even in respect to free children.

106

Correspondingly, slaves might be perceived as being in a perpetual state of childhood since they were felt to have, in some respects, a comparable social status to children. Neither slaves nor children, for instance, were regarded as capable of self-regulation, nor were they permitted to take a full part in Greek society. The difference was that the free (male) child could look forward to one day graduating from childhood, while the slave could not.[50] This ideological similitude between slaves and children is aptly expressed by the 'dual use' of the word *pais,* which could be used for children as well as for slaves of any age.[51] An equivalent practice of humiliation has occurred in other slave societies – in the slave-holding American South, for instance, male slaves were commonly referred to as 'boy', regardless of their age.

The barbarian slave

Another way of expressing the inferiority of the slave was to illustrate slaves with barbarian characteristics, which in turn might further help to explain representations of slaves as inherently cowardly and lazy. Although depictions of barbarian slaves to a certain extent reflect a historical reality – by the classical period, there was a Greek reluctance to enslave fellow Greeks – importantly for the present discussion, foreignness could function ideologically to create an even greater gulf between slave and free.[52] The barbarian slave was an 'Other' twice over, since he or she was not only unfree but also non-Greek. While the perceived inferiority of barbarian populations has been attributed to several factors, including cultural and political differences with Greeks, it is less often stressed that corporal difference was also a factor in how barbarians were perceived. Yet this should not be surprising considering the strong connection Greeks made between character and body.

Unlike the practitioners of racial slavery of the eighteenth and nineteenth centuries, the Greeks did not associate any particular skin-colour with slaves because, with the notable exception of the Spartans and their helots, they did not enslave people from only one region. While it is exceedingly difficult to demonstrate that the Greeks had a concept of race as it exists in modern times, let alone racism (though it should be noted that today the biological validity of the concept of race is increasingly questioned), judging by the available evidence, the Greeks did have a concept of physical difference, or perhaps 'proto-racism'.[53] The Aristotelian *Physiognomics* for instance, attributes cowardice to people with very (*agan*) curly and very dark hair, skin and eyes, as well as to those with the other extreme of very pale skin, hair and eyes (812a13-b30). Earlier on, Hippocrates had associated black hair with a lack of courage and endurance (*Airs, Waters, Places* 24), and Aristotle similarly associated woolly-haired Ethiopians with diminished intelligence (*On the Generation of Animals* 5.3.782b-83a).

The association between certain physical characteristics, cowardice and other non-ideal character traits, however, was usually explained by reference to cultural and geographical differences than to race. The view that very dark skin is indicative of cowardice is perhaps connected with the idea that too much sun exposure might result in a lack of energy, while pale skin was associated with too little sun exposure, as it was connected with weakness and effeminacy. A good example is found in Xenophon's *Agesilaus*, where he writes that since the Spartan soldiers saw that the Persians were 'white because they never undressed, and fat and lazy through always riding in carriages', they were no longer afraid of them, believing that 'the war would be just like fighting with women' (1.28).[54] Hippocrates, who was a notable proponent of the idea that the natures and bodies of people are affected by their location (termed 'environmental' or 'geographical determinism' by modern scholars), claims that the inhabitants of hot climates are flabby, weak and sickly (*Airs, Waters, Places* 12). This corresponds with Cyrus' statement in the final chapter of Herodotus' *Histories* that 'soft countries breed soft men; it is not the property of any one soil to produce fine fruits and good soldiers too' (9.122).[55] Cyrus' words strongly imply a characteristically Greek contrast between the 'soft' Persians and the 'hard' Greeks – that is, the former's disposition was thought to be due to their warm climate and correspondingly fertile land and the latter due to the poverty of their land and variable, harsher climate (cf. Herodotus 9.82; Thucydides 1.2).[56]

Artists would sometimes contrast slaves and masters by depicting slaves with physical characteristics associated with non-Greeks, such as light-coloured or reddish hair, non-Greek ethnic facial features, dark skin, and/or tattoos. An example of an artistic expression of the physical contrasts between Greeks and barbarians is a mid fifth-century Attic red-figure head-kantharos (Fig. 5.3) depicting two faces often thought to represent a Greek woman and her black slave. It is, however, unclear whether the man was meant to be representative of a slave or whether the vase was intended simply to 'exploit the contrast of racial differences', as Claude Bérard argues.[57]

While it is true that there does not appear to be anything disparaging about the way in which the black man is depicted (both faces are beautifully sculpted and equally attractive), the scenes above each of the two heads might provide a further clue for how this vase should be interpreted. The scene painted above the white female's head depicts three figures fully dressed in conventional Greek clothing associated with members of the elite – each is wrapped in a long himation, and the bearded figure also wears a wreath around his head. The two male figures, moreover, stand in characteristically composed postures, while the female figure elegantly gestures towards them. The scene above the head of the black man, however, depicts figures who can be classified as 'Others': a satyr and a warrior dressed in barbarian (possibly Thracian) garb. The pair's ani-

108

Fig. 5.3. Red-figure head-kantharos depicting a Greek woman and an African man; Attic, mid-fifth century BCE. Hearst Castle, San Simeon, CA.

mated pose and the warrior's non-Greek clothing draw a striking contrast with the comparatively calm Greeks on the other side of the vase. This is further stressed by the fact that the (Thracian?) warrior is running from his attacker in a decidedly cowardly and thoroughly 'non-Greek' way. While it is impossible to know whether this vase was meant to contrast a free Greek woman with a black slave, it does at the very least illustrate a characteristically Greek contrast between 'civilised' Greeks and supposedly wild and exotic 'Others'.

An iconographic example of what can more decisively be identified as a black slave is found on an Attic white-ground lekythos attributed to the Bosanquet Painter (Fig. 5.4; 440 BCE).[58] While the slave, who carries a small bottle and a stool on her head, does not have dark skin, her facial features indicate that she is African; her snub-nose and thick lips draw a strong contrast with the idealised profile of the woman, probably her mistress, on the other side of the vase.[59] Another notable representation is a fifth-century Attic red-figured skyphos depicting Heracles and his Thracian nurse Geropso, who is shown with prominent tattoos on her face, arms, and feet.[60] While tattooing was not a popular practice among the Greeks, it appears to have been widely practised by some other ethnic groups, most notably the Thracians, and Thracian women in particular. In Thracian culture, tattoos were decorative and might signify religious as well as other cultural practices. Herodotus comments that for Thracians 'to be tattooed is a sign the well-born, while to not be tattooed is a sign of the baser-born' (5.6.2). The Greeks, on the other hand, associated tattoos with barbarians and runaway slaves, who were sometimes punished with penal stigmata, and so considered tattoos signs of degradation.[61]

109

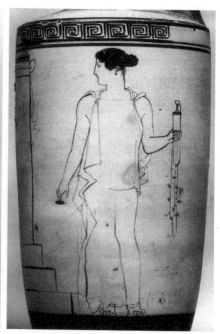

Fig. 5.4. White-ground lekythos depicting a female slave and her mistress attending an altar. Attic, 440 BCE. Antikensammlung, Staatliche Museen, Berlin, Germany.

Foreign characteristics were not necessarily considered ugly. Greek mythology includes black persons, such as the Ethiopian king Memnon, who aided Priam during the Trojan War, and Epaphos, son of Zeus and Io. Herodotus famously describes Ethiopians as the most beautiful (*kallistoi*) of all people (3.20). Yet, as Rankine has pointed out, the Greeks named the Ethiopians after their skin colour, so they 'did know colour'.[62] Greeks more typically represented barbarians as inferiors – free and slave barbarians are frequently mocked in comedy for the way they look and speak and are often depicted as rather stupid and silly. One noteworthy example is Aristophanes' Scythian Archer, with his poor grasp of Greek and correspondingly limited intellect (*Thesmophoriazusae* 1001-1225).[63] Tragedy also emphasises the barbarian provenance of some characters – in Aeschylus' *Agamemnon*, Clytemnestra clearly views Cassandra as her inferior, not only because she is a war captive but also because she does not understand Greek and speaks in a barbarian tongue (1060-5). Bérard has argued, moreover, that while there are a number of examples of black people depicted in Greek art, Memnon was never depicted as black and concluded that 'the artists were not able to conceive of a prestigious heroic figure as bearing the mark of negritude'.[64]

In short, when foreignness was represented in the fifth and fourth centuries BCE, it does not appear to have been something that was usually incidental or extolled but was more often used as an expression of degradation or, at the very least, 'Otherness'. While there were clearly political reasons for propagating the fiction of the intellectually and physically inferior barbarian, particularly subsequent to the Persian Wars, this idea was also useful, for obvious reasons, in the context of slavery. It must also be remembered that while many Greeks, such as soldiers and merchants, had actual experience of foreigners and were perhaps less likely to 'buy into' the typology, many more Greeks experienced foreigners primarily as slaves.

The good slave and idealisation

It is noteworthy, however, that some images illustrate not only characteristics associated with barbarism and difference, but also qualities that were deemed useful in slaves. The lekythos discussed above (Fig. 5.4) shows a slave obediently serving her mistress during a visit to a tomb, a characteristic one can imagine owners would want in their slaves. These types of images might reflect representations of domestic slaves in Greek tragedy, where they are often depicted as deeply loyal and caring. It is important to be aware, however, that some of the most faithful slave characters might also be represented as excessive gossipers, who pass on information that they should keep to themselves, or who do not follow orders properly. Some are so indiscreet that they bring ruin to their households, as in the case of Phaedra's nurse in Euripides' *Hippolytus*. Therefore, slaves might be represented as caring and loyal, although they are often put in positions of trust, they are less often depicted as trustworthy (as epigraphy and the forensic speeches also attest).[65]

Although the artists of the scenes on the pots discussed above tried to configure slaves as physically different from their owners, in other works the bodies of slaves do not appear any less idealised than those of free persons. A case in point is a fifth-century Attic red-figured *chous* depicting a bearded reveller urinating into a pot held by a male figure who is almost certainly a slave (Fig. 5.5). The figure's servile status is suggested by the fact that he is carrying the reveller's belongings, and, not least, by his assistance with the pot. Yet the slave's body in isolation is virtually indistinguishable from images of young free Greek males – his servile status is only made apparent by his depiction as assisting with the pot, and perhaps also by his short stature and nakedness, both of which, as mentioned earlier, could be used to signify low status and vulnerability. Although it is difficult to determine what exactly the artist had in mind (other than the joke that this vessel might have an alternative, less palatable, use), the purpose of depicting the slave with a nubile, unclothed body might be explained by the komastic context of the image. In addition to their many duties at symposia, slaves were required to be part of the entertainment, which could involve anything from dancing and singing, to sexual activity. A possible erotic overtone is further emphasised by the

Fig. 5.5. Red-figure chous by the Oionokles Painter depicting a reveller and a male slave; Attic, *c.* 470 BCE. J. Paul Getty Museum, Los Angeles, CA.

partially ithyphallic reveller. Attractive slaves would be very useful in the sex-trade – slave courtesans, for instance, are often represented as beautiful, a quality that would doubtless make them more lucrative assets and thus more valuable to their owners.

Another possible reason for depicting slaves as physically ideal is that beautiful slaves, like other beautiful belongings, were a potent advertisement of the wealth and good taste of their masters. It was certainly no accident that the noblest and most famous of heroes in the Homeric epics and later in Athenian tragedy were rewarded with the most beautiful 'well-girdled' war captives. Exotic-looking slaves, moreover, might have been considered indicative of the owners' wealth, as they were in Roman times. One can imagine that attractiveness would have been particularly important for domestic slaves, who would be the most likely to come into contact with guests. Slave narratives from the antebellum American

South comment upon domestic slaves, often chosen primarily for their beauty (which was usually defined in terms of their looking more European and therefore less different from their owners). Although such examples might suggest the reality that some slaves were, indeed, attractive (as some must have been), their beauty can be seen primarily as advantageous to the slave-owners' perception of their own importance and prestige.

The non-ideal as ideal

Non-ideal physical characteristics, however, might also be sought out by slave owners. Greek terracottas typically thought to depict slave nurses show strong matronly females with large breasts and hips and rather aged and pronounced facial features. Although such exaggerated features might be representative of comic costume (and so might represent comic nurses), their bodies have more realism than obviously comic figurines – they do not appear to be wearing costumes or masks. These figures might represent characteristics that owners would desire in their slaves, although which characteristics were desired, of course, depended upon the context in which the slaves were to be used. Slaves best suited for the role of a nurse, whose primary responsibility was to care for young children, would indeed be likely to be chosen first and foremost for their matronliness, loyalty, and perhaps also for their mature age. Beauty, on the other hand, would probably not head the list of desired characteristics and might even be considered a distraction (at least, to the masters and perhaps also to the other household slaves). Ischomachus in Xenophon's *Oeconomicus* provides some evidence for this in his list of desired attributes for the head female domestic slave – although he states that she should be temperate in eating, drinking, and sleeping, as well as modest, loyal and caring, he does not mention that she should be beautiful (9.11).

Ingomar Weiler assembles documentation to support the view that in antiquity there was even a demand for deformed or handicapped slaves and that these were sold in 'monster markets' – some slaves might have been intentionally maimed by their owners in order to increase their value.[66] Although considered relatively useless for hard labour,[67] 'monstrous' or handicapped slaves would be desired largely for their capacity to entertain, for instance, as dancers, musicians and jesters. The author of the Aristotelian *Problems* claims that some deformities could be induced in animals and humans, such as stunted growth through lack of nutrition or narrowly confined spaces (10, 12, 892a). There was apparently a market for thieves and other villainous people in Athens, the *Kerkopôn agora* (named after the Cercopes, the two monkey-like or gnomish thieves in the Heracles myth); it is conceivable that this would also be the market for malformed slaves.[68] By the Roman period, extraordinary and exotic-looking slaves were sought after by wealthy households, 'whose principal duty', Robert Garland writes, 'appears to have been to undergo degrading and painful humiliation in order to provide amusement at dinner parties'.[69] In short, what might ostensibly be considered non-ideal physical features could in fact be viewed as ideal in the context of slavery.

Conclusion

Although I have only been able to scratch the surface of the complex topic of slave representation, an examination of the ways in which the Greeks depicted the slave's body can tell us a great deal about how representation was used to illustrate ideas about slaves, as well as their uses (and abuses). As Hunter writes, slave ideology functioned 'to maintain both the domination [of the slave-owning class] and their legitimacy'.[70] Depending upon the purpose of the writer or artist, there were a number of ways of expressing the inferiority of slaves, and each of these plays into Greek prejudices, for instance, those against manual labour, lack of body rights, and foreign ethnicity. Considering that it was the wealthy who owned most, if not all, of the slaves, the representations are, in turn, coloured by elitist values, concerns and perceptions.

Regardless of what characteristics are applied to them, however, the sources largely depict slaves in the manner that owners wanted to see them. In this way, they aided in the construction of slave identity as well as in the oppositional identity of the master. Negative characteristics, such as ugliness and lack of self-control, actually become positive characteristics in the context of slavery – if the slave is ugly, this makes the master look better; if the slave lacks control, this is because only the master should have control; if the slave is foreign, this Otherness makes the Greekness (indeed, the civilised nature) of the owner explicit. On the other hand, positive portrayals, although occurring less frequently, might be seen as expressing precisely the characteristics one can imagine owners would want in their slaves – love, loyalty, industriousness, beauty and, in some contexts, even lack of beauty. In fact, when considered in this way, it is rather inaccurate to view slave representations in terms of negatives and positives, as each might be seen as benefiting the master, whether by making him appear superior to his slave and the slave deserving of slavery, or by illustrating the master's wealth and prestige. The institution ultimately depended upon such distinctions, regardless of how true they were in practice. It might even be argued that belief is in some respects more powerful and important than reality. After all, as Rankine observes, 'although these categories are artificial constructs, they are very real and they matter in the imagination and in the lived experiences of entire populations'.[71]

Notes

1. Stewart (1997) synopsis, inside front cover.

2. For a brief but informative discussion of *kalokagathia* and the opposite concept, 'inverted *kalokagathia*', see Weiler (2002) 11-28. For a more detailed and comprehensive discussion, see Bourriot (1995).

3. Benardete (2001) 3 n. 1 provides a suitable definition of *kalos* as 'everything outstanding in body, mind, or action'.

4. Halperin (1990) 99.

5. For a discussion of dwarfs in ancient art, see Dasen (1993).

6. Stewart (1997) 12. See Klees (1998) for a detailed study of the evidence for the experiences of slaves in ancient Greece.

7. Fisher (2001) 7.

8. Austin and Vidal-Naquet (1977) 18-19: 'Greek history ... intensified inequalities by developing simultaneously the notion of the free citizen and that of the chattel slave who was bought on the market ... and who (in theory, at least) had no rights at all.'

9. As Goff (2004) 9-10 noted in her discussion of ideology, 'what is socially determined, to the advantage of one identifiable group and at the expense of another, is said to be natural, and moreover, to benefit all groups'.

10. Patterson (1982) 35.

11. Ischomachus in Xenophon's *Oeconomicus* uses the metaphor of the bee hive; it is the duty of the Queen bee (his wife) to look after the 'hive' (house) and make sure that the 'bees' (slaves) do not remain idle (7.32-3).

12. On these terms in Aristotle see also above, pp. 72-3.

13. For a discussion of the usage of the word *sôma* for 'slave', see Ziesler (1983) 135-8.

14. Vogt (1974) 130.

15. For these 'anonymous opponents of slavery', see Cambiano (2003).

16. Patterson (1982) ix.

17. See Shaw's preface to the revised and expanded version of Moses Finley's *Ancient Slavery and Modern Ideology* (1998) which provides an illuminating discussion of the relationship between industrialisation and the abolition of slavery.

18. Hunt (1998) 161.

19. Similarly, as Hunter (1992) 36 states, 'ideology is not pure illusion: it does allude to reality and to real conditions of life. What is distorted in the imagination is the relationship of the individual to that reality and to those conditions' (276).

20. Millett (2007) 183, in line with Aristotle, writes that the slave's 'whole function is to be a tool and possession of his master; and, since he performs only physical tasks, he is part only of the master's physical nature'. See Aristotle, *Politics* 1.1253b24-54a13.

21. For the banking slaves Pasion and Phormion (and others), see Demosthenes 36. Cohen (2000) 130-54 provides the most detailed, if somewhat overstated, discussion of the evidence for 'wealthy slaves' at Athens, including banking slaves (134-5).

22. The real environment of workshops was doubtless quite different from the 'harmonious stillness' of those seen in vase-paintings and funeral reliefs. See Burford (1972) 70-1.

23. Millett (2007) 195.

24. Pollux describes the different types of theatre masks, including the red-haired slave mask, in his *Onomastikon* 4.119, 120. Slave characters are sometimes

given names connoting certain physical characteristics, such as Xanthias (red-haired; e.g. Xanthias in Aristophanes' *Frogs*). Consult Fragiadakis (1986) for a full list of slave names and the sources in which they appear. Some pots and terracotta sculptures also depict red-haired slave characters. Cf. Wrenhaven (forthcoming).

25. For further discussion, see Marshall (1999) 191.

26. See McNiven (2000) for a detailed discussion of how the Greeks used behaviour to distinguish between themselves and the 'Other' in art.

27. For comparison, see McNiven's (2000) analysis of artistic depictions of *sôphrosynê* in the context of women running and the comparatively stoic suitors from whom they are running (81-3).

28. See Worman (2008) 9 for the possibility that comedy developed from street revels, where the lower classes mocked the upper classes. Mockery of the elite body was likely part of a wider discourse of abuse, which, as she writes, 'appropriates various "low" perspectives as a means of reinforcing distinctions between friends and enemies, insiders and outsiders' (11).

29. On the theme of slavery in *Frogs* and its relationship to the constituency of its audience, which may have contained many recently emancipated slaves, see Hall (2006) 196-206. See Wrenhaven (forthcoming) for further discussion of comic slaves and their costumes.

30. duBois (2007) 437.

31. The essays collected in Serghidou (2007) notably explore this, from a perspective which associates violence against slaves primarily with fear of them.

32. Hunter (1994) 164, citing Wiedemann (1981) 10.

33. Arnaoutoglou (2007) 138. See Hunter (1994) 154-84 for a detailed discussion of the public and private punishment of slaves at Athens.

34. The abridged Liddell and Scott defines *mastigias* as 'one that always wants a whipping'.

35. Patterson (1982) 4.

36. See Hunter (1994) 168-9 for further discussion of the whipping of Greek slaves.

37. Sumner (1979) 267.

38. See Rhodes and Osborne (2003) 112-18 for the inscription and commentary. Glotz (1908) 571 has argued that the number of strikes slaves would receive was equivalent to the number of drachmas a free person would be fined for the same offence. For further discussion, see Hunter (1994) 155, 158-9, who disputes this idea, arguing instead that there were other reasons for limiting the strikes to fifty (such as considerations of clemency, cost and effectiveness).

39. Arnaoutoglou (2007) 138.

40. See Arnaoutoglou (2007) 138 for a discussion of this inscription.

41. For the references, see Demosthenes 29.5; 45.61; 52.22; Isaeus 8.12; Antiphon 1.13, 2.7, 6.25; Isocrates 17.54. See Hunter (1994) 91-5, who charts the 'instances of torture' mentioned in the forensic speeches. Gagarin (1996) 7 states that the effectiveness of *basanos* was never once disputed.

42. Finley (1998) 163.

43. For a wide-ranging discussion, consult duBois (1991) 9-34. She argues that the process of *basanos* might in part be seen as cleansing: 'The *basanos* reveals the good, separates base metal from pure gold, aristocrat from commoner' (15).

44. See Figueira (1995) 52.

45. An exception can be found in Antiphon 5.47 where a non-Athenian who appears to have been socially indistinguishable from a slave was tortured for evidence. See also Lysias 13.59, where it is implied that a man could be tortured

because he is not an Athenian. There is also some suggestion that Athenian citizens could be tortured under special circumstances, namely when it involved the safety of the state (for instance, when someone was accused of treason), though even in this case torture does not appear actually to have taken place. For a discussion, see Hunter (1994) 174-6.

46. This is further reflected in tragedy when in Sophocles' *Oedipus Tyrannus* the Theban herdsman (a slave) refuses to provide information until his arms are painfully twisted behind his back (1154).

47. Oakley (2003) 182-3.

48. Red-figure plate by Paseas. New Haven, Yale University Art Gallery 1913.169. For the image and a discussion, see Bonfante (1989) 560. There are other representations of this same scene where Cassandra is not depicted as abnormally small. An example is a red-figure kylix by the Codros Painter (440 BCE) now in the Louvre (Inv. G. 458).

49. Athens National Museum 934. For a drawing of the relief, see Clairmont (1993) 0.930 (Plates Volume) and the accompanying description (Vol. 1). The inscription, *IG* II.2 7816, reads 'Deinias Ôathen [*sic*]', who was evidently of citizen family. Other members of his family appear on a loutrophoros (2.852 = *IG* II.2 7825.)

50. Of course, ideology and reality do not always intersect. Some slaves found themselves in a liminal status between slave and free and were permitted to run businesses as well as their own households. The phrase *chôris oikountes* is used by modern scholars to describe slaves who were already living apart from their masters in a quasi-free, self-supporting condition. There is evidence for slaves who lived apart from their masters, supporting themselves with their earnings and paying their masters what was probably a monthly fee. Syros in Menander's *Epitrepontes* is one example (379-380); see further Proffitt, below, Chapter 8. Similarly, Demosthenes mentions a slave called Lampis, who had a wife and children (34.37). Consult Cohen (2000) 130-2 for a discussion of *chôris oikountes* slaves and the related scholarship.

51. For a discussion of the term *pais*, see Golden (1985) 101, where he argues that the dual use of *pais* can be understood as a consequence of the slave and the youth's 'similar status within the Athenian social structure'.

52. While there are instances of Greeks enslaving other Greeks, by the fifth century, at least, these appear to have been exceptions to the rule. Herodotus, for instance, expresses surprise that the Lesbians once enslaved the Arisbians 'even though they were blood-relatives' (1.151). For a discussion of the foreign sources of Greek slaves, see Cartledge (1993) 136-40.

53. This is the term used by Isaac (2006) in his study of the development of racism in the ancient world.

54. Translation adapted from Marchant and Bowersock (1925). Cf. Bonfante (1989) 555.

55. Tr. de Sélincourt (1954).

56. The Greeks of Asia Minor, on the other hand, were thought to have characteristics of both Greeks and barbarians, due to their liminal location between Greece and Persia. This intermediate position suits the Ionians' lack of consistent commitment to either side during the Persian War (as illustrated by Herodotus) and might help to explain, to a Greek audience at least, why they were unwilling 'to undergo *ponoi* during the Ionian Revolt'. Quote from Thomas (2000) 105-6. In Herodotus, moreover, the Ionians are accused of 'living soft' (6.11).

57. Bérard (2000) 409.

58. Oakley (2000) 245. Compare Thalmann's discussion, above pp. 87-8 and Fig. 4.6.

59. See Oakley (2000) 239 fig. 9.6 for a similar example of a black female servant and her mistress.

60. Attributed to the Pistoxenos Painter, *c.* 460 BCE. Schwerin, Kunstsammlungen, Staatliches Museum 708. For the image, see Tsiafakis (2000) 374 fig. 14.4. In his study of 'stigmata' in the ancient world, Jones (1987) finds that tattooing 'was associated above all with the Thracians' and gives several literary and iconographic examples (145-6).

61. On slaves and tattooing see also pp. 85-7, 109. There is some evidence that the Greeks adopted penal tattooing from the Persians. In Greek society, it was used it as a way to punish and mark out runaway slaves. See Jones (1987) 146. In Aristophanes' *Birds*, a runaway slave is referred to as a 'multi-coloured grouse' (760-1). Cf. Aristophanes, *Lyistrata.* 330-1 for another references to tattooed (female) slaves.

62. Rankine (2006) 5. The Greek term *aithiops* means 'Burnt-Face'.

63. See Hall (1989) 38-54 for a detailed discussion of the scene and its importance in the study of ancient slavery.

64. Bérard (2000) 402.

65. See Hall (1997) 110-17.

66. Weiler (2002) 23-4.

67. Pericles allegedly commented when he saw a slave fall from a tree: 'There's another *paidagôgos*' (Hieronymos of Rhodes ap. Stobaeum, *Florilegium* 31.121).

68. Suda s.v. *Harpokration* and Hesychius s.v. *agora Kerkopon*; Diogenes Laertius 9.114; cf. Weiler (2002) 23. The Roman equivalent might have been the so-called *teratôn agora* (see Plutarch, *Moralia* 520c); Garland (1995) 47.

69. Garland (1995) 46.

70. Hunter (1992) 276.

71. Rankine (2006) 7.

References

Arnatoglou, I. (2007) 'Fear of slaves in ancient Greek legal texts', in A. Serghidou (ed.) *Fear of Slaves – Fear of Enslavement in the Ancient Mediterranean.* Paris.

Austin, M.M. and Vidal-Naquet, P. (1977) *Economic and Social History of Ancient Greece: An Introduction.* London.

Benardete, S. (tr.) (2001) *Plato's Symposium*, with commentaries by A. Bloom and S. Benardete. Chicago, IL & London.

Bérard, C. (2000). 'The image of the other and the foreign hero', in B. Cohen (ed.) *Not the Classical Ideal.* Leiden.

Bonfante, L. (1989) 'Nudity as a costume in Classical art', *American Journal of Archaeology* 93, 543-70.

Burford, A. (1972) *Craftsmen in Greek and Roman Society.* London.

Bourriot, F. (1995) *Kalos Kagathos. Kalokagathia: D'un terme de propagande de sophistes à une notion sociale et philosophique: Étude d'histoire athénienne.* Hildesheim.

Cambiano, G. (2003) 'Aristotle and the anonymous opponents of slavery', in M.I. Finley (ed.) *Classical Slavery*, new edn. London.

Cartledge, P. (1993) *The Greeks: A Portrait of Self and Others.* Oxford.

Clairmont, C.W. (1993). *Classical Attic Tombstones*, vol. 1. Kilchberg, Switzerland.

Cohen, E.E. (2000) *The Athenian Nation.* Princeton, NJ.

Dasen, V. (1993) *Dwarfs in Ancient Egypt and Greece.* Oxford.

5. Greek Representations of the Slave Body: A Conflict of Ideas?

De Sélincourt, A. (tr.) (1954) *Herodotus: The Histories*. London.

duBois, P. (1991). *Torture and Truth*. New York & London

—— (2007) '*The Coarsest Demand*: utopia and the fear of slaves', in A. Serghidou (ed.) *Fear of Slaves – Fear of Enslavement in the Ancient Mediterranean*. Paris.

Figueira, T.J. (1995) '*KHRÊMATA*: acquisition and possession in archaic Greece', in K.D. Irani and M. Silver (eds) *Social Justice in the Ancient World*, 41-60. Westport, CT.

Fragiadakis, C. (1986) 'Die attischen Sklavennamen von der spätarchaischen Epoche bis in die römische Kaiserzeit: eine historische und soziologische Untersuchung', Diss. Mannheim

Finley, M.I. (1998) *Ancient Slavery and Modern Ideology*, expanded and republished with an introduction by B. Shaw. Princeton, NJ.

Fisher, N.R.E. (2001) *Slavery in Classical Greece*. London.

Glotz, G. (1908) 'Les esclaves et la peine du fouet en droit grec', *Académie des inscriptions et belles lettres, comptes rendus* 52, 571-87. Paris.

Goff, B. (2004) *Citizen Bacchaee*. Berkeley, CA & London.

Golden, M. (1985) '*Pais*, "child" and "slave"', *Antiquité classique* 54, 91-104.

Gagarin, M. (1996) 'The torture of slaves in Athenian law', *Classical Philology* 91, 1-18.

Garland, R. (1995) *The Eye of the Beholder: Deformity and Disability in the Graeco-Roman World*. London & Ithaca, NY.

Hall, E. (1989) 'The Archer Scene in Aristophanes' *Thesmophoriazusae*', *Philologus* 133, 38-54, revised version in Hall (2006) ch. 8.

—— (1997) 'The sociology of Athenian tragedy', in P.E. Easterling (ed.) *The Cambridge Companion to Greek Tragedy*, 93-126. Cambridge.

—— (2006) *The Theatrical Cast of Athens*. Oxford.

Halperin, D. (1990) *One Hundred Years of Homosexuality*. London & New York.

Hunt, P. (1998) *Slaves, Warfare, and Ideology in the Greek Historians*. Cambridge.

Hunter, V. (1992) 'Constructing the body of the citizen: corporal punishment in Classical Athens', *Échos du monde classique/Classical Views* 36, 271-91.

—— (1994) *Policing Athens*. Princeton, NJ.

Isaac, B. (2006) *The Invention of Racism in Classical Antiquity*. Princeton, NJ & Oxford

Jones, C.P. (1987) 'Stigma: tattooing and branding in Graeco-Roman antiquity', *Journal of Roman Studies* 77, 139-55.

Klees, H. (1998) *Sklavenleben im klassichen Griechenland*. Stuttgart.

Manring, M.M. (1998) *Slave in a Box: The Strange Career of Aunt Jemima*. Charlottesville, VA & London

Marshall, C.W. (1999) 'Some fifth-century masking conventions', *Greece & Rome* 46, 188-202.

Marchant, E.F and Bowersock, G. (tr.) (1925 [1968]) *Xenophon: Scripta Minora – Hiero. Agesilaus. Constitution of the Lacedaemonians. Ways and Means. Cavalry Commander. Art of Horsemanship. On Hunting. Constitution of the Athenians*, Loeb Classical Library. London & Cambridge, MA.

McNiven, T. (2000) 'Behaving like an Other: telltale gestures in Athenian vase painting', in Beth Cohen (ed.) *Not the Classical Ideal*, 71-97. Leiden.

Mirhady, D. (2000) 'The Athenian rationale for torture', in J.C. Edmondson and V. Hunter (eds) *Law and Social Status in Classical Athens*, 68-70. Oxford.

Millett, P. (2007) 'Aristotle and slavery in Athens', *Greece & Rome* 54, 178-209.

Oakley, J.H. (2000) 'Some "other" members of the Athenian household: maids and their mistresses in fifth-century Athenian art', Beth Cohen (ed.) *Not the Classical Ideal*, 227-47. Leiden.

—— (2003) 'Death and the child', in J. Neils and J.H. Oakley (eds), *Coming of Age in Ancient Greece: Images of Childhood from the Classical Past*, 163-94. New Haven, CT & London.

Patterson, O. (1982) *Slavery and Social Death: A Comparative Study*. Cambridge, MA & London.

Rankine, P.D. (2006) *Ulysses in Black*. Madison, WI.

Rhodes, P.J. and Osborne, R. (2003) *Greek Historical Inscriptions 404-323 BC*. Oxford .

Serghidou, A. (ed.) (2007) *Fear of Slaves – Fear of Enslavement in the Ancient Mediterranean*. Paris.

Stewart, A. (1997) *Art, Desire, and the Body in Ancient Greece*. New York & Melbourne.

Sumner, Colin (1979) *Reading Ideologies: An Investigation into the Marxist Theory of Ideology and Law*. London.

Thomas, R. (2000) *Herodotus in Context*. Cambridge.

Tsiafakis, D. (2000) 'The allure and repulsion of Thracians in the art of Classical Athens', in Beth Cohen (ed.) *Not the Classical Ideal*, 364-89. Leiden.

Vogt, J. (1974). *Ancient Slavery and the Ideal of Man,* tr. T. Wiedemann. Oxford.

Weiler, I. (2002) 'Inverted *kalokagathia*', in T. Wiedmann and J. Gardner (eds) *Representing the Body of the Slave*. London.

Worman, N. (2008) *Abusive Mouths in Classical Athens*. Cambridge.

Wrenhaven, K.L. (forthcoming) 'A comedy of errors: the comic slave in Greek art', in B. Akrigg and R. Tordoff (eds) *Slaves and Slavery in Ancient Greek Comic Drama*. Toronto.

Ziesler, J.A. (1983) '*Sôma* in the Septuagint', *Novum Testamentum* 25, 133-45.

Slavery and Freedom in Euripides' *Cyclops*

Boris Nikolsky

One of the distinguishing features of the early nineteenth-century Russian liberal movement was the twofold nature of its objectives. It strove both for the abolition of slavery in its specific Russian form of serfdom and for a constitutional reform that would put an end to monarchial absolutism. These two aims were fundamentally interrelated on a conceptual level: it seemed futile as well as irrational to seek political rights and a constitution without abolishing serfdom and granting human rights to everyone.[1]

In addition to the logical relationship between these endeavours, there was another way in which they were connected. Two types of oppression, social in the form of serfdom and political in the form of absolutism, were considered comparable to each other and it was the same metaphor and imagery of slavery that was applied to both of them. The words 'slavery' and 'slave' in both senses, social and political, are found in the political literature of that period, as well as in liberal poetry, for example, in Pushkin's lyrics of the late 1810s. In his *Ode to Liberty* (1817), the main theme of which is the obligation of rulers to obey to the authority of laws, the words 'slavery' and 'slaves' are applied to the condition of people living under a tyrannical regime.

> Tremble, you tyrants of the earth!
> Fate's random minions, heed and cower!
> Awake, you bondsmen of their power!
> Rise up, I say, and show your worth!
> Looking around I ever face
> Whips upon whips and fetters groaning,
> Laws' peril in a world's disgrace,
> And helpless slaves for the ever moaning;
> Arrayed on every hand I mark
> Dense superstition, fatal craving
> For fame, and genius for enslaving,
> And unjust power thunder-dark.

In his ironic eclogue 'The Village' (1819) Pushkin used the motif of slavery and freedom in both of its senses, contrasting the 'slavery' of the serfs to the 'freedom' of the hero taking refuge in his village 'to adore Law in his free soul'.

There is, moreover, yet another sense in which Pushkin used this motif. One year earlier, in 1818, he had written the poem 'The Triumph of Bacchus', which pictured the procession of Bacchus victoriously returning from India. This joyous and sonorous Bacchic festival provides a stark contrast to the gloomy and silent world of tyranny depicted in the *Ode to Liberty*. Bacchus himself, with his regal insignia, holding his thyrsus as a sceptre and in his crown of vine leaves, constitutes a positive counterpart to the despotic rulers from the *Ode to Liberty*. In this context it is particularly significant that, at the very beginning of the poem, freedom is introduced as one of the main characteristics of the Bacchic festival. Thus, Bacchic freedom contraposed to political slavery under tyranny is implied by the political meaning of the imagery of freedom in contrast with slavery. This juxtaposition of different significations of 'freedom' and 'slavery', which is a characteristic of early nineteenth-century Russian liberal thought and poetry under monarchy and serfdom, was derived from Western sources, and therefore ultimately is derived from Greek and Roman antiquity. Although the ideal of *eleutheria* is a feature of some archaic poetry, it was in the ideological discourse of classical, democratic Athens that the polarisation of the terminology of slavery and freedom acquired a specifically political metaphorical sense, being applied to the condition of freemen under tyranny (for example, in Persia) and democracy (in Athens and many of her allied states) respectively. But the intimate association between democratic freedom and emotional release in the cult of Dionysus *eleuthereus* dates back from the same era, the fifth century BCE. In this article I analyse the function of these metaphors in a text that was produced for the fifth-century theatre, Euripides' satyr play *Cyclops*, and try to demonstrate their essential significance for the interpretation of the play.

Satyr drama has often been overlooked by classical scholars, and not only because *Cyclops* is the only complete surviving example. The genre was often dismissed as merely a lightweight frolic appended to the serious trilogies of tragic dramas which were indeed significant investigations of important issues in the classical city-state. But since an important article using an anthropological perspective by François Lissarrague, scholars have been increasingly inclined to accept that the satyrs replay the same serious social issues as tragedy, but 'in a different key'.[2] The 'serious' economic and social implications of the encounter between satyr, giant and man in *Cyclops* have indeed been analysed by David Konstan; he argues that the contrast between them presents, in Odysseus, 'the human community ... as the positive realisation of social relations', in contrast with both the monadic *Cyclops* and the unindividuated satyric collective.[3] Edith Hall, in her illuminating article on satyric drama, noted the significance of the motif of slavery and was the first to put forward the specific question as to 'whether the motifs of slavery and release function as fantasy-correctives to the class-ridden city-state of Athens, found on slave-labour'.[4] She has subsequently pointed out a text in which slaves and satyrs are very explicitly associated, *The Interpretation of Dreams* (*Oneirocritica*) by the dream critic Artemidorus (see further her chapter in this volume). He diagnoses dreaming of actually dancing in honour of Dionysus as 'inauspicious for all but slaves. For most men, it foretells folly and harm because of the ecstasies of the mental processes and the frenzy.'[5]

Seeing satyrs as sharing some of their identity, on the level of myth and fantasy, with slaves, presupposes an essentially social and class-oriented interpretation of the motif. The same class-based interpretation forms the basis of the hypothesis proposed by Mark Griffith, who suggested that 'the annual self-presentation of satyrically cross-dressed choruses of citizens played into Athenian anxieties and prejudices about slaves'.[6] These ideas were the point of departure for my own study of the motif of slavery in Euripides' *Cyclops*, but my investigation, in the event, ultimately proceeded along somewhat different lines. Satyr play is interested in slavery, but it is metaphorical slavery, in the sense of subjection to a tyrannical sovereign power. I will therefore argue for a different – political and not class – interpretation of this motif in *Cyclops*, and try to show that the notions of slavery and freedom as represented in the play should rather be understood in their derivative or secondary political sense, and that the general meaning of the play relates to discussions of democracy that were being held by thinkers in contemporary democratic Athens.

The contrast of freedom and constraint is evident from the beginning of the play, indeed from its introductory prologue. Silenus describes the predicament in which he and his fellow satyrs find themselves as Polyphemus' slaves, the word 'slaves' (*douloi*) being underlined by a strong enjambment (23-4): 'instead of our Bacchic revels we now herd the flocks of this godless Cyclops' (25-6). A large part of Silenus' speech in the prologue is devoted to recounting their unpleasant duties – Silenus has to sweep and rake the Cyclops' cave, while the satyrs pasture the Cyclops' sheep. As the chorus of slave satyrs enters, hard at work, Silenus laments that they used to dance to the music of the lyre in attendance upon Dionysus (39-40).

We find this stark opposition of enslavement to Polyphemus and free Dionysian pleasures in the ensuing parodos, where the satyrs, as they pen the sheep, deplore their lot and remember their former Bacchic lifestyle, with its dances, wine and sex (63-72). It is remarkable that this contrast between Dionysian freedom and constraint is transferred even to the sheep. They try to escape, rushing away while being driven into the cave, and the satyrs ask them why they are trying to find a way to the cliffs, when they and their young are provided with grazing and drinking-troughs near the Cyclops' cave (41-8). These phrases, both in their meaning and in their syntactic structure, resemble one passage in Euripides' *Hippolytus* where the nurse attempts to stop Phaedra craving for the world of the wild countryside inhabited by her beloved Hippolytus (223-7):

Why, my child, these feverish thoughts?
What has hunting to do with you?
Why do you crave streaming spring water?
For there is a dewy slope right next to the city wall
With a continuous supply of drinking water.

Since in *Hippolytus* it is the image of a Bacchic woman which serves as a model for Phaedra's desire to escape, we can assume that in *Cyclops* it is implied that the desire of his sheep to escape is consciously assimilated to Bacchic emotions. Thus Dionysian escapism, being transferred to the sheep, is pictured as a natural though bestial feeling. In its naturalness it is opposed to Polyphemus' way of life, which, since it involves anthropophagy, is contrary to nature.

From his first mention in the text, constraint and domination are the defining features of Polyphemus. His name first appears in the prologue surrounded by such words as 'slaves', 'compulsion', and 'master' (*anagkaiôs echei, despotên* 29-35). In the parodos he is named as the master of the stall from which the sheep are longing to escape (54). When Polyphemus appears in the *orchêstra*, he begins at once to dictate orders and prohibitions (203-11). His cannibalism, which is constantly connected with the theme of constraint, becomes itself a particular and extreme expression of repression and violence. Moreover, under his rule even his slaves, the satyrs, are themselves forced to become dictators. In the parodos, despite all their love for freedom, they are driving the sheep into the cave by throwing stones at them (51). More than that, the satyrs and Silenus have to participate in an extreme form of Polyphemus' violence – they are compelled to attend to him at his cannibalistic feasts, as Silenus had earlier complained, by 'assisting this godless Cyclops at his unholy meals' (30-1).

It is this world of constraint and violence that Odysseus enters in the first episode. His situation in the Cyclops' land, and his desire to get away from it, are described in a way very similar to the description of the satyrs' situation, i.e. also in terms of compulsion and liberty. Even the circumstances under which he and the satyrs arrived on the Cyclops' island are very much the same. The satyrs and Silenus wanted to liberate Dionysus after he had been kidnapped by pirates (112), while Odysseus was fighting against the Trojans, aiming to punish them for the abduction of Helen (280-1). It is their struggle against constraint and violence, expressed by the word *harpagê* (violent 'seizure', 'abduction', or 'appropriation'), that makes both cases similar. Indeed, the noun and its cognate verb *harpazein* are thematic words in the play, expressing the idea of violence and often applied to Polyphemus' agency. For example, it is used when Polyphemus snatches up Odysseus' comrades to devour them (400), or commandeers Silenus and drags him off in order to rape him (586). A further parallel is furnished by the fact that both Odysseus and the satyrs have been forcibly driven to the island by a storm, which is also described with words signifying violence (*bia*) as well as the recurrent *harpazein* (109, 111). Thus the notions of violence and force accumulate a thematic significance in the drama which extends even to its evocation of natural and elemental phenomena. Having found himself subject to the rule of the Cyclops, moreover, Odysseus, like the satyrs, has to suffer violence, culminating in the Cyclops' killing and devouring of his comrades. Odysseus, like the satyrs, is compelled to assist Polyphemus at his unholy meal, and the hero's complaint about this cruel destiny is quite similar to that of Silenus in the prologue (406, 30-1).

Odysseus is contrasted with the Cyclops not only as the object of his constraint, but also in his fundamental attitude to the world. While the Cyclops represents the principle of coercion, Odysseus consciously advocates the principle of voluntary action in all interactions. For example, early in the drama he explains his trade with Silenus as being carried on 'willingly and with willing customers: there was no violence in this business' (258). He demonstrates the same principle in practice at the end of the play, when the satyrs, out of fear, refuse to take part in blinding the Cyclops. Odysseus does not force them to collaborate with him, but allows them to help him as they wish and can – with their songs and dances (649-53).

While Odysseus and the satyrs have in common their desire for freedom, there is nevertheless one particular and substantial difference in their characterisation. The word 'free' (*eleutheros*) is applied only to Odysseus. He pronounces it himself, declaring his decision to speak freely before Polyphemus, that is, to take up what in democratic Athens would be called his *parrhêsia*, or right equivalent to any other free citizen's to voice his opinion (286-7). The principal traits in Odysseus which combine to define him as an *eleutheros* are his love of freedom, his manliness and his martial prowess. He does not just crave freedom, but always struggles to attain it and is always successful in so doing. His permanent condition in the play is to act in defence of freedom and opposition to violence: even his role in the Trojan War is presented in this way, becoming a model for his heroic deeds in the land of the Cyclops. The two conflicts, against the Trojans and against the Cyclops, are explicitly compared in the text. When Odysseus first meets Polyphemus, Silenus advises him to hide in the cave, but Odysseus refuses, recalling his victory over the Trojans (198-202). Declaring his willingness to 'die nobly', he uses the word *eugenôs* that expresses the specifically moral implications of this hero's love of freedom.

In the case of the satyrs and Silenus, on the other hand, their desire for freedom is not combined with any virtue, manliness, martial prowess or nobility. Like Odysseus, Silenus is proud of his participation in a war: in his case, it is the war of Gods against Giants. However, his idea of his role in the war and of his victory over Enceladus is no more than illusion (5-8). The reason for the introduction of the story is the setting of the play's action, which locates the Cyclops' cave on Etna, which is where Enceladus was buried. There is a suggestion that Silenus' battle with Enceladus is somehow a prototype of his conflict with Polyphemus, just as Odysseus' role in the Trojan war prefigures his struggle with Polyphemus. But Odysseus is a real hero and the victor in both struggles, while Silenus and the satyrs win their victories only vicariously through the agency of others. It was actually Athena who killed Enceladus and it is Odysseus who will blind the Cyclops. The scene of blinding the Cyclops further demonstrates the satyrs' cowardice; in other situations, they may display mendacity and perfidy, for instance, when Silenus falsely accuses Odysseus of robbery and advises Polyphemus to devour the hero who has just become his friend (176). These faults are in contrast with the bravery, honesty and fidelity of Odysseus, who, for example, rejects the idea of escaping from the Cyclops alone and leaving his friends in danger (478-9).

These contrasting phenomena show how an opposition is established between the moral character of Silenus and the satyrs and that of Odysseus. While he is *eugenês*, noble, they are *ponêroi*, base: this is how Odysseus evaluates them when they exhibit their cowardice and refuse to help him in blinding the Cyclops (642). While Odysseus is *eleutheros*, the satyrs are slaves in a fundamental, ontological sense. For even after their escape from enslavement to Polyphemus, they will remain slaves – they will always be the slaves of Dionysus. Thus, slavery is not only their temporary position but also a permanent status rooted in their very being.[7]

We may conclude that the motifs of slavery and freedom in the drama have two different fundamental meanings. First, they can describe a situation and a set of relationships; freedom in this sense is opposed to coercion and violence (*bia*). In respect of this kind of freedom, both Odysseus and the satyrs are similar; all of them find themselves in the Cyclops' power and strive for liberation. Secondly, they express permanent moral qualities of dramatis personae; *eleutheria* in this sense correlates with *eugeneia* (nobility), and *douleia* with *ponêria* (baseness).

These two meanings of the 'freedom' motifs, the one positional or relational, and the other moral, correspond with the semantics of the words and notions *eleutheros* and *doulos* as they were used in classical Athens. But the two aspects, relational and moral, coexisted in these Greek words from early times. In their primary, direct meaning, they designated the position of two social classes, freemen and slaves. On the other hand, the adjectives *eleutherios* and *doulios*, derived from them, denoted qualities proper to members of each class, having the meaning 'fit for a freeman' and 'characteristic of a slave,' and by the early fifth century, certainly, the word *eleutheros* itself also acquired this meaning (Pindar, *Pyth.* 2.57, Aeschylus, *Persians* 593).

The words *eleutheros* and *doulos* also acquired indirect, wider and metaphorical meanings, with which they were used to polarise different groups of free men as well as free *versus* slave. Both aspects of the concepts they denoted, relational and moral, were part of this semantic development. Moral *eleutheria* thus became an important aristocratic value correlating with *eugeneia* and subsequently it was included, alongside other aristocratic values, in the nexus of ideal democratic principles, having lost its social aristocratic implications and become applicable to all citizens. However, while in the aristocratic world this kind of *eleutheria*, integrally associated with competitive values, cannot be separated from the idea of domination and power-holding, in the democratic society of Athens it was conjoined with *eleutheria* in the relational sense of freedom. This relational *eleutheria*, indeed, is a very specifically democratic value, as we can from infer from such Thucydidean passages as Pericles' Funeral Oration and Nicias' exhortation to the Athenians before the battle against the Syracusans (Thucydides 2.37 and 7.69 respectively). Here, in the latter example, we find a conjunction of the notion of freedom and the idea of moral virtue; moreover, this moral virtue appears to be one of the aristocratic hereditary virtues (*patrikai aretai*), namely *eugeneia*, which correlated with *eleutheria* in its moral meaning. This hereditary nobility certainly received a new democratic interpretation, in which usage it lost its social, hierarchical meaning and retained only a moral one. The idea of combining the aristocratic 'freedom' of status with this new democratic freedom, may, in its turn, have been aimed at defining the proper sphere of moral activity in democratic society, i.e. that it must be concerned with freedom. We may assume, therefore, that this conjunction of relational, democratic *eleutheria* and the moral, aristocratic *eleutheria* existed as a model in Athenian democratic ideology, and that the image of Odysseus in the *Cyclops*, combining the two aspects of *eleutheria*, reflects this type of public discourse.

The same conjunction of the two aspects of *eleutheria* can be found in another play by Euripides, the tragedy *Children of Heracles*, where it appears as an integral part of the thematic structure. The plot of the tragedy enacts a story about the support and protection given by the Athenians and their king, Demophon, to the children of Heracles, when they were persecuted and pursued by their deceased father Heracles' deadly enemy Eurystheus. Attica is recurrently called 'a free land' (*eleuthera gê*) in the tragedy, and the term is used to stress that Attica can save the children of Heracles from violence and coercion. Although the tragedy has an ironic tone which does not unquestioningly reproduce the clichés of Athenian democratic public discourse, by identifying some of its central themes it allows us to see them operating in a way that would have been familiar to an audience in the later fifth century. Demophon, for example, is depicted as trying proving his nobility (*eugeneia*) by this glorious act of protection of asylum seekers, and the notion of nobility here implies both noble behaviour and noblility of birth (323-6). Heracles' daughter Macaria voluntarily offers herself for the human sacrifice when Persephone demands one, and her deed, we are told, is noble in itself, and derived from her hereditary nobility (302-3). On the other hand, it has a many-sided connection with freedom: her self-sacrifice secures freedom for the Heraclids and for Attica from Eurystheus, it saves Macaria herself from slavery (one of the stated aims also of Polyxena when she freely submits to being sacrificed in Euripides' *Hecuba*), and is in itself a voluntary act, thus constituting the opposite of a coerced one. The language used by Macaria as she expresses her decision to die and to kill herself by her own hand (550-1, 559) underlines this contrast of voluntariness and coercion in terms very similar to those found in *Cyclops*. In response to her decision, Iolaos remarks upon the 'nobility' of her speech (553). Thus nobility and freedom appear to be mutually interdependent: a noble deed brings freedom and a free act reveals nobility.

Odysseus in *Cyclops* therefore exhibits the same combination of striving for relational freedom with moral nobility, or moral *eleutheria*, which we find in democratic thought and which is represented in the ostensibly more 'serious' genre of tragedy. As for the images of the satyrs and Silenus, on the contrary, they represent a marked separation of the two aspects of *eleutheria*. In them it exists only as a relational value, as freedom from hierarchical dominance, and even licence; it is not a moral quality. This aspect of their portrayal is indeed a *topos* of satyric drama; in the existing remnants of the genre, they are always cowardly and *ponêroi*. The motif of their captivity, enslavement and subsequent liberation is also widespread in satyric dramas. In such plays as Aeschylus' *Lycurgus*, *Sphinx*, and *Circe*, for example, it seems to have determined their entire plots. This accords with the widespread ideological conviction in fifth-century and other ancient sources that slaves are 'by nature' morally inferior to the free. However, in view of the civic implications that the motif of freedom and the image of Odysseus holds in *Cyclops* (civic implications which are to do, rather, with the ideological underpinning of the sovereignty of the Athenian *dêmos*), we may possibly detect some political meaning in the image of the satyrs as well.

The separation of the two aspects of *eleutheria*, similar to that found in the image of the satyrs, is present in the oligarchically inclined authors of the fourth century BCE, especially in their description of Athenian democracy. These authors gave a negative interpretation of the democratic concept of freedom, and indeed use it as a criterion of criticism and weapon against democracy. In their view, what the democrats called freedom was actually not freedom but licence. We find such a view, for example, in Isocrates' *Areopagitica* 7.20 and his Panathenaic oration 12.131. This negative notion of *eleutheria* is contrasted by the oligarchs with a positive one, the aristocratic *eleutheria* in its sense of nobility regarded as a moral and even more as a social virtue.[8] In their view, it is only *aristoi* who are truly free because of being inherently and congenitally noble, while the non-aristocratic members of the *dêmos*, considered to be free from the democratic point of view, may be regarded as unfree, or indeed slaves, because of their inherent moral inferiority.[9] It is true that this literature dates from the early fourth century BCE, that is, from rather later than Euripides. But it probably derived its concept of *eleutheria* from the oligarchic thought of previous decades. This was, in fact, argued by Raaflaub on two grounds, the first of which is some parallels with the 'Old Oligarch'. This ancient author equates democratic freedom with poor government (1.8), and draws a distinction between the *ponêroi* and the 'best people' (*chrêstoi*), a distinction which is both moral and social at the same time (1.1). The second ground adduced by Raaflaub is the distinction between free and unfree trades or professions (*eleutherioi* and *aneleutheroi technai*) that dates from the late fifth century BCE. If this is correct, we may assume that this oligarchic separation of the democratic notion of *eleutheria* in the 'relational' sense of freedom in terms of position in a hierarchy, and moral *eleutheria* in the sense of nobility interpreted in an aristocratic fashion (i.e. as a virtue both moral and social at the same time), was indeed seen as opposing the fusion of the two aspects of *eleutheria* in democratic thought. Moreover, the democratic fusion of the two may be regarded as a response to the oligarchic view, with its negation of democratic, relational freedom and its defence of the true, aristocratic *eleutheria* of inner character.

Some scholars have argued that Polyphemus' viewpoint in *Cyclops* caricatures some strains in contemporary anti-democratic ideology, especially his view that riches (here taking the form of comestibles) can substitute for divinity (316, 336), and that man-made rules and laws are redundant (338-40). In this Polyphemus is strongly reminiscent of Callicles in Plato's *Gorgias*, who argues that civic laws are devised by the weak majority: natural law dictates that strong individuals should satisfy their desires at the expense of such man-made legislation. Yet of all the oligarchic literature of the fourth century BCE, it is Plato's *Republic* that contains the closest parallels to the *Cyclops*, notably those parts of books 8 and 9 in which the author describes democracy and tyranny. A tyrant is several times depicted as a cannibal, an image which inevitably brings to mind the image of the archetypal cannibal, Polyphemus, and his tyrannical characterisation in Euripides' play.[10]

An analogous image, but used to signify democracy, is a Bacchic one, which appears several times in *Republic* book 8. For example, Plato links the change into democratic man with the satisfaction of unnecessary and vain desires, which is called 'bacchising' (*ekbakkheuthe,* 8.561a9). Subsequently, the first desires of a democrat are identified as wine-drinking and *aulos* music (8.561c7). Wine also serves as a metaphor for democratic freedom (8.562c8-d1). These specifically Dionysian associations – wine and the sound of the *aulos* – of democratic freedom are, on the one hand, reminiscent of Euripides' satyrs. On the other hand, they are based on the idea recurrent in other oligarchic writers that democratic freedom is decadent licence rather than true freedom. Moreover, in Plato *eleutheria* in another sense is contrasted with this licentious democratic freedom: this is the concept of moral and aristocratic *eleutheria* proper to systems that are presented as better than democracy and included in Plato's list of moral virtues.

All these parallels between the Euripidean *Cyclops* and oligarchic literature, parallels both in images and ideas, make it possible to argue that while Odysseus epitomises a democratic view of democratic freedom, which combines the relational and moral aspects of *eleutheria*, the satyrs may represent the same democratic freedom, but with the crucial difference that it is presented from the oligarchic point of view, which separates and polarises these two aspects. If so, then the satyr play displays the inherently contradictory nature of democratic freedom, by approaching it from two radically disparate viewpoints. This leads us to ask what might be the aim and the meaning of such ambivalence?

The first function of this ambivalence may be psychological and may be assumed to be a specific feature of the genre of satyric drama. In Athenian theatrical performances, a satyric drama followed three tragedies, thus acting as a conclusion of an extended dramatic sequence. Tragedies often depict the world as ambiguous, casting doubt on conventional notions and values and causing a crisis in the audience's conceptions. Sometimes conventional values themselves, and other times human ability to follow them are called in question. This tragic crisis usually arises in the course of the dramatic action, at the moment of reversal, when the initial view of the heroes and the dramatic situation that seemed to be evident suddenly changes. Such a dynamic ambivalence is inherent in many of Euripides' tragedies; it plays a significant role in *Children of Heracles*, in which democratic freedom is a central theme.

At the beginning of this tragedy, the thematic function of each character seems to be relatively straightforward and fixed: Eurystheus epitomises violence, constraint and moral baseness, while the Athenians, the children of Heracles, as well as Iolaos and Alcmene, on the contrary, epitomise freedom and nobility. However, after the reversal, when Eurystheus has fallen into Alcmene's hands, these functions fluctuate. The former persecutor becomes a victim; now it is not Eurystheus but Alcmene who becomes the agent resorting to violence. Thus Alcmene's image becomes infected by associations with violence, formerly a characteristic of Eurystheus, whereas Eurystheus revives his inborn nobility (988) and is even presented as becoming absolved to some extent of responsibility for his crimes, as he shows that they have been caused by the intervention of Hera (990).

If we consider the structure of *Cyclops*, it becomes apparent that in some ways it reproduces the same elements as are contained in tragedy, including tragedy's typical role reversal. At a certain point, Polyphemus turns into a victim and Odysseus into an avenger. The similarity of the Cyclops' role before the reversal and Odysseus' position after it is emphasised by the use of the same verbal motif, in the form of the term *anthrax* (coal) and its cognates. The coals on which Polyphemus cooks his profane meals become transformed into the instrument with which Odysseus blinds him. Nevertheless, this paratragic reversal does not produce any ambiguity in the situation and in the main roles and functions of the characters. Polyphemus continues to epitomise the idea of violence and coercion right to the end of the drama, an idea which becomes especially evident in the last scene. When Odysseus and the satyrs are in flight from his island, he tries to stop them by throwing a stone at them (704-5), a gesture which recalls the stone which the satyrs cast at the sheep in the parodos (51), and which itself functioned as a symbolic expression of the theme of constraint. Thus, *Cyclops* displays dynamic stability in marked contrast to the dynamic ambiguity of the not wholly dissimilar tragedy.

On the other hand, the absence of dynamic ambivalence in the developing action is compensated for here by another kind of ambivalence, a more static, conceptual one. There are two opposed perspectives on freedom in *Cyclops*, and they are not produced in the course of its action. They exist unchanged from its very outset. Whereas the dynamic ambivalence of tragedy produces a crisis, this static ideological ambivalence of *Cyclops*, on the contrary, ends in a kind of harmony. Odysseus and the satyrs are finally united as they escape from Polyphemus' tyranny. If this kind of ideological resolution and closure were typical of the genre, we may assume that it was through such blurring of ideological faultlines in the democracy that satyric drama offered its audience a relief from a tragic crisis.

This ambivalence of satyr drama and its ultimate resolution probably had a religious meaning, demonstrating the unity of Dionysus' two faces – high and low, or heroic and slavish – two faces discussed by Charles Segal in his analysis of Aristophanes' *Frogs*.[11] However, here, in *Cyclops*, this ambivalence receives a particular political meaning. The drama displays two opposing views on democratic freedom but ultimately harmonises them by bringing them together into conflict with the image of tyranny.[12] Slavery, ever-present in the Athenian democracy, is nevertheless effaced through metaphorical transference into the creation of free men's identity. It therefore serves a complex role in the Athenian slaveholding democracy's self-definition, even through the superficially simple stories enacted in satyric theatre.[13]

Notes

1. An important role in defining the fusion of these two strains in the liberal case for reform was played by the works of Nikolai Turgenev (no relation of the novelist Ivan), especially *Russia and the Russians* (1847, published simultaneously in Russian and French).

2. Lissarrague (1990) 235-6.

3. Konstan (1990) 227.

4. Hall (1998) 23.

5. 2.37, translated by White (1975) 118.

6. Griffith (2005) 164.

7. See above, pp. 122-3 and n. 6. On the satyrs as slaves see esp. Konstan (1981).

8. On the emergence of this notion in oligarchic literature see Raaflaub (1983). On the emergence of the metaphorical political sense of *eleutheros* and *doulos* see now Raaflaub (2004).

9. Cf. the disenfranchisements under the 'Thirty Tyrants' which stripped previously inalienable citizen rights such as trial by jury from many Athenians, thus diminishing their position.

10. Cf. O'Sullivan (2005) 119-59.

11. Segal (1961) 207-42.

12. If we accept *Cyclops*' assumed connection with the Sicilian expedition (which is quite possible, considering numerous references to Sicily as the scene of action of the play and particularly because tyranny was Euripides' typical way of representing Athens' enemies in the Peloponnesian War), then we may regard the concrete social function of the play as that of harmonising opposite opinions on Athenian democracy by contrasting both of them with the image of the enemy.

13. I am indebted to Gregory Dashevsky, Edith Hall, David Konstan, Patrick O'Sullivan and Deborah Boedeker for the careful reading of a previous version of this paper. Their valuable suggestions have helped me greatly in improving my style and argumentation.

References

Griffith, M. (2005) 'Sophocles' satyr-plays and the language of romance', in I. de Jong and A. Rijksbaron (eds) *Sophocles and the Greek Language*, 51-72. Leiden.

Hall, E. (1998) 'Ithyphallic males behaving badly, or, satyr drama as gendered tragic ending', in M. Wyke (ed.) *Parchments of Gender: Deciphering the Bodies of Antiquity*, 13-37. Oxford. Revised version now published as Hall (2006) ch. 5.

Konstan, D. (1990) 'An anthropology of Euripides' *Kyklôps*', in J.J. Winkler and F. Zeitlin (eds) *Nothing to Do With Dionysus? Athenian Drama in its Social Context*, 207-28. Princeton, NJ. Revised version of article original appearing in *Ramus* 10 (1981) 87-103.

Lissarrague, F. (1990) 'Why satyrs are good to represent', in J.J. Winkler and F.I. Zeitlin (eds) *Nothing to Do with Dionysos? Athenian Drama in its Social Context*, 228-36. Princeton, NJ.

O'Sullivan, P. (2005) 'Of sophists, tyrants and Polyphemos: the nature of the beast in Euripides' *Cyclops*', in G. Harrison (ed.) *Satyr Drama: Tragedy at Play*, 119-59. Swansea.

Raaflaub, K. (1983) 'Democracy, oligarchy and the concept of the "free citizen" in late fifth-century Athens', *Political Theory* 11, 517-44.

―――― (2004) *The Discovery of Freedom in Ancient Greece*. Chicago, IL.

Segal, C. (1961) 'The character and cults of Dionysus and the unity of the *Frogs*', *Harvard Studies in Classical Philology* 65, 207-42.

Turgenev, Nikolai (1847) *La Russie et les russes*. Brussels.

Navigating Race, Class, Polis and Empire: The Place of Empirical Analysis in Aristotle's Account of Natural Slavery

S. Sara Monoson

Scholars have long favoured language like 'incoherent', 'very weak', 'feeble' and 'battered shipwreck' to describe Aristotle's theory of natural slavery in *Politics* book 1.[1] These words stress its perceived logical incompatibility with the rest of his moral philosophy as well as scholars' dismay at Aristotle's failure to recognise it as such, or possibly even fury at what they detect as a measure of philosophical dishonesty or blatant personal bias. Studies of Aristotle on slavery thus often focus attention on exposing the contortions he has to perform in order to fit a case for slavery into his otherwise admirable philosophical system. He is often assumed to have been motivated to defend slavery by an un-philosophic attachment to widespread, exclusionary practices common in his day.[2] Given that Aristotle acknowledges current arguments against slavery and explicitly positions his discussion as an intervention in a contemporary controversy over its justice (*Pol.* 1.1253b15-23), the modern reader's disappointment is intense. Accordingly, Aristotle's discussion of slavery has for some time stood as a prime example of how even the finest mind can be corrupted by class interests, ethnic or race prejudice, or just the common orthodoxies of his time.

Recent work on Aristotle by two eminent political philosophers suggests another way of reading his handling of the question of slavery in *Politics*. Both of course find the Aristotelian justification of slavery every bit as repulsive as all other cases for the just ownership of human beings. But they also find the argument to be, from an Aristotelian vantage point, philosophically sound. Malcolm Schofield takes on the charge that Aristotle's theory of slavery is a prime example of false consciousness at work. He argues that the account of natural slavery in the politics is 'not to any interesting extent ideological', 'at least potentially a critical theory', and that 'the doctrine of living tools is a defensible piece of Aristotelian philosophy'.[3] Though for different reasons, Richard Kraut similarly proposes that Aristotle's justification of slavery is 'internally consistent' and even 'contains a limited amount of explanatory power'. Kraut continues, 'It was a coherent way of looking at the social world'.[4] Both explain

Aristotle's theory of slavery in a way that requires us to distinguish between a philosophical muddle and a failure of critical imagination.

In this chapter I examine the theory of slavery developed in *Politics* book 1 for what it suggests about the contours of Aristotle's political imagination. How far does it reveal Aristotle's view of the possibilities that inhere in the material world? Building on the work of Schofield and Kraut, I start by reviewing why it is possible to conclude that Aristotle presents an internally consistent theory of a 'natural slave'. My main focus, however, is on the next step in Aristotle's thinking – his attention to 'whether or not anyone exists who is by nature of this character' (*Pol.* 1.1254a18).[5] What part does an appeal to evidence play in the construction of his argument? We must tackle that issue in order to expose some of the defining peculiarities of a distinctively Aristotelian way of thinking about slavery, and indeed about politics generally. I then draw out the measure of critical potential that his theory of natural slavery contains from the perspective of his own culturally specific experiences and the standpoint of lasting theoretical power. I conclude with some reflections on why this argument about slavery as practised in the fourth century BCE has informed and encouraged modern racism.

Why isn't the theory of natural slavery a philosophical muddle?

The central claims of Aristotle's theory of natural slavery are simply stated. Nature produces a plurality of sorts of people. This variation has moral and political import. As theorists, we can decipher these differences and conduct a normative inquiry into the best way to order them hierarchically and into partnerships so as to form a just state and thus produce the conditions necessary for human happiness and virtue ('goods') to come into being in the world. As theorists, we can identify 'slave' (along with male, female, and ruler) as a natural character (a kind of 'being'[6]) and an elemental part of a state. We can further understand that a partnership between a natural slave and natural ruler can form a simple compound that, when joined with other simple compounds (male and female, father and children), will produce an *oikos* (household) which will, in turn, combine to form more complex social organisms – villages and cities (*poleis*) – that are necessary for the practice of virtue and happiness. To best understand the distinct purposes and excellence of the most complex form, a *polis*, in Aristotle's view a theorist must investigate in detail the character of its component parts, starting with the master/slave relationship.

Aristotle explicitly positions his account of mastership (*despoteia*) in opposition to contemporary critics of slavery who maintain 'that for one man to be another man's master is contrary to nature, because it is only by convention that makes the one a slave and the other a freeman and there is no difference between them in nature, and that therefore it is unjust, for it is based on force' (1.1253b23-6). He quickly offers definitions that capture the sociological condition of a slave.[7] A slave is an ensouled article of property (*ktêma ti empsuchon*, 1.1253b32[8]), an instrument for action (life) separable from its owner, and a person who is not merely the slave of the master but who 'wholly belongs to the master' (1.1254a12-13). He concludes, 'one who is a human being belonging by nature not to himself but to another is by nature a slave'. But the force of 'by nature' and thus his answer to contemporary opponents is not yet clear. To make it so he adds that a slave by nature is one who is 'capable of belonging to another' (*ho dunamenos allou einai*, 1.1254b2). How can he account for this capacity? Aristotle stresses that natural slaves indeed have the traits that distinguish humans from animals – speech and reason. But in the case of a natural slave the person's reasoning faculty is in a significant way deficient. He can conduct productive reasoning leading to the mastery of a craft but not deliberation leading to practical wisdom. Accordingly, the master/slave relation can be, for the natural slave, just and advantageous. It is advantageous because the relationship supplies rational direction and a pathway to participation in excellence. The relation addresses the deficiency of reason this type of person suffers in a way that is mutually beneficial to both parties. The master gains release from labour and access to leisure and thus to the practice of politics or philosophy. A natural slave gains certain kinds of skills and forms of knowledge appropriate to his service activities (1.1255b30), an opportunity to practise a variant of the moral virtues like courage and temperance (1.1259b20ff.), and even a type of friendship with the master (1.1255b13). This relation is just, then, because being rooted in nature, it advances the high purposes of the polis (not just life but good life) and, when properly practised, amounts to an exercise of authority that tends to the well-being of the ruled as well as the ruler (though not in equal measure, 1.1259b18-20).

Many see a great big muddle here. This sophisticated philosopher has conjured up a stilted and weak account of a soul deficient in reason and of how best to tend to this soul's well-being so that he can cast familiar patterns of human behaviour that his own moral theory would otherwise easily recognise as oppressive and exploitative from the point of view of the slave and disgraceful from that of the master as activity that sustains relationships of *mutual* benefit to masters and slaves. Some question whether his readers should even assume that Aristotle sincerely believes what he presents as his own view. Perhaps he is in the grip of ideological thinking? Isn't he really just manufacturing philosophical cover for an institution that denigrates labourers and barbarians so that there can be a leisured sector (of which he is a member) to practise political action or undertake the contemplative life? Surely he is a self-conscious partisan of the upper classes abusing philosophy for political ends? Or perhaps a reflexive embrace of a form of racism can explain the mess? He proposes, after all, that 'natural slaves' populate barbarian lands in Europe and

Asia, not Greece. Perhaps the theory of slavery is a deliberate or even unwitting mystification of Greek arrogance?

Schofield and Kraut both plunge right into these difficult questions. Both show that, however repulsive, basing an account of natural slavery on a conception of a soul deficient in reason does not produce a stilted and weak argument inconsistent with Aristotle's theory of well-being. Kraut systematically examines such things as Aristotle's understanding of the cognitive capacities and dysfunction peculiar to the natural slave, why slavery and not another condition (wage earner) best suits such a character, the idea of slave virtue and friendship between master and slave, and how it is possible to imagine that slaves are not harmed by their enslavement – and he shows how all of this is even consistent with the possibility that a master can legitimately offer a slave his freedom as a reward for good behaviour over time.[9] Schofield too examines Aristotle's elaboration of the diversity in nature, including the likelihood that there are some persons who are better off being ruled than ruling, the distinguishing features of such souls, how they participate in virtues like temperance, why it is not necessary to attribute feeblemindedness to them, why master/slave and not a form of paternalism benefits them, and, most importantly, how the master/slave relation models a distinctive form of authority that stands in stark contrast to both domination by force and political rule. Like Kraut, he concludes that this conception of a natural slave sits comfortably in the Aristotelian philosophical system.

But why is Aristotle interested in slavery at all? Are there philosophical reasons to take up the topic in general and the assessment of contemporary practices of slavery in particular? Schofield maintains that Aristotle has no philosophical interest at all in justifying contemporary institutions of slavery, only in dismantling wrongheaded ways of understanding the practice of political rule. In particular, Schofield sees Aristotle's introduction of a the theory of slavery not as an effort to defend an institution but as the 'launch' of a philosophical case for a plural view of the nature of rule in opposition to Plato's 'Unitarian conception'.[10] In his view, Aristotle 'gratuitously' peppers forceful theoretical arguments about rule with unfortunate expressions of an 'unargued' personal attitude towards the institutions of contemporary slavery. These unreflective comments indicate that Aristotle indeed assumed that most slaves in his own society were natural slaves. Schofield accepts that his comfort with this assumption was 'no doubt' due ultimately to 'the bias we might expect in a slave-owning culture which looked outside its own borders and ethnic identity for its supply of slaves' and he straightforwardly calls these passages evidence that Aristotle exhibits 'a nasty case of false consciousness'. But, he insists, it does not 'infect' Aristotle's theory of slavery itself.[11] Instead, the presence of unargued expressions of bias regarding contemporary institutions only obscures the real driving concern in the passage – undermining 'the equation of domination with political rule'.[12] Schofield has a strong case. The opening of the *Politics* makes it very clear that Aristotle's paramount concern in this work is to demonstrate that his signature mode of inquiry can make it manifest that a pervasive view of the nature of political rule is wrong (*ouk alêthê, Pol.* 1.1252a18). The erroneous view that so exercises him is one that holds that the statesman, king, head of household and master of slaves have identical natures and that the difference between them is only one of degree (the size of the group over whom they rule), not one of kind (1.1252a7-12). For Schofield, the discussion of slavery kicks off Aristotle's account of why it is instead the case that the differences among these forms of rule are indeed matters of kind and not degree.

Schofield sees that some practical concerns and an orientation toward contemporary institutions do follow from a crisp distinction between mastership and political rule (rule of free men). Specifically, it clarifies the aims of true politics for the already politically ambitious, urges the virtuous who ordinarily scoff at political engagement to give it a try, and challenges people's attachments to commonly held attitudes that identify domination with happiness. But, in Schofield's view, a defence of the particular form slavery took in his own society does not follow from Aristotle's philosophy of rule. When Aristotle takes up that concern (that is, praises contemporary Greek institutions and suggests reforms), in Schofield's view he is not arguing about the nature of rule but rather is *un*philosophically reproducing common biases.

Kraut has a different account of Aristotle's interest in slavery in the *Politics*. On his view, Aristotle does indeed have reason to elaborate a philosophically rigorous defence of slavery as an institution. If he could not justify slavery, Kraut points out, he 'would have been forced to announce to the Greek world that its political institutions ... rested on resources that could not be justly acquired or used'.[13] Aristotle recognises, Kraut suggests, that any defence of the polis as a viable, natural and indeed ideal political formation had to include a case for slavery. I would add that Aristotle also recognises that any argument for the polis as a locus for the practice of moral excellence had to cast the ubiquity of slaves in its daily life in an approving light.

That an attachment to the polis motivates Aristotle's attention to slavery may seem to confirm that a form of unthinking bias (parochialism) is at work in the *Politics*. And this does indeed seem to be the way Kraut interprets his own observation. He suggests that Aristotle's defence of the polis and of its practices of slavery are dispiriting signs that even Aristotle sometimes succumbs to the 'all too human tendency to avoid upheavals of thought' and that he might very well be a 'victim of these complacent habits of mind'.[14] But I think it is a sign of something else. Though the *Politics* is often read as (notoriously) oblivious to the contemporary Macedonian conquests and current threats to the polis as a durable form of political organisation,[15] his sustained attention to slavery both as a concept and institution suggests otherwise. For example, in the era of Macedonian military and political ambitions and their attendant embrace of Hellenising cultural goals, what precisely might have been the reach of the 'Greek world' to which Kraut worries Aristotle would have to announce the incoherence of the polis as a political form? And of what importance might such a revelation be to the 'barbarians'? Did he defend the polis philosophically to avoid an uncomfortable disturbance in his own thought or actively to do combat with contemporary advocates of rival formations?

Aristotle's *Politics* does on occasion betray a heightened sense of the imperilled state of the polis as a political formation. We find evidence of this in the anxieties that attend his treatment of the apparently innocuous issue of the significance of population size in the discussion of the ideal city in *Politics* book 7. He explicitly says that he wishes to reduce the importance of population size in the analysis of politics. Population size alone, he insists, cannot signal greatness. A great state (*megalê polis*) is not the same thing as a state with a large population (*poluanthrôpos polis*, 7.1326a25). Why would this variable be of such special concern to him? It is I think an indication of Aristotle's awareness of the challenging new forms of political organisation emerging in his time and his interest in showing that his mode of political science can pinpoint their defects as well as the excellence of a well-ordered polis. This concern is evident, for instance, in his critical discussion of a new form of kingship in which a single person is sovereign on every issue and governs at his own discretion, and stunningly, is able to exercise authority over a whole city a whole race and possibly over several races (*poleôs kai ethnos enos ê pleonôn*, 3.1285b33). This passage suggests the example of Alexander's ambitions.[16] Aristotle may also have contemporary experiences of Philip's ambitions and Alexander's conquests in mind when he worries about the intense pressures on contemporary Greek political communities to be huge in size in order to enjoy prosperity as well as a reputation for greatness and success. He explicitly wonders whether this new size requirement will mean that the only type of polis still able to come into being is one with a democratic constitution (3.1286b20-5).

Because Aristotle describes at length the peculiar pathologies likely to infect the kind of democracy that is 'last in point of time to come into being' (4.1293a1-2), we can infer why this limiting condition for the future of the polis disturbs him. He views large democratic cities as prosperous communities in which the rich are very busy managing personal estates and the poor are at leisure to participate in deliberative activities because they will receive pay for service (from the public treasury). As a consequence of the poor citizens being both numerous and politically active, in Aristotle's view, in this type of polis the multitude's preferences, not the laws, will become sovereign (*kurion*, 4.1293a11) to ill effects.[17] Later in the *Politics* he addresses another peculiar pathology that characterises an excessively large city with a democratic constitutional structure and political culture (both are implied by the term *politeia*). Owing to the lack of personal knowledge of one another, visiting foreigners and metics (resident aliens) will be able to escape detection and 'share' in the *politeia* (assume the privileges of citizenship) (7.1326b15-25). In practice, that is, subversions of birth as the usual, formal criteria for citizenship will likely occur, rendering the *politeia* vulnerable to precipitous change.[18] It is striking that Aristotle so clearly identifies a practice that could favour him personally – he was himself a metic during his years of residence at Athens – as a sign of a diseased polity. In this case, the prospect of personal benefit does not generate a bias that interferes with his philosophical reasoning. Instead, without hesitation he applies his theory of 'the causes that destroy each form of constitution' (5.1301a22) articulated in *Politics* book 5 (and derived from analysis of the collection of constitutional histories of 158 Greek cities produced under his direction at the Lyceum) to this circumstance. In fact, he shows no inclination at all to obstruct observation of this subversive activity. It occupies pride of place in *Constitution of Athens* attributed to him, which is the only surviving example of the storied collection of constitutional histories. Specifically, it opens the account of the 'present constitution' (*Ath. Pol.* 92) with an explicit account of the manner in which the Athenians try to manage precisely this problem (secretive subversions of birth as a criteria). It recounts the process that accompanies the presentation of young men for enrolment in the (deme-based) registry of citizens when they come of age, highlighting the several opportunities it provides for the exposure of imposters.

Aristotle's work betrays interest in the vulnerability of the polis as a living form in another way as well. In his discussion of how the legal structure and mores of a polis can be shaped to produce an ideal city (*Politics* book 7), he seeks to undermine the influence over ideas of greatness exercised by known examples of sovereign entities that control huge populations and vast territories. In particular, he argues that when most people imagine that a prosperous state must be large (*megalê*) they mistakenly identify *megalê* with the 'numerical magnitude of the population' (7.1326a12). He concedes, however, that in all probability it is today impossible to escape the identification of the size of a population with a community's greatness (7.1326a17). Since this is so, he offers, it is necessary to attend to the correct indicator (*sêmeion*, 7.1326a23) of great size. To judge size correctly, he proposes, requires more than counting the bodies residing within a sovereign territory. It requires the critical analytical skills of a theorist and empirical political scientist. Specifically, it requires distinguishing between the special component parts of which a state consists and understanding their relation to the practice of excellence. And so, the inevitably large numbers of slaves, metics and foreigners that will populate a polis cannot account for its greatness (7.1326a18-20). Instead, the sign (*sêmeion*) of greatness must be the size of that portion of the population that practices statesmanship or political

139

rule (7.1326a20-2). The remaining discussion of the ideal city in *Politics* book 7 addresses whether the various necessary sectors of a population, specifically, leisured property holders, citizens of modest wealth, artisans, tradesmen, farmers, labourers, etc., should be citizen, free or slave, that is, whether they should count among the active citizens, the portion of the population that determines the true size of the state. And, though he concludes that in an ideal polis only a fraction of the whole population domiciled in its territory will be citizens and thus count in the calculation of true size, the upshot of this story is that no matter how small this number, it will be sufficient to establish the superiority of a polis to all other known and newly emerging forms of political organisation. These rival forms would include the ones that appear too many to be especially distinctive and indeed impressive precisely for their exceptional size. Aristotle's theory of natural slavery and the distinction between master-ship and political rule enable him to deny any standing as an empirical indicator of greatness to an uncritical calculation of population size and territorial expanse. Instead, on his view, a vast empire in control of a large population of natural slaves or sovereign over of a mixed population in which the natural rulers among them enjoy little opportunity to practise true political activity or philosophy will, at best, rank as a very small, not particularly great state, if indeed it qualifies as a state at all.[19]

How does Aristotle determine precisely who qualifies as a natural slave?

So far I have tried to show that Aristotle's theory of natural slavery is not a tangle of assertions at odds with basic tenets of his moral and political theory but a set of reasonable (though repugnant), intertwined proposi-tions that fit with and at times shore up his philosophical system. But is his idea of precisely who qualifies as a slave a great muddle and just a function of bias? In this section I examine how Aristotle conducts that part of his investigation, reaching the conclusion that natural slaves populate the European and Asian (barbarian) nations.

Aristotle takes it as manifest (*phaneron*, 1.1255a3) that among the persons that inhabit the earth, some are slaves by personal constitution and character of soul (that is, by nature) and some are by nature free. To craft a just state, for Aristotle, then, it is necessary to sort people into these categories. But, he also takes it to be manifest that the intentions of nature (*bouletai hê phusis*, at 1.1254b27) are not perfectly clear in individual empirical cases. A condition of soul is not easily visible. It must be inferred from empirical observation. To make correct inferences requires the kind of 'practised faculty' of judgment that Aristotle identifies as the product of wide personal experience coupled with the enlarged experience that study of collections of empirical data can provide (*Nicomachean Ethics* 10.1181a10-14, b1-20). To get it right requires, that is, a grasp of political science. And so, he takes it to be a chief task of political science to make the intension of nature apparent to rational people. The practice of political science must enable the location of a sign in the empirical evidence that allows a reliable inference. And that is the way his discussion of how one can determine precisely who qualifies as a slave proceeds.

Aristotle begins by dismissing body type as a reliable indicator of free or slave by nature even though natural slaves will be especially suited to hard physical labour. As a matter of fact, he acknowledges, 'slaves often have the bodies of freemen' (1.1254b33). Moreover, it does not even occur to him to consider skin colour as a useful sign. He does not trust physical markers much at all. Instead, he assumes that an observable form of human activity must supply the basis for a reasonable inference about the slavish or free condition of a human soul. The activity to which he devotes the most extensive attention is victory and loss in war. Is victory in war – that is, the successful use of force – a reliable sign of the superior justice of a particular state (and thus superior condition of its members' souls) and is loss in war is a reliable sign of a state populated by naturally slavish souls (1.1255a12-15)? Answering yes, he suggests, lies at the heart of a common and problematic belief in the justice of the widespread conventional practice of obtaining slaves from a pool of prisoners of war or of selling such prisoners into slavery. Answering no, on the other hand, lies at the core of a belief that slavery is only a legal condition dependent upon misfortune or accident and that it therefore cannot be just. And so, when Aristotle rejects conquest as a sign of just rule and natural freedom, Aristotle is agreeing with contemporary opponents of slavery to a certain extent. He even seems to have some fun exposing the logical contortions that contemporary proponents of slavery by conquest must perform in order to assert what they really want to assert, that is, that barbarian prisoners of war positively deserve such status but that Greek prisoners of war must merely endure it (1.1255a25-b5). Credibly to propose that anyone – Greek or barbarian – *deserves* slavery, Aristotle argues, one must locate a more reliable indicator of condition of soul than prisoner of war status.[20] Conquest as an indicator produces an unacceptable measure of ambiguity (*dichôs*, 1.1255a3) in the determination of individual cases.

Though Aristotle does not argue for it explicitly and systematically in the context of the discussion of slavery in *Politics* book 1, a key later passage suggests that he believes that he has indeed located a reliable sign. In particular, he asserts that one can infer that barbarians are 'servile in nature' from the observable fact that they 'endure despotism without resentment' (*hupomenousi tên despotikên archên ouden duscherainontes*, 3.1285a22). The endurance of despotism without resentment signals a critical lack of deliberative capacity on the part of this population. Not surprisingly, this sign of slavish nature dependably excludes Greeks. Indeed, Aristotle uses this criterion to compare Greeks and barbarians, concluding that barbarians are 'more servile' (*doulikôteroi,*

3.1285a20). But even though the assertion appears rooted in bias, it is still the case that this proposition intelligently fits with key principles of his moral and political theory and does not create a muddle. As Kraut has observed, 'The thesis that by their very nature Asians and Europeans lack the capacity for deliberation suits his purposes perfectly; it locates the superiority of the Greeks in their capacity to deliberate, a capacity made evident by the greater maturity of Greek politics, as compared with the primitive [despotic] politics of Asia and Europe.'[21]

The ability of endurance of despotism to signal natural slavishness is also the assumption lying behind Aristotle's invocation of tragic poetry. Very near the start of the *Politics* (1.1252b5-10), he cites line 1400 from Euripides' *Iphigenia at Aulis*, ''Tis meet that Greeks should rule barbarians.' What is the implication here? What does this relation satisfy? The line suggests, Aristotle explains, that the poets understand that barbarians and slaves are 'the same in nature'. They know this because they recognise that barbarians equate all forms of rule exercised in the household (over slaves, children and wives) with domination. They hold exactly the erroneous view of rule (*archê*) that the *Politics* sets as its main task to dispute and disrupt – that is, that various forms of rule differ in only degree, not kind. The poets understood, he proposes, that the way barbarians run their families suggests that they are a nation bereft of 'natural rulers'. That is, they are bereft of free men who, through political struggle, design structures that require ruling and being ruled in turn and enable the practice of moral excellence. How else, Aristotle might have reasoned, can one explain the absence in their histories (as far as he knew) of any resistance to tyranny and of stories of political battles that aimed to establish forms of rule other than domination?

The surprisingly extensive quotations from Solon's lyric poetry in the Aristotelian *Constitution of Athens* (*Ath. Pol.* 5-12) also suggest an interest in identifying evidence among the Greeks of endurance of, or resistance to despotism and in interpreting that evidence as signifiers of slave or free conditions of soul. According to the account in the *Constitution of Athens*, the very origin of the Athenian *politieia* resides in the Athenians' response to a civil crisis over the pervasive presence of relations of mastership (*despoteia*) among the various strata of the local freeborn Athenian population. But, the *Constitution of Athens* demonstrates, the Athenian populace did not suffer domestic despotism lightly or without resentment. Athens has a long and illustrious history of civil strife over the relative power of the rich and poor, as evidenced by Solon's poetry. Indeed Aristotle stresses that Athens was the site of intense civil unrest dating at least to the time of Solon (the earlier chapters of the text are lost) owing to the fact that the poor were the 'slaves of the rich'. And he does not mean this in a metaphorical sense. At that time debt bondage was commonplace. If the ordinary people could not pay their debts, Aristotle reports, they and their children could be seized and sold into slavery (2.2). He extensively cites

Solon's poems to provide evidence for what he treats as the organising principle of Athenian political development – the Athenians resolved strife and achieved a measure of domestic peace by struggling politically to introduce order and justice, not by suffering the establishment of an all-powerful, dominant authority. Aristotle recounts the episodes of tyranny at Athens (Peisistratids, the Thirty) but recalling them works to celebrate their overthrow and the city's adoption of ever-stronger measures against tyranny resurfacing. Tyrant slaying is part of the Athenian civic self-image (e.g. veneration of Harmodius and Aristogeiton[22]) marked by their overthrow. In Aristotle's view, Athenian history supplies evidence of the free nature of the Athenians. We can only suppose that he could have based a generalisation regarding the free nature of all the Greeks on some familiarity with similar indications of histories of resistance to despotism in the constitutional histories of various Greek poleis. Perhaps that was one point he took away from his examination not only of Athenian history but of the (now lost) constitutional histories of 157 other Greek cities that his Lyceum is said to have compiled under Aristotle's supervision expressly as aids to the conduct of political analysis (*Nicomachean Ethics* 10.1181b20).

Another notorious passage about Greek superiority also exhibits Aristotle's empirical mode of inquiry concerning the determination of the identity of natural slaves. Aristotle (in)famously attributes Greek superiority at least in part to the fact that 'the Greek race' (*tôn Hellenôn genos*, *Pol.* 7.1327b29) occupies 'a middle place geographically' (not too cold and not too hot when compared with too cold Europe and too hot Asia) and that its population is thus both spirited and intelligent in nice proportions. The European peoples (*ethnê*), on the other hand, are 'more spirited but somewhat deficient in intelligence and skill so that they continue comparatively free but lacking in political organisation and capacity to rule their neighbours' while the Asian peoples 'are intelligent and skilful but lack spirit so that they are in continuous subjection and slavery' (7.1327b20-30). But notice that having already determined that the barbarian races' endurance of despotism is a good sign of their slavish natures, what he is doing in this passage about climate is trying to account for the observable variety among slavish natures. Indeed, that his main concern here is to identify a variable that accounts for a good deal of the observable variety of states in the world is evident from the fact that he considers climate to be a differentiating force not only among the states populated by slavish natures but among the free Greek states as well. He does not leave this implicit, but says, 'the same diversity also exists among the Greek races (*ethnê*) compared with one another' (7.1327b34-45). This troubling passage about the influence of climate on human nature is thus not part of Aristotle's argument about the empirical basis for inferring, on a case-by-case basis, whether a soul is free or slave. He does not claim that climate is anything like a reliable sign of that. But he does accept that it can account for some of the clearly visible variety inside that class. And this variety is important to examine, in Aristotle's view, because it can suggest which specific populations from among the naturally occurring diversity of slavish natures will likely be more or less 'manageable' when placed in a relation with a class of natural rulers, that is, when brought to Greece.

Is there a measure of critical potential in the theory of natural slavery?

Perhaps surprisingly, Aristotle never appeals to the apparent omnipresence (through history and cross-culturally) of slavery in one form or another to support his view that it is a condition rooted in nature. This is likely because, as a sensitive observer and scientist, he suspects that many factors might account for such a condition in the world, chief among them being the prevalence of war and the pervasive practice of enslaving (or selling) prisoners, as well as the frequency of violent crime, banditry, abandonment and abductions and the development of a legal and illegal slave trade. His concern is to infer from the largest possible data set why slavery it is a natural condition, not why it is a widespread one. Whether it is also widespread and whether it is so justly are, in principle, separate questions. Conveniently for him, of course, the proper examination of the question, 'Who deserves to be a slave?' issues in an answer, 'barbarians', that corresponds to a sufficiently large set of (close by) persons so as to provide the relatively easy delivery of an adequate supply of labour to the Greek city-states. And so it appears that, however philosophically interesting, his account of slavery does not generate much of a critique of contemporary practices.

That is not exactly right, however. He does deliver a strong critique of slavery by force, which practice was indeed common in his time (that is, a critique of slavery by an imposed legal standing deriving from some legally acceptable misfortune like debt or loss at war). As a result, we can imagine that Aristotle's view could motivate an upstanding slave owner to ask 'Is my slave deserving?' His view does not require the slave-owner to conduct such an inquiry, of course. Aristotle's theory is comfortable with the identification of empirical signs that support a reasonable inference about groups of persons. For example, it proposes that the barbarians' observable endurance of despotism makes that class of people a good bet for slaves by nature. Accordingly, in Aristotle's view, free men can legitimately treat certain group memberships as proxies for identification as slave by nature. Nevertheless, his theory does leave room for the possibility of interrogating the inference.

The logic behind this small measure of critical potential resident in his theory of slavery is most visible in Aristotle's discussion of whether hereditary citizenship is just (3.1275b23ff.).[23] In that section of the *Politics*

144

he reiterates that citizenship involves participation in the policy-making and judicial functions of a state and should be limited to those who have a certain character of soul (capacity for deliberation) but observes that, in practice, citizenship is usually limited to the children of citizens. He asks, 'Are such children rightly or wrongly given citizenship?' Is descent a legitimate proxy for a free nature?[24] Aristotle even identifies descent as a politically efficacious but still *hasty* practical definition of citizenship (*politikôs kai tacheôs*, 3.1275b25). He draws attention primarily to the question of colonisation and the participation of metics, foreigners and freed slaves in the peopling of new cities (3.1274b27).[25] Later generations of citizens of these colonies can, he notes, be descendents of classes of non-citizens. The first citizens of these colonies had to have been made citizens on some basis other than birth. And so, in some cases it appears allowable to interrogate the usual criterion, descent. In this case it is likely that Aristotle is thinking about how foreigners, metics and freed slaves of Greek ethnicity could start a new hereditary line of citizens, surely an attractive possibility for these often accomplished and ambitious members of the polis (and recall that this group would have included Aristotle himself). It is unlikely that he is here challenging the capacity of barbarian heritage to be a convenient and reliable sign of slavish nature. But the point remains that since Aristotle's view of individual cases rests on inferences, his conclusions remain, at least potentially, empirically falsifiable. Indeed Kraut goes so far as to stress that since Aristotle thinks it is unjust to enslave anyone who has the capacity to deliberate, once we drop the assumption that there are whole peoples in whom this incapacity is widespread as untenable, we emerge with the result that slavery is an unjust institution. 'This is not Aristotle's conclusion,' Kraut reminds us, 'but it is the one to which his political philosophy is driven, when it abandons the empirical claim of the natural slavishness of Europeans and Asians.'[26]

Kraut also rightly stresses that Aristotle valorises self-sufficiency, citizenship and philosophical activity so highly that his theory cannot be accused of glossing over the impoverishments of a life of slavery. It highlights what a life in slavery lacks no matter how comfortable a slave's material existence may be, how knowledgeable and sophisticated a slave might become regarding the exercise of certain technical skills, nor how indispensable a part of the achievement of excellence of the polis his contributions might be. This is an especially important point in regards to Aristotle because a key element of his theory of natural slavery is that slaves by nature benefit greatly from slavery. The critical potential of his theory comes to the fore, Kraut points out, when we compare it to Stoic philosophy, which argued that a fully flourishing human life was indeed compatible with slavery.[27] In Aristotle's view, in contrast, whatever benefit slavery offers the natural slave it cannot compare to the enjoyment of freedom experienced by a natural ruler. As the distinguished sociologist of slavery Orlando Patterson has noted, Aristotle's view renders apparent the fact that a slave enjoys 'no independent social existence'. Aristotle makes it plain that a slave exists 'only through, and for, the master; he is, in other words, naturally alienated … and in a perpetual state of dishonor'.[28] Aristotle's theory highlights this assessment of a slave's life even as it defends the justice of the institution.

Aristotle exhibits a brilliant, nearly unfettered sociological imagination in his political works and yet it never even occurs to him that a free society could be based on anything but slave labour. What accounts for this failure of imagination? I don't think that an arrogant sense of Greek superiority and concomitant need to assert the lowly condition of barbarian peoples can explain this failure. Neither can the claim that he did not escape the profile of his own times. His discussion of the sociological conditions that would most likely lead to citizens being able to navigate the sources of revolution and thus enable their constitution to persist through time includes a striking act of political imagination. He proposes that a 'community administered by the middle class' is best (4.1295a20-96a22). Nowhere in Greek history could Aristotle point to such an empirical reality. He could observe that perhaps the most exemplary individual citizen in the history of Athens possessed a middle quantity of wealth (e.g. Solon at *Ath. Pol.* 5.3[29]) and could point to the presence of some middle-class citizens in large cities (*Pol.* 4.1296a12), but he could not point to economic forces or structures that could drive the development of a sizeable population of 'middle class citizens', let alone identify a city in which such a class held sway over political life. The rule of the middle class was a wishful fiction.[30] Rather, what best explains Aristotle's inability to conceive of a free society based on anything but a slave economy is his contempt for physical labour and utter rejection of any possibility that a fully virtuous and good life could be consistent with any experience of manual labour or service to another. Citizen virtue, he says in no uncertain terms, does not belong to every citizen or every free man, 'but only to those who are released from menial occupations' (3.1278a10). Substantial leisure, he holds, is an essential condition of political freedom. Sadly, Aristotle does not seem to have used his acute powers of observation to uncover the pathologies that would likely attend a slave economy, including the violence and cruelty that accompany the trade in human bodies and souls. Sadly, it was enough for him that in an ideal city all mercantile activity, and presumably that means the slave trade, would be carried out by the lower orders of free men (foreigners, metics, former slaves).

Is Aristotle's theory of natural slavery pernicious?

Moses Finley reminds us that the presence of a defence of slavery in this most famous philosopher's body of work rarely added much more than 'learned embroidery' to the main argument for modern slavery, which 'rested on Scripture'.[31] This is largely true, save for some propaganda produced during a brief period leading up to the US Civil War. In this case, American advocates of race-based slavery explicitly appeal to Aristotle to argue that that slavery is not simply a 'necessary evil' (as compatriots had maintained for years) but is instead, as John C. Calhoun the Senator from South Carolina put it, a 'positive good'.[32] Some Southern intellectuals even argue that the modern case for slavery represented a significant advance over Aristotle, while remaining firmly Aristotelian in spirit. In particular, some argue that Aristotle's theory of natural slavery remains compelling except for one detail – his empirical data was faulty and thus he made a wrong inference regarding the identity of the group that best qualifies as natural slaves. In their view, Aristotle erred when he abandoned the possibility that an easily visible physical trait like race could indeed be a reliable indicator of the (inferior) character of soul. For example, in 1850 George Frederick Holmes published an article entitled, 'Observations on a Passage in the *Politics* of Aristotle relative to Slavery' in the prestigious *Southern Literary Messenger* in which he proposed not simply that Southern practice was in keeping with Aristotle's understanding of slavery (specifically, that 'the relation of master and slave is, in the full extent of Aristotle's proposition, both natural and expedient'), but that 'in our own day' we better understand how to read the empirical evidence precisely to determine who qualifies as natural slaves and masters. He lauds Aristotle and the Greeks generally for 'paying strict attention to the characteristics of different races' in their efforts to classify people into categories (by nature slave or free). He also immediately notes, however, that the Greeks were 'erroneous' in the application of that 'great principle'. Only in 'modern times', he stresses, have the different 'functions' of the different races become 'definite and clear'. He appeals to a notion of the march of history as well as to specific characteristics of contemporary society. He offers a narration of ancient and contemporary history as evidence for the Negro race's 'utter incapacity' to live in freedom. In contrast, he suggests, observation of history shows that 'the various Caucasian races ... have wholly or in part been subject at times to a servile condition, but with the progress of civilization they have uniformly advanced, and have extricated themselves from slavery by the exhibition of an aptitude for freedom'.[3] These Southern intellectuals found it possible to follow Aristotle's mode of inquiry to produce an update of the content of what they consider to be an Aristotelian conclusion. These intellectuals found reasoning with Aristotle attractive also because they share his unequivocal opposition to the very possibility that political freedom could be consistent with a working life (which they always associated with labouring generally and not just drudgery). They drew on Aristotle to attack Northern elites for allowing free white brethren to suffer 'wage slavery' instead of embracing Negro slavery as a path to white freedom.[34] These examples show that interest in Aristotle among Southern intellectual elites is not superficial. As Harvey Wish observed in 1949,

'Aristotle proved a major prop to antebellum Southern romanticism for the leisured class ideal'.[35]

While it was intended in its own time to be a (reformist) critique of unjust forms of slavery by force, a part of a theory of rule, and as an essential element in the articulation of foundation for the polis (in contrast to other emergent imperial political formations) as the best basis for a free society in which a leisured elite would engage in equal citizenship, Aristotle's theory of natural slavery and empirical case for the identity of slavish natures may have actually inaugurated a particularly pernicious way of thinking about slavery. As the French philosopher Alexis de Tocqueville observes in his writings about his travels in the United States in the 1830s, the fact that slavery in America is not based on legal standing alone (which could allow a freed slave's former status to go undetected), but instead on the observation of race and its interpretation as a signal of an inferior condition of soul that is said to render one fit for and capable of benefiting from enslavement, makes it likely that this nation's specific experience with slavery will have terribly persistent and horribly debilitating sociological and psychological effects long after it (eventually) achieves abolition, legal equality and even effective black enfranchisement.[36] He was, of course, dead right. But the point I want to stress in bringing to mind these modern references is that we must scrutinise Aristotle's mode of inquiry – and not simply his record of having accepted contemporary opinions regarding Greek superiority over the barbarians – in order to gain access to the peculiarities of Aristotle's reading of slavery and the shape of his political imaginary and its reception in modern times.

Notes

1. Williams (1993) 117; Patterson (1991) 162; Garnsey (1996) 125, 107.
2. Dietz (2009) 3 summarises this perspective: 'Aristotelian political theory exemplifies a conventional acceptance of Greek cultural prejudices in the service of an exclusionary, racist, sexist, slave-owning political status quo.' She goes on to interrogate that view.
3. Schofield (2005) 91, 100, 105.
4. Kraut (2002) 278.
5. Translations from the *Politics* are from Rackham (1977).
6. See Frank (2005) and Mara (1995) for discussion of the central role of activity in Aristotle's understanding of nature.
7. That Aristotle offers a remarkably insightful account of the sociology of the master/slave relation and of slavery as a condition of 'social death' is not contested. See Patterson (1991), 162: 'what he has left us is a first rate sociology of it [master/slave relation]'.
8. Citations of the Greek text are from Ross (1957), available online at *Thesaurus Linguae Graecae* (2009). On this Aristotelian phrase see also Thalmann, above p. 72.
9. Kraut (2002) 295-6.

10. Schofield (2005) 106.

11. Schofield (2005) 110.

12. Schofield (2005) 109.

13. Kraut (2002) 279.

14. Kraut (2002) 279.

15. Aristotle is assumed to have failed to absorb the 'transience of the polis' (MacIntyre [1981] 149). I owe recollection of MacIntyre's phrasing to Dietz (2009) 4.

16. For discussion of how this exceptional and emergent form Aristotle terms *pambasileia* (e.g. *Pol.* 3.1287a9) recalls the ambitions of the Macedonian kings, see Dietz (2009).

17. Aristotle identifies the control of judicial and legislative functions by the poor as the defining characteristic of the final, most thoroughly democratic, incarnation of the Athenian *politeia* (*Ath. Pol.* 41.2). Aristotle surmises from observations like this that the best kind of population for a democracy is an agricultural one. He stresses that in this case the many are enfranchised and content but far too busy to tend to political affairs, which they leave to the leisured elite by default. See *Pol.* 1318b5.

18. A instability in the effective criteria for citizenship status can harm a *politeia* by making it vulnerable to revolutionary change (as when a city with a depleted population due to war or disease enfranchises resident foreigners and freed slaves and becomes more democratic, or when civil strife leads to partisans trying to shape the demographic balance of a city by (in some cases) enfranchising non-citizen populations who fought with them or (in other cases) disenfranchising lower status compatriots who dilute their influence). See *Pol.* 1.1275b37.

19. It may be become an *ethnos*, but it is unlikely to become a *polis* because a multitude assembled by conquest cannot easily establish and come to possess a *politeia* (*Pol.* 7.1326b5-6).

20. The question of desert comes up again when he discusses rule and imperial expansion. 'It is not proper', he argues, 'to attempt to exercise despotic government over all people [i.e. mastership on a grand scale], but only over those suited for it, just as it is not right to hunt human beings for food or sacrifice, but only the game suitable for this purpose' (*Pol.* 7.1324b35-40). The theory of slavery suggests a critique of the imperial designs of the Macedonians over Greek *poleis*.

21. Kraut (2002) 303.

22. I address the part of Harmodius and Aristogeiton in the Athenian civic self-image in Monoson (2000). Note that Aristotle's *Ath. Pol.* lingers on this episode and it remembrance by the Athenians, arguing that its interpretation is a paramount importance. See Frank and Monoson (2009).

23. It also drives the discussion of the enfranchisement of metics, foreigners and former slaves as part of revolutionary change in a *politeia* (Cleisthenes' enrolment of many non-citizens in his tribes after the expulsion of the tyrants and Thrasybulus' attempt to enfranchise many after the defeat of the Thirty) or as the result of a problematic depletion or expansion of the citizen population due to prosperity, disease or war (e.g. Pericles' reform of citizenship laws). See *Pol.* 3.1275b35ff.

24. He also challenges parentage and descent as good indicators of the measure of moral virtue a child can be expected to exhibit (*Pol.* 1.1255a1-5).

25. Subversion of the restrictions on membership and shifting practical opportunities for metics and former slaves to gain full membership in an existing polis are considered sources of the destruction of a *politeia*. See discussion of the pathologies that threaten large-scale poleis on pp. 138-9 above.

26. Kraut (2002) 303.

27. Kraut (2002) 304-5.

28. Patterson (1991) 10.

29. 'Solon was one of the leading men by birth and reputation but middle class in wealth and position', *tê d'ousia kai tois pragmasi tôn mesôn, Ath. Pol.* 5.3, tr. Moore (1975), reprinted in Everson (1996).

30. The constitution of the 5000 described in *Ath. Pol.* (30-3) might be thought to provide an example in history of such a possibility. But Aristotle clearly says the restriction of power to this class did not actually occur and that the constitutional reforms needed to empower them never made it out of draft form (31.1). The *Ath. Pol.* identifies the rule of the 5000 with an idea that failed precisely because of the absence of the material conditions (in this case a particular stock) necessary for its realisation.

31. Finley (1980) 18.

32. Calhoun's 'Speech on the Reception of Abolition Petitions' delivered in the US Senate on 6 February 1837, reprinted in McKitrick (1963) at 13. That Aristotle had a direct influence on Calhoun's thinking is evident from a letter he wrote in 1840 which included the following: 'I would advise a young man with your views ... to read the best elementary treatise on Government, including Aristotle's, which I regard as among the best.' Quoted in Harrington (1989) 65. On Calhoun and the impact of Aristotle on American pro-slavery arguments see further the Introduction by Hall and especially the chapter by Monoson in Alston, Hall and McConnell (2011).

33. Holmes (1850) 200.

34. Fitzhugh (1854); Hammond (1858).

35. Wish (1949) 254.

36. de Tocqueville (2003 [1835/1840] 326-50.

References

de Tocqueville, Alexis (2003 [(1835/1840)] *Democracy in America*, tr. H. Reeve, with an introduction by E.W. Plaag. New York.

Dietz , M. (2009) 'Between polis and empire: Aristotle's *Politics*', paper prepared for the Political Theory Workshop, University of Chicago, 9 November.

Everson, S. (ed.) (1996, ed.) *Aristotle: The Politics and the Constitution of Athens.* Cambridge.

Finley, M.I. (1980) *Ancient Slavery and Modern Ideology.* London.

Fitzhugh, G. (1854) *Sociology for the South, or The Failure of Free Society.* Richmond, VA.

Frank, J. (2005) *A Democracy of Distinction: Aristotle and the Work of Politics.* Chicago, IL.

Frank, J. and Monoson, S.S. (2009) 'Lived excellence in Aristotle's *Constitution of Athens*: why the encomium of Theramenes matters', in S. Salkever (ed.) *Cambridge Companion to Ancient Greek Political Thought*, 243-70. Cambridge.

Garnsey, P. (1996) *Ideas of Slavery from Aristotle to Augustine.* Cambridge.

Hammond, J.H. (1858) Speech to the US Senate, March 4. Online at 'Africans in America', pbs.org.

Harrington, J.D. (1989) 'Classical antiquity and the proslavery argument', *Slavery and Abolition* 10, 60-72.

Holmes, G.F. (1850) 'Observations on a passage in the *Politics* of Aristotle relative to slavery', *Southern Literary Messenger* 16, 193-205.

Kraut, R. (2002) *Aristotle: Political Philosophy.* Oxford.

MacIntyre A. (1981) *After Virtue: A Study in Moral Theory*. London.

Mara, G. (1995) 'The near made far away: the role of cultural criticism in Aristotle's political theory', *Political Theory* 23, 280-303.

McKitrick, E. (1963) *Slavery Defended: The View of the Old South*. Englewood, NJ.

Monoson, S.S. (2000) *Plato's Democratic Entanglements: Athenian Politics and the Practice of Philosophy*. Princeton, NJ.

————— (2011) 'Recollecting Aristotle: proslavery thought in antebellum American and the arguments of *Politics* book I', in R. Alston, E. Hall and J. McConnell (eds) *Ancient Slavery and Abolition*, ch. 9. Oxford.

Moore, J.M. (1975) *Aristotle and Xenophon on Democracy and Oligarchy*. Berkeley, CA.

Patterson, O. (1991) *Freedom in the Making of Western Culture*. Cambridge, MA.

Rackham, H. (tr.) (1932) *Aristotle, Politics*, Loeb Classical Library. London.

Ross, W.D. (1957) *Aristotelis politica* (Greek text). Oxford.

Schofield, M. (2005) 'Ideology and philosophy in Aristotle's theory of slavery', in R. Kraut and S. Skultety (eds) *Aristotle: Critical Essays*. Lanham & Oxford. Reprinted from Günter Patzig (ed.) (1990) *Aristotles' Politk: Akten des XI. Symposium Aristotelicum*. Göttingen.

Williams , B. (1993) *Shame and Necessity*. Berkekey, CA.

Wish, H. (1949) 'Aristotle, Plato, and the Mason-Dixon Line', *Journal of the History of Ideas* 10, 254-66.

Family, Slavery and Subversion in Menander's *Epitrepontes*

Laura Proffitt

According to Orlando Patterson in his seminal *Slavery and Social Death* (1982), the fundamental fragility of family bonds is one of the constituents of slavery in any slaveholding society. Defining the concept of 'natal alienation' he argued: 'Not only was the slave denied all claims on, and obligations to, his parents and living blood relations, but, by extension, all such claims and obligations on his more remote ancestors and on his descendants. He was truly a genealogical isolate.'[1] That is to say that slaves in any society, Classical and Hellenistic Greece being no exception, have no formally or legally recognised family, regardless of actual blood-kinship or any affective relationships which may exist between them. Any provisions for slaves to live with their 'spouses' or children[2] have always been entirely at the whim of the owner, with separation and sale always possibilities.

That to be a slave is to be 'natally alienated', to suffer under the weight of the most fragile of family bonds, was a concept already familiar to the Greek cultural imagination by the fifth century, explicitly articulated as the stuff of tragic drama in, among other plays, Euripides' *Andromache* and *Ion*. In both these tragedies, the eponyms' enslavement is marked by a profound sense of familial alienation and its attendant lack of identity. This is most explicit in Ion's case; entirely unaware of his parentage, he is fatherless, motherless, homeless, and, at least at first, nameless. Their ultimate passages from slavery into freedom are accompanied by their restoration to formally recognised familial relationships: Andromache as the wife of Helenus, and mother of the royal son she very nearly lost to Menelaus and Hermione's murderous plot, and Ion as the son (in name and public recognition, at least), of Xuthus, and as the natural son of Creusa and Apollo. The foundling-child plot pattern,[3] a staple of myth and folk tale, and subsequently of tragedy, was very often centred around an abandoned boy-child, raised as a slave before being reunited with his natal family,[4] and restored to his true – inherited – status, usually royal.

For a dramatised slave to lay claim to a family of sorts therefore takes on a complex cultural significance. My aim is to trace a map of this discursive field as articulated in the extant sections of Menander's *Epitre-*

pontes. During the course of what survives of this comedy, pseudo-familial relationships (most crucially that involving the slave-prostitute Habrotonon's care for the foundling child) are brought into close contact with discourses of slavery and freedom, with the result that such relationships exhibit an implicit and unsettling liberatory potential.[5] This potential is tempered but never fully erased either by discourses that naturalise the slave-free divide and support the interests of the slave-owning classes, or by the comedy's (probably) normative and superficially conservative ending.

Given the almost total inaccessibility of Greek slaves' subjective voices, a cultural-historical approach to the sources, a study of representations and discursive practices, is by far the most fruitful approach to the subject, and has been responsible for several excellent publications in the field of ancient comedy, both Greek and Roman.[6] It should be clear from the outset that I make no presumption to be able to recover the subjectivity of ancient slaves, or even their 'typical' experiences – to do so could only be at best epistemologically dubious, and at worst dangerously unethical. Meanings are by no means the record of subjective experiences, although they can and often do set conditions as to the possibilities of such experience. As Catherine Belsey argues in relation to seventeenth-century fiction, '[literature] like architecture and painting is a signifying practice which can be understood in its period to the extent that it shares the meanings then in circulation. This is quite distinct from the claim that fiction reflects the practices of the period.'[7]

It is important, however, not to lose sight of the existence of real and tangible slaves behind these representations; the issues and conflicts explored in such artistic creations as *Epitrepontes* were played out in various permutations not just on stage but in the daily interactions between slaves and the free. We may never be able to recover exactly *how* they affected everyday life, but should nevertheless recognise that they did; slave and free alike lived from day to day with the ramifications of 'natal alienation', with the close proximity of slaves to the free members of the *oikos* (in whose case familial claims on each other *were* formally recognised), and with the responsibilities of caring for and training enslaved children.[8] The issues represented and navigated in this comedy were no cultural abstracts but existed in a dynamic relationship with lived reality. I shall argue that *Epitrepontes* is a rich repository of conflicting and competing meanings, some of them decidedly subversive, surrounding Greek slavery. It is a cultural site where slave characters are portrayed quite openly voicing discontent with their lot, taking control of their own futures by actively striving for – and achieving – freedom, and controlling the supply of crucial information to the free. Yet it was written by a free man and enjoyed by free audiences all over the Hellenistic world. It is essentially a play divided against itself, 'dynamised by a profound struggle between conflicting impulses'.[9]

I do not intend to suggest that Menander deliberately sought to undermine the all-pervasive institution of slavery by subtly enacting resistances through his slave characters. Such a claim requires that we believe both in a certain anachronistic, 'abolitionist' self-consciousness on the part of the dramatist, and that a free, slaveholding audience with an interest in maintaining the status quo would find such self-conscious criticisms entertaining. Neither, however, do I argue that such criticisms were cynically 'intended' as part of an ideological project to reaffirm the primacy of the free Athenian ruling class by being erased by the effect of the play's conservative resolution. The latter is a stance taken, in more or less sophisticated permutations, by a number of scholars working on ancient comedy,[10] and one that has been roundly criticised by Kiernan Ryan with respect to Shakespearean scholarship.[11] The contradictions within discourses surrounding ancient slavery are what make it such a fruitful area of research; better to investigate these than simply interpret literature as justifying the domination of the master-class. It is more helpful to see the potentially subversive discourses voiced by Menander's slave characters as an expression of social tensions showing, as it were, 'through the cracks', and that, in striving to create sympathetic, well-developed and believable characters, the dramatist has given these voice despite himself.[12]

Perhaps the most useful analytical tools for theorising the polyvalent and tension-ridden reading of *Epitrepontes* that I wish to offer are those developed by Mikhail Bakhtin (under the influence of Marxist aesthetics) with reference to the development of the novel as a genre.[13] Crucial to all of Bakhtin's theory, and invaluable to my investigation of *Epitrepontes,* is the notion of dialogism – the epistemological mode whereby every single utterance, every meaning, must be understood, not in isolation[14] but as part of a greater whole, where there is a constant interaction between meanings, all of which have the potential to condition others. This amounts to far more than simply the expression of contradictory opinions. According to this principle, where there is dialogue, there can be no one single 'monologue', no one overarching, unilateral meaning existing at the expense of all others. This can only exist where there is an authoritative voice. When words and discourses become repositioned relative to competing definitions, as does the discourse of a taken-for-granted moral superiority of free over slave in *Epitrepontes,* it cannot be ultimately authoritative or absolute. Consequently, the play exhibits a plenitude of competing meanings; the intended meaning – whatever it may be – is only ever one of those communicated. Although Bakhtin developed these theories with specific reference to the novel, I believe that his work somewhat over-stresses the uniqueness of that genre and the supposed one-dimensionality of drama; Menandrean comedy is as polyphonic as any novel discussed by Bakhtin, with any controlling authorial voice (which could serve to fix its discourses and arguments within a set ideological frame) obscured.[15]

In *Epitrepontes*, characters as diverse as a free head-of-household and an enslaved prostitute speak openly and disagree with one another (consider Smikrines' and Onesimos' conversation towards the end of the fragments, in which the latter informs the former of the child's parentage, or Onesimos' Charisus' and Habrotonon's discussion in Act IV during which the slaves wrangle with their master in order to make him realise that he is in fact the child's father). Not just the free characters but also the slaves (Daos, Syros, Onesimos and particularly Habrotonon) act in accordance with their own interests and desires. The slaves' words do not simply reflect a ruling-class ideology seeking to shore up the authority of the master classes, but simultaneously present the possibilities of another world-view, where slaves can voice discontent with their lots and ultimately achieve freedom as a consequence of their own actions.[16] In short, *Epitrepontes* is a play that demonstrates empathy with diverse viewpoints. Like the novel's characters in Bakhtin's assessment, they have their 'own perceptions of the world incarnated in [their] actions and discourse'. The 'other' is here essentially manipulated by Menander as a self. What emerges is 'a plurality of independent and unmerged voices and consciousnesses, a genuine polyphony of fully valid voices'.[17]

Another Bakhtinian concept that can shed light on the unsettling and destabilising strains articulated in *Epitrepontes* is his insight that to situate an artistic image in the present can invest it with a sense of open-endedness and progression into the future.[18] It follows that the meanings negotiated in such a work are by no means fixed. The final word, as it were, has not yet been spoken:. 'Every object of artistic representation loses its completedness, its hopelessly fixed quality and its immutability [qualities that had been crucial to epic]. Through contact with the present, an object is attracted to the incomplete.'[19] By the 'present', Bakhtin means not necessarily contemporary 'reality' but 'live action', whichever era this may be set in, as opposed to a narrative of past action. Although originally referring to the difference between the genres of novel and epic, this notion of progression and potential – the 'what will happen next?' question – is in fact no more pertinent than when applied to drama. The specific 'future orientation' of drama, as opposed to, for example narrative, lyric, or even film, has been succinctly discussed by Hall (2004). Drawing on the work of Susan Langer,[20] she recognises the political potency of this orientation, arguing that it can 'make the future seem controllable or at least susceptible to intervention ... This sense of empowerment gives theatre [Ernst Bloch's] utopian tendency or signature. This designates its potential for transcending in fictive unreality the social limitations of the moment of its own production.'[21] If such future orientation is a hallmark of all drama, then Menander's comedy can be said to display it markedly. In comparison to tragedy, comedy had little in the way of further tradition to look forward to; no knowledge based on previous experiences of literature and myth of the sort that informed the audience, for example, of Euripides' *Medea,* that its anti-heroine would go on to cause murderous havoc in Athens as she had done at Corinth. This 'thinking in the present tense' also offers the audience a far more immediate affective engagement than would a more remote narrative or lyric recitation. The inherent inconclusiveness afforded by the plays' temporal orientation contributes towards the suitability of New Comedy to the negotiation of social tensions.

Ryan's work on Shakespearean comedy can prove immensely useful here. He reads into *Twelfth Night* a recognition that its superficially conservative conclusions – the reunion of the siblings Viola and Sebastian and their marriages to Orsino and Olivia respectively – 'cannot be achieved within the social or sexual framework they present or presuppose'.[22] It takes such 'removals from regular roles and familiar circumstances' as exile in Illyria, Viola's foray into transvestism and living as a man, and Olivia's falling in love with her to ensure that the reunion and marriages can take place at all. 'The desirability of these endings as solutions is undermined in advance by the richer definitions of identity and possibility established or adumbrated in the course of the play as a whole.' To Ryan, the 'utopian conclusions'[23] of Shakespearean comedy and romance can never entirely escape the intrusion of irrepressible and unredeemed realities stressing the 'fragile fictionality and incompleteness of the otherwise uncompromised state of concord'.[24]

Ryan's radical thesis nevertheless recognises that such endings, with their 'distinct sense of the world's intransigence', are never allowed to dissolve into escapist fantasy. The alternative worldviews and possibilities of social relations which are implicitly presented are situated in the future; such journeys are yet to be – if, indeed, they ever will be – completed. That such possibilities are marked out as still unrealised invests them with an ambiguity; they can be read both in favour of and against the status quo simultaneously. Such endings as those of *Twelfth Night* and *Epitrepontes* therefore contain within them the semantic potential to communicate both subversive and conservative messages, each in dialogue with and inseparable from the other. For example, Onesimos' manumission may, on one level, add to the celebratory atmosphere of the play's normative ending. On another, however, the fact that a slave character is so easily and instantaneously freed, with no implication that anything permanent or innate is tying him to his position, carries major implications for the arbitrary nature of slavery. The possibility of social change is here at once both raised and postponed; yet the one must, however implicitly, make reference to the other in order for it to have meaning – Bakhtin's 'word with a sidewards glance'.[25]

The discourses running through the entire drama are also unstable. Where both free and slave (or male and female, rich and poor) interests and worldviews are given equal weight and authority by the dramatist, they cannot help but imply and unsettle the other whenever they are expressed. Even where *Epitrepontes* expresses a viewpoint that straightforwardly seems to naturalise the slave-free divide and support the status quo – such as Smikrines' painting of Habrotonon as a stereotypical comic *hetaira*, greedy and conniving – it cannot 'simply' reflect badly on her. That the audience have already witnessed Habrotonon's planning to have the child recognised as free, her own unhappiness and desire to better her situation, her interiority, essentially (within the confines of the play) her *subjectivity*, means that this side of the *hetaira* is implied by contrast even when she is being denigrated.

The great advantage of New Comedy as a vehicle for this kind of unsettling discourse is that it both depends on conflict and differing worldviews for its narrative structure, and, like all comedy, requires a great deal of familiarity with cultural norms and expectations in order to produce humour.[26] To quote Bakhtin:

> Laughter has the remarkable power of making an object come up close, of drawing it into a zone of crude contact where one can finger it familiarly on all sides, turn it upside down, inside out, peer from above and below, break open its shell, look into its centre, doubt it, take it apart, dismember it, lay it bare and expose it, expose it freely and experiment with it. Laughter demolishes fear and piety before an object, before a word, making it an object of familiar contact, and thus clearing the ground for an absolutely free investigation of it ... laughter delivers an object into the fearless hands of investigative experiment ... and into the hands of free investigative fantasy.[27]

According to this theory, the object – which in this case would be *Epitrepontes,* its staging and constituent discourses and meanings – is 'broken apart, laid bare, and its hierarchical ornamentation is removed ... What takes place is a comic act of dismemberment.'[28] Even if one does not accept the total removal of hierarchy in comedy which Bakhtin describes,[29] the recognition that laughter creates a space in which the dissection of the object and its constituents is enabled, is extremely suggestive. The play itself can be broken down into many constituents (of which issues of slavery and freedom are two), all of which can be examined 'up close' and treated with free familiarity.

When it comes to previous classical scholarship on Menander, the focus has tended to be on linguistics and stylistics, dramatic functions, conventions and aesthetic ideals.[30] Much of the literature, ultimately deriving from Aristophanes of Byzantium's famous exclamation (see n. 7), discusses the extent to which Menander's comedies are indeed unmediated reflections of 'reality'.[31] Work on Menander's treatment of slaves and slavery is sparse considering the numerous important, active and vocal slave characters permeating his comedies. The only full-length publication to deal specifically with the topic is Marta Krieter-Spiro's *Sklaven, Köche, und Hetären* (1997). Essentially a reference work, it catalogues the slave characters in Menander, describes their functions regarding plot, and offers linguistic commentary on the etymologies of their names and patterns of speech. She deals little with wider cultural-historical issues. Methodologically, she conflates dramatic sources with what is known of extra-literary 'reality', as in her speculation on the legal status of the union between Syros, *Epitrepontes*' charcoal-burning slave, and his 'wife'.[32] Wiles' article in Archer (1988) discusses slave characters from the perspective of their masks, and does recognise the lack of linguistic distinction between slave and free in Menander, with all characters speaking a uniform Attic Greek.[33] His short article, however, cannot offer a detailed theoretical analysis, and assumes that New Comedy sought to 'legitimise' slavery in the eyes of the free.[34] Discourses which might suggest world-views other than those advantageous to free slave-owners are, Wiles implies, opened and played out, only to be neutralised by the comedy's conclusion and because they are contrary to expectations; they become the exceptions that prove the rules.[35]

There seems to have been an unwillingness, with a few notable exceptions, to tackle any ideological negotiations and wider social issues. The first of these exceptions was Konstan's 1995 *Greek Comedy and Ideology*, which aimed to 'interpret the texts as vehicles of social or ideological tensions in the classical city-state, which show up in the plays as complex or overdetermined elements in plot or characterisation'.[36] In his work, which addresses 'ways in which the plays respond to cultural issues, shaping the narratives by which Athenians defined and understood themselves', he treats a diverse selection of Greek comedy, and its adaptation in later cultures and languages. One of the greatest strengths of the book is its recognition that Greek comic drama was an open space for ideological exploration. I am indebted to Konstan's approach insofar as I too am concerned with investigating *Epitrepontes* as a cultural site where 'social tensions or contradictions are enacted, and … the seams and sutures in the construction of ancient comedy become visible'.[37] Indeed, his astute insight concerning *Epitrepontes*, that the comedy displays a 'double impulse towards utopian inclusiveness and the reassertion of conventional social boundaries',[38] is an important *a priori* assumption of this chapter.

Yet Konstan's work has little to say about specific issues of slavery. He judges *Epitrepontes*, despite its slaves' frequently voiced desires for freedom, to be primarily concerned with the exploration of conflict in gender relations, specifically male anxiety concerning pre-marital female sexual experience and the legitimacy of children. The issue at stake for Konstan is one of Athenian citizenship, but I would argue that this element should not be overestimated, particularly when one considers Menander's popularity not just in Athens but across the Greek-speaking world. The slave-free division could have conveyed as much, if not more, meaning than the distinction between Athenian citizen and non-citizen to its diverse audiences over several centuries; in its most basic form (of course, the technical specifics of slavery will have varied from state to state) it was relevant to the entire Hellenistic world.

Likewise, Lape's *Reproducing Athens* (2003), which has raised the bar in Menander scholarship, is focused on the intersections of gender roles and citizen identity at a time when political upheaval was presenting a threat to the Athenian democratic ethos. New Comedy, she argues, consolidated democratic identity while Athenians struggled against the effectively autocratic puppet governments imposed on them by the Macedonians, against which they sporadically revolted.[39] She understands Menander's comedy as a producer, rather than product, of ideology;[40] to Lape, it exhibits countervailing tendencies towards both the reproduction of democratic Athenian culture and, in the face of an external enemy, the subversion of internal status boundaries 'between citizens and non-citizens and men and women'.[41] Lape's strengths lie in her unusual recognition of the implicit political content of New Comedy,[42] and her treatment of the sources as 'active participants in the cultural and political negotiations of their times'.[43] Since texts are in a constant process of negotiation, we cannot expect them to be politically or ideologically coherent; gaps and slippages are inherently revealing.[44] Like Konstan, Lape breaks away from the interest in stereotypes, patterns and stock-types that had limited much of the previous scholarship, and recognises the complexity and diversity – within generic conventions – of Menander's drama.[45] She recognises the potential of comedy to voice subversive discourses, and the empowerment, during the course of the play, of female characters who would be marginalised in 'reality', or at least in other genres such as oratory. This, she argues, is not necessarily negated by New Comedy's conventional, formulaic endings, which are necessary to contain the authority achieved by these women. To Lape these plays succeed in installing the figure of (in her case) the empowered woman into the cultural imagination. Yet she, too, fails to address slavery as a serious topic of discussion in itself, mentioning it only when it impinges on other elements of her argument.[46]

Given this absence of a cultural-historical study of slavery in Menander, we must turn to scholarship on Roman Republican comedy for theoretical insights. McCarthy's *Slaves, Masters and the Art of Authority in Plautine Comedy* (2002) is the one of the most useful.[47] McCarthy specifically reads tension and unresolved multiplicity into Plautine master-slave relationships. She recognises the opposition within comedy between the 'socially conservative values of familial plots' and the 'charmingly subversive intelligence of the clever slave'. Working with the Bakhtinian notion of dialogism (although ultimately rejecting its original, optimistic sense), McCarthy identifies two modes of comedy operating within all the plays, the one 'naturalistic' and conservative, and the other a 'farcical' mode more subversive and cynical. The 'complex instability' produced by the interaction of these two modes, which never entirely succeed in disengaging themselves from one another, is, she argues a major source of comedy's meaning.[48]

McCarthy argues that the mixing of the two modes offered 'dreams that are at once liberatory and grounded in traditional authority'.[49] For the elite free, they allayed anxieties surrounding potential slave rebelliousness by painting slaves as simple, playful figures unconscious of free people's quotidian cares.[50] Plautine comedy, she argues, ultimately worked to 'create, defend and shore up'[51] the basis of free domination even as it voiced words of subversion; these words, by providing rebellion fantasies, ultimately worked too in the interests of the master class. Publicly funded drama, she argues, can never function as the voice of an otherwise silenced group. Instead, such productions are part of the 'public transcript', a script used by dominant and subdominant groups when together: 'The contribution of subordinates to this transcript is circumscribed by the imperative that the transcript as a whole preserves a view of the existing social order as both natural and just.'[52] Her analysis, though sophisticated and nuanced, makes little mention of the sizeable involvement that slaves had in Plautine comedy, which distinguished Roman theatre from the performances at Athens. Roman slaves could participate as both actors and spectators;[53] the comedian Terence was a freedman. Her readings of Plautus, however, focus exclusively on the 'master' elements of the production and audience; an acknowledgement of the active participation of slaves as both performers and spectators would profoundly change the dynamic of authority for which she argues.

McCarthy holds up Menander as a prime example of the 'naturalistic' mode, indeed, as the prototype for this mode where it appears in Roman comedy.[54] It would follow, therefore, that to McCarthy, Menander uses the 'farcical mode' rather little,[55] preferring to represent the familiar world of the spectators,

> but with all the rough edges smoothed away ... The mode presents itself as somehow 'truer' than real life, as though we are seeing the workings of both social life and divine will. The plot device of recognition (*anagnorisis*) is virtually constitutive of this kind of comedy and perfectly expresses its worldview: we find out in the end that the identities we took seriously were merely optical illusions, caused by the flux of appearances, and the real identities remained all the time hidden beneath this veneer ... The overall effect is to make the dramatic illusion as powerful as possible, as if we are spying on the characters through a one-way mirror, rather than watching a play scripted by an author and performed by actors.[56]

In terms of its ideological stance, the naturalistic mode 'affirms the real contemporary social code ... As with this mode's attitude towards plot and style, its moral perspective is a better version of real life (a version in which people actually observe the laws they claim to value), but does not replace the values of real life with a new and different set of values.' To McCarthy, this mode presents itself as disinterested reality, enabling the values it champions to take on the appearance of immanent truth. By the plays' conclusions, recognitions have 'drawn our attention away from the long time that everyone was living in error ... and focus instead on the moment of realignment with the underlying persistent truth'. Ultimately, plays in which this mode dominates function as hegemonic discourse, legitimising the status quo by making the world seem to 'be the one destined by divine, (or at least superhuman) will'.[57] McCarthy also denies the liberatory potential of Bakhtinian dialogism in the interaction of the two modes, by arguing that, in Plautine comedy, 'dialogic openness is part of an ongoing successful domination [by providing rebellion fantasies that work to the benefit of the free], and therefore dialogism is not necessarily connected to a more humane social practice'.[58]

An attempt to read McCarthy's 'naturalism' into *Epitrepontes*, however, soon runs into difficulty. In what follows I argue that this comedy challenges stereotypes at every turn. The notion of a naturalised free-slave divide exists in dynamic interaction with the possibilities of alternative ways of life, where slave and free can be moral equivalents and where slaves can challenge their subservient position and be ultimately rewarded with freedom. The metatheatrical nature of this play – not just in the famous 'arbitration scene' but notably in Habrotonon's 'rehearsal' and role-play – destabilises the dramatic illusion and any 'naturalism' that this might imply. Lastly, and crucially, I propose that the tiny, mute and helpless foundling child serves as a locus for the majority of this play's discourses surrounding slavery and freedom.

Where previous scholarship has dealt with *Epitrepontes*, two foci have tended to emerge. The first treats the famous arbitration scene between the slaves Daos and Syros as a source for the historical institution of private arbitration in Hellenistic Athens.[59] The second examines the play's sexual politics and gender relations; no small task given the act of rape which serves as the plot's catalyst, the remarkable scene of Charisios' breakdown and about-turn over his wife's supposed infidelity.[60] It has also, along with the rest of Menander, been the subject of dramaturgical research inspecting its plot structure[61] and its relationship with other works of literature and drama,[62] as well as traditional linguistic commentary and analysis,[63] most recently Martino's huge three-volume Italian edition (2000). Martino examines the play's slaves insofar as they feature in his catalogue of characters, but his analysis only addresses their dramatic functions, character traits, name etymologies, and possible staging, including masks. His focus is concentrated on the play's practical performative rather than ideological aspects.

The importance of the child to the play has been almost universally neglected.[64] A 2002 article by Heap argues that child-figures were central to the plots of several of Menander's comedies, especially *Epitrepontes* and *Samia*, despite lacking any personal characteristics of their own; she focuses on ways in which babies contribute towards the characterisation of the adult characters with whom they come into contact. Ideological issues again take a subsidiary role while she looks at the creation of emotional affect and pathos. She does, however, recognise that power and powerlessness are crucial to *Epitrepontes*,[65] that the abandoned baby is 'at the centre of an argument about status',[66] the complexity of the slave-prostitute Habrotonon and the double-edged nature of her tenderness towards the child,[67] and the thematic centrality of the arbitration scene.

Although the slaves Syros and Daos,[68] the eponymous 'arbitrants', feature only in this scene and nowhere else in the play, their appearance, in close contact with the child and his fate, establishes the tensions underlying the entire surviving drama.[69] They are both slaves, and their scene introduces the conflicting conceptions of 'natural' versus arbitrary slavery which are to play off one another subsequently. The child, as a free citizen in danger of being raised a slave, symbolises one side of this tension; Onesimos and Habrotonon, as slaves striving for their own freedom (and in the case of the former, achieving it), represent the other. The charcoal-burner Syros responds to Smikrines' sharp-tongued and reproachful enquiry as to why he is 'debating law whilst dressed in slave's clothes' (228-30) with an appeal to the common lot of humanity and equivalence between free and slave where matters of justice are concerned.[70] Likewise, in his contention that the birth-tokens should be returned to the child, he argues that 'life is precarious by nature – we must have foresight and protect against events by all means possible' (343-6) – the specific danger being implied in this case being, of course, enslavement. Such statements and their implications, however, sit alongside a 'naturalising' discourse of slavery. The child, though set to be raised as a slave by Syros and his 'wife', may grow to despise these servile folk, and exhibit free (*eleutheron*) traits. He may, Syros argues, seek his own level, by wanting for example to go lion-hunting, to carry weapons and to run in athletic competitions, much like the heroes of the many abandoned-baby tragedies of the fifth century. The twin brothers Neleus and Pelias, mentioned here in a metatheatrical reference to a lost play (possibly Sophocles' *Tyro*[71]) were only two of these.

This acknowledgement that anyone might find themselves enslaved is used, paradoxically, to substantiate an argument based on the premise that freedom is less a legal status and more an innate quality which will win out regardless of upbringing. Syros' speech, with its concern for the precarious status of the helpless child, simultaneously betrays a recognition of the arbitrariness of slavery and an attempt to attenuate it with a naturalising discourse, neither of which can be invested with ultimate authority. This contradiction goes unresolved through the remainder of the fragments. Both Onesimos and Habrotonon become focal points for its thematic development subsequently (see below). The real prospect that the freeborn may be raised in slavery is never erased. The inverse is likewise true, since this inconclusiveness also contains within it the possibility that slaves can traverse the boundaries of legal status, moving towards freedom. This is, in fact, realised with Onesimos' manumission towards the end of the surviving fragments. The naturalising discourse, based around the argument that Pamphile's abandoned child might go on to display 'naturally free' characteristics, is shaky at the least. As long as Syros shows concern that the external, material tokens of status, may be the infant's only key to freedom, the suggestion of an innate difference between free and slave cannot dominate.

The attitudes of Daos and Syros towards the child of which they both seek 'guardianship'[72] are entirely consistent with the conflicting themes expressed elsewhere in Greek discourses where issues of family and slavery intersect. The child provides an ideological focus for notions of what it meant to be both a slave and a parent. Patterson's theory of natal alienation proves useful here, finding articulation in Habrotonon's complex exploitation of the child in an attempt to secure her own freedom (see below). Yet, in keeping with the polyvalence of this play's discourses, it is never entirely separable from sentiments similar to those expressed by Daos in this scene; to be a slave and to have the responsibility of caring for a child is a tiresome economic and emotional burden.

Daos reports how he had wondered to himself, on taking the child home, 'What do I want with the trouble of raising children? Where will I find the money? Why give myself the worry?' (253-5). His concerns are far more immediate and practical than the long-term trauma of raising a child to be someone else's property. In keeping with his portrayal as self-interested and shallow, his only interest in the child is material: he seeks to sell the tokens. Yet such complaints were standard rhetorical tropes in the mouths of enslaved tragic heroines, some one hundred or more years before Menander.[73] The attitudes expressed by Syros, the charcoal burner, are more ambiguous. When Syros entreats Daos to take care of Pamphile's abandoned child, as a substitute for his own, dead, slave-born baby, he implies a certain desperation stemming from something more than a bereaved father's grief.[74] In Daos' description of Syros' entreaty, the dead child is mentioned perfunctorily and only once (278); stress is laid, rather, on his anxiety to take home the foundling. He calls down countless blessings on Daos, and kisses his hands when the goatherd capitulates and hands over the child. It is any child, not the specific child he lost, for which he seems to long. Surely the suggestion of the liberatory potential of family in slavery underlies this representation of Syros' joy. As he takes it from Daos he actually wishes that his fellow slave may, 'be lucky, be free' (266-7).

Habrotonon later draws a similar connection between the child and the possibility of freedom when she devises her plan to impersonate the child's mother in the hope that (among other things) Charisios will manumit her. This possibility is developed at length and explicitly in Habrotonon and Onesimos' plotting scene. Moreover, given Daos' negative portrayal as ignorant and self-interested, the suggestion that freedom may come in conjunction with the removal of the child from *his* care actually reinforces the notion of the infant as a symbol of freedom. Daos is utterly uninterested in his own status, seeking only short-term material gains. His

163

relinquishing of this child speaks of this; a degree of irony can be heard here in Syros' wish for his fellow-slave. Unlike the materialistic and self-interested Daos,[75] Syros' contact with the child implies that he is deeply unhappy with his position, preparing us for more in-depth characterisations of discontented slaves in Onesimos and particularly Habrotonon. Syros is clear that the child, even in his care, is being wronged. He is deeply concerned that the foundling, if free, should be recognised as such, and be spared the misery of slavery – he believes it utterly wrong that Daos should steal his 'hope for the future'.[76]

Syros' reference to the tragic twins Neleus and Pelias in relation to the trinkets left with the child has been seen as a play on the idea of dramatic illusion,[77] or as making a 'clever internal contrast between the false world of heroes and the "real" one of arbitrations', a contrast which stresses the 'reality' of the arbitration scene and invites the historian to examine it as a tangible historical source that implies the possibility that the baby is the product of a prosperous family.[78] But its relevance to the issue of slavery has not been appreciated, even though it places *Epitrepontes* firmly within the tradition of foundling-child plotlines, with their fascination with issues of status, family and innate freedom. It also paints Syros as a slave conversant in the tragic tradition. Perhaps, in the light of Theophrastus' roughly contemporary references to slaves at the theatre,[79] the audience would not be surprised by a slave-connoisseur of tragedy. He is not, after all, the play's only culturally refined slave – Onesimos later threatens Smikrines that he will declaim an entire speech from Euripides' *Auge* (another play concerned with foundling children) if the old man fails to realise that the child is his grandson.[80]

The mythical tradition as developed in fifth-century tragedy bore some decidedly conservative connotations where slavery is concerned. Free foundling children are invariably restored to their natal status, sometimes with fatal or ominous consequences (in Sophocles' *Oedipus Tyrannos* and Euripides' *Alexandros*), and sometimes with near-misses leading to melodramatic 'happy endings' (Euripides' *Ion*). Such children exhibit innately 'free' characteristics (Amphion and Zethus in *Hypsipyle*, Ion in his name-play) setting them apart from other slaves.[81] Moreover, speaking slaves (other than enslaved aristocrats) have either assimilated the master-class's viewpoint and interests (Medea's nurse), or become unselfconsciously deviant (Phaedra's nurse, Creusa's old slave). But they do not voice explicit unhappiness with their position, and desire to change it, as do Menander's slaves. The weight of the tragic discourse on slavery tends to fall, though not unequivocally, on the side of 'naturalisation'. The invocation of Neleus and Pelias adds to the naturalising strain which runs through the scene. On the other hand, the child in *Epitrepontes* is quite unlike the tragic foundlings such as Oedipus and Ion since he is not an agent in his own liberation. He is a focus but not a producer of discourse, and has no chance to display his biologically 'free' qualities. Instead, it is the efforts of resourceful, unhappy slaves that bring about his recognition as the child of his parents, and these slaves improve their own statuses in the process.

The metatheatricality of the tragic reference also has subversive implications.[82] As Ryan has argued in relation to Shakespearean comedies, they have the 'profound inclination' to 'cite their own status as a staged event, a scripted performance fiction reflecting, yet not to be conflated with ... reality lived beyond the charmed circumference of the Globe'.[83] Comedy's reference to its own fictionality, according to this view,

> stimulates in the spectator a critical awareness of the extent to which the stage world and the lived world of which it is a projection are provisional versions of human experience which invite revision rather than inviolable instances or definitive editions of what life might be like. The audience are obliged to assess the validity of theatrical representations in the light of the actualities with which it begs comparison, and to re-examine the rationale of the real social production in which they have been cast.[84]

The challenging potential of metatheatre is certainly realised in the remarkably complex slave *hetaira* Habrotonon, hired by Charisios to distract him from his wife's supposed infidelity. Habrotonon becomes an actress within a play, rehearsing her part in front of Onesimos before she plans to act it out to Charisios. In assuming the role of the child's putative mother, she displays an eclectic mix of power and helplessness, compassion and cynicism, altruism and selfishness. Like Syros, she lays claim to a child as a means of alleviating her own unhappiness in slavery, but her strategy is both more overt and less straightforward than the uneasy joy of the boy's 'adoption' by the charcoal-burner.

Scarcely any of the substantial scholarship on this fascinating character has recognised her complexity; instead it has concentrated on passing unilateral judgements on her moral status. She has been deemed either a selfish, vacuous, exploitative harlot,[85] or an empathetic, compassionate and charming mother-figure,[86] as though the two were mutually exclusive.[87] To Arnott, she is a prime example of Menander's achieving 'realism' through the challenging of dramatic stereotypes. She is both the stock one-dimensional, ruthless, selfish, vain, avaricious courtesan he sees in the 'traditional' *hetairai* of the comic stage,[88] but also an individual characterised by linguistic quirks such as the effusive use of superlatives and by 'vivid and insightful details which ... suddenly bring a character alive and charge a situation with its own electricity, the little detail which implies a lot more'.[89] One of these details, he notes, is her care for the child – Arnott argues that it absorbs her attentions, 'humanising the *hetaira* and turning her into an individual'.[90] Heap similarly stresses how Habrotonon's interactions with the foundling develop her character. Although much of her discussion depends on a good girl/mother – bad girl/prostitute polarity (i.e. whether Habrotonon is motivated by altruistic compassion or the 'selfish' pursuit of her own freedom), Heap does recognise the complexity of her character, not least through the suggestion that she has only recently been prostituted.[91]

In her quest for manumission,[92] Habrotonon acts the role of mother; the slave takes on a child in pursuit of freedom. The entirety of her plot to have the child recognised as free is underpinned by the implication that her becoming a parent, however temporarily, is a means to liberty. This topos operates on a deeper level than simply by suggesting that 'real' slaves could be manumitted on becoming parents, or that Habrotonon, through her efforts, hopes to impress Charisios sufficiently to win her manumission. It works too as a deep-seated recognition of the potential of parenthood and family to provide comfort and solidarity – a degree of 'freedom' – in slavery. In this respect, perhaps Arnott's argument that the child 'humanises the *hetaira*' is not too far off the mark, although in ways slightly differing from his intended meaning.

In Habrotonon's interaction with the child, the simple desire for the affective ties that motivated Syros to take on the foundling seems absent; the exploration of the child-as-freedom trope is both more explicit and also more symbolic. On one level, her dealings with the infant are unambiguously teleological; she has a definite end towards which she is working. That the child is a viable means to actual civic freedom is never questioned; Onesimos puts it bluntly when, having heard Habrotonon's plan, he complains, 'She realises that she can't use her sex appeal to win freedom, so she's taking the other route. But I'll stay a slave forever, snivelling, helpless, never able to pull off a plan like this!' (557-62). In this respect, the foundling boy becomes a symbol of what Habrotonon wants for herself; in securing him his freedom, she hopes to secure her own. Likewise, for the time in which his status is precarious, the child's closeness to the slaves serves to highlight his alienation from his real parents.[93]

The scholarship which has taken a dim view of Habrotonon's morality for exploiting the child to her own ends has failed to recognise her desperation to escape slavery. Lying behind her plot to reveal the child's parentage, it is possible to read not just the interplay between her cynicism and conscientiousness, but also her deep unhappiness, not least in her insistence that Onesimos would deserve death were he to let the child be raised as a slave like themselves (468-70). The conflict at the heart of Habrotonon's characterisation is the struggle between power and powerlessness. In taking her fortune into her own hands and taking actions which she hopes will improve her position, she is a remarkably empowered character, particularly in contrast to Daos.[94] Yet the paradox underlying this over-determined conflict is that in order to pursue her own interests, she must act in the interests of a free family. She can only improve her situation through helping a non-slave child escape slavery, and returning him to his rightful place as his father's heir and future head of his *oikos*. This paradox can be illuminated by reference to Aristotle's discussion of slavery in the *Politics*, in which he refers to the community of interest between slave and master (1.1255b):

> For the same thing is advantageous for a part and for the whole body or the whole soul, and the slave is a part of the master – he is, as it were, a part of the body, alive, but yet separated from it; hence there is a certain community of interest and friendship between slave and master in cases where they have been qualified by nature for those positions, although when they do not hold them in that way but by law and by constraint of force the opposite is the case.[95]

In short, what benefits the master must benefit the slave, for the latter is but an appendage to the former. Aristotle's qualification that this applies only when the slave is 'naturally' servile is here irrelevant; what matters is the light it sheds on Habrotonon's powerlessness. In the face of the slave-owning class's absolute and arbitrary power, her only hope for freedom is to work within the system which prostitutes and oppresses her. Violent rebellion could lead to punishment. Although no passage providing details of Habrotonon's manumission has survived, a subjective improvement in her status, in the regard in which she is held by the play's other characters, is apparent in a fragmentary part of Act 5, when one of the characters (possibly the now-free Onesimos) says, 'She's no common little prostitute, now. What's going on here is no coincidence – all of a sudden she has a child. She has a free person's mind' (984-7).

Neither Habrotonon nor the other slaves meddle or connive in order to improve their status. Indeed, the absence from *Epitrepontes* of the conventional 'scheming slave' stereotype is striking. Habrotonon, in actually designing a strategy, is as near as this play gets to either the tricky schemers of later Roman comedy, or even such Greek comic rebels as Xanthias and Sosias in Aristophanes' *Wasps*. McCarthy argues that the scheming slaves of Plautus work in favour of the status quo by offering in their squalid morals an ideological justification for the free-slave hierarchy. She thinks they are infantilised by their trifling intrigues; they may be either punished or forgiven, but their status does not change. In *Epitrepontes*, Daos has the potential to provide an example of this type of role, but he is foiled. His role is also overshadowed by Habrotonon's proactive approach and by Onesimos' rejection of scheming immediately after the arbitration scene. As the play's most prominent household slave, Onesimos would be the character most likely to be portrayed as the stereotypical schemer, but, on the contrary, he castigates himself for even mentioning the ring to Syros and has to be persuaded by Habrotonon even to go along with her plan. After she leaves, he explicitly disavows meddling in other peoples' affairs (573-5). Charisios' accusations of eavesdropping and mischief only serve to reinforce, through contrast, his characterisation as non-manipulative. Onesimos' repudiation of malice precedes his manumission (which has taken place by Act 5), the moment when the play's liberatory dimension became most pronounced. His high-mindedness, even 'free-mindedness', and subsequently his manumission reveal the boundaries between free and slave as essentially contingent, subject to negotiation and dissolution. His moral character subverts the grounds for his own subjection. Simultaneously, however, he is rejecting behaviour which inconveniences and irritates the free – like Habrotonon, he must behave in ways which serve his master's interests in order to achieve his goal.

Far from expounding the conservative ideologies which have usually been read into it, *Epitrepontes,* in conclusion, makes use of a number of profoundly unstable ideological positions and can be read in the opposite way. The enslaved, both in their words and actions, challenge and improve their positions. Even where conservative, naturalising discourses emerge, they cannot win out totally and often work to imply the existence of other more subversive viewpoints. The mute foundling, the son of Pamphile and Charisios, provides a locus for much of the play's questioning import, since it is through interaction with him that the slaves Syros, Onesimos and Habrotonon voice discontent with their subservient statuses. To Habrotonon especially, the child becomes a means to the pursuit of both civic manumission and 'freedom' in the broader sense of exercising a degree of personal autonomy. Her insistence that the child be regarded as free implies too her own hatred of her position. A deep liberatory significance can be read into her impersonation of the child's mother. The child represents to the slave characters nothing less than a symbol of freedom.

Notes

1. Patterson (1982) 5.

2. Such as the arrangement detailed in Hyperides' speech *Against Athenogenes,* whereby a slave lived and worked with his two sons away from their owner's home (Hyp. 3.3-6)

3. Of which the plot of *Epitrepontes* and a number of other comedies by Menander (notably *Perikeiromene* and *Sikyonioi*) are modifications. The extant fragments of the latter contain a heart-rending description of a very young free girl kidnapped and sold at a slave market (2-19, Arnott).

4. A tradition much exploited by Euripides, whose fragmentary *Alexandros, Antiope* and *Melanippe Desmotis* definitely dealt with abandoned boys raised as slaves, as does his extant *Ion*. So, in all likelihood, did Sophocles' lost *Tyro*, on which *Epitrepontes'* famous arbitration scene is thought to have been modelled (see below). Euripides' *Hypsipyle* dealt too with issues of family and slavery, this time inverting the foundling-child pattern; a free mother sold into slavery is reunited with her (free) sons and father upon gaining her freedom.

5. King (1995) 18, studying antebellum American slave children, has recognised the importance of familial and fictive-kinship bonds as a palliative against the cruelties of slavery.

6. E.g. Lape (2004), Omitowoju (2002), McCarthy (2000), Fitzgerald (1999), Konstan 1995.

7. Belsey (1985) 4. This recognition is particularly pertinent given that a good deal of Menandrean scholarship, for example, Krieter-Spiro (1997) 9-10, is still caught up in the 'Menander and life' question, to be referred back at least as far as the grammarian Aristophanes of Byzantium's famous comment rhetorical question, 'O Menander and O life, which of you was it that imitated the other?' (Syrianus *in Hermogenem* 2, 23).

8. The personal letter from the young male Lesis, written on lead and found in the Athenian agora, serves a reminder of this, if he is actually a slave. See Harris (2005) for a convincing argument in favour of this identification.

9. To use the phrase of Ryan (1989) 17 concerning *The Merchant of Venice*.

10. i.e. Wiles (1988) *passim*; McCarthy (2000) *passim*; Omitowoju (2002) 181.

11. Ryan (1989) 6-7 argues that some early New Historicist critics seem to be cynically seeking to expose drama only as a piece of ruling-class machinery. Their stance envisages a process whereby 'plays only open authority to question along the way in order to vindicate it all the more completely in the last analysis' (6-7). The possibility that plays might actually be read to signify just the opposite is entertained only to be dismissed as an unwarranted delusion. But we should, he argues, be open to the possibility that drama might just call into question the taken-for-granted values of its society, and to the degree and respects in which 'the text can be seen to point towards the possibility of more desirable ways of organising human life and relationships'.

12. Howard (1994) 7 has argued a similar thesis with respect to Renaissance literature: 'Rather than as signs of aesthetic failure, these incompatibilities can be read as traces of ideological struggle, of differences within the sense-making machinery of culture.'

13. See Holquist (1990) for a good introduction.

14. See Bakhtin's diatribe against reductive stylistic and linguistic analysis of literature in (1981*a*), 259. Again, this is a theory primarily concerned with criticism of the novel, but is also applicable to drama.

15. Hall (1997) 118ff. offers a succinct discussion of this polyphony with reference to tragic drama, arguing that it reflects 'the contemporary development of rhetoric in democratic Athens'.

16. Here, 'freedom' refers both to a degree of psychological or personal autonomy on the part of the slave characters, and also, in the case of Onesimos at least, concrete and civically enacted freedom; he is manumitted by his owner, Charisios.

17. Bakhtin (1981*a*) 412.

18. Bakhtin (1981*b*), 30-1.

19. Bakhtin (1981*b*) 30-1.

20. Langer (1953) 215, 258-79, 307.

21. Hall (2004) 78-9. A revised version of this article is published in Hall and Harrop (2010).

22. Ryan (1988) 92-3.

23. Ryan (1988) 93. In relation to Menander, however, it should be noted that very few endings actually survive. Although we can be reasonably sure that *Epitrepontes* ended in marital reunion and familial reconciliation, only three plays – *Samia*, *Dyskolos* and *Misoumenos* have their (similar) conclusions intact.

24. Ryan (1988) 94.

25. Jameson (1981) 289-90 makes this point more generally in recognising that the even the expression of seemingly hegemonic, ruling-class discourses can contain a certain 'utopian' quality by recognising the potential for solidarity and rebellion on the part of the oppressed.

26. See Apte (1985) 16-17.

27. Bakhtin (1981*b*) 23.

28. Bakhtin (1981*b*) 24.

29. See McCarthy (2000), especially ch.1, for a more sceptical reading of comedy's subversive potential.

30. The canonical bibliography by Gomme and Sandbach (1973), Webster (1974), Katsouris (1975), Goldberg (1980), Arnott (1979), Frost (1988), Zagagi (1994) and Cusset (2003) focuses on Menander's use of earlier dramatic, literary and mythological traditions.

31. E.g. Webster (1974) 42, 'Menander gives a convincing picture of rich society and poor society insofar as it impinges on rich society.' This stance has now been more or less discredited although does persist in some more recent publications, such as Krieter-Spiro (1997).

32. Krieter-Spiro (1997) 40-1.

33. Wiles (1988) 58: 'The politics of form in Menander are interesting, with all of the play in iambic trimeter, which was neither sung nor accompanied, leaving no room for a star singer. Also, a uniform Attic dialect was, as Wiles notes, spoken by Menander's free and slave characters alike. There was no lyric/iambic distinction between the slave-born (although not the enslaved) and the free as in tragedy, on which sociology of form see Hall (1997) and (2006) ch. 10.

34. This somewhat simplistic view is in many ways similar to that criticised by Ryan (1988).

35. Wiles (1988) *passim*.

36. Konstan (1995) vii.

37. Konstan (1995) 4-5, where he recognises that 'where society is riven by tensions and inequalities of class, gender and status, its ideology will be complex and unstable, and literary texts will betray signs of the strain involved in forging such refractory materials into a unified composition'.

38. Konstan (1995) 141.

39. Lape (2004) ch. 1.

40. Lape (2004) 11.

41. Lape (2004) 38.

42. For Menander as apolitical see e.g. Gomme (1937) 249-95; Goldberg (1980) 109-21; Bain (1983) xii-xxvii. For an argument against this approach see Omitowoju (2002) 137-40, who focuses on representations of sexual violence in Menander.

43. Lape (2004) especially 11-12. However, the political resistance which she sees in Menander is far more self-conscious and explicitly articulated than that which I read into *Epitrepontes*; it is also an essentially 'reactionary' resistance, seeking to defend the waning democratic status quo in the face of oligarchic threats. Moreover, the premise of her thesis is Athenocentric, not taking into account the 500-year-long and geographically and culturally diverse tradition of performances of Menander.

44. See also McCarthy (2000) 16-17, for a similar approach to Plautine comedy.

45. Exemplified by Webster (1974), with his interest in typologies of whole plays, plot-patterns, and types of characters, and by Wiles (1988). Pollux's catalogue of New Comedy mask-types discussed by Wiles may be to some extent held responsible for this interest in stock-types and conventions.

46. E.g. Lape (2004) 5, where Lycurgus' horror at the assembly's decision to free slaves and enfranchise foreigners after the battle of Chaeronea (Lyc. 1.41) is used to back up the thesis that the myth of autochthony was crucial to Athenian citizen

identity. Like Konstan, however, Lape pays attention to class and gender divisions among the free.

47. Along with Fitzgerald (1999), which succinctly recognises conflict and slippage in the literature representing Roman slavery (especially 10-11).

48. McCarthy (2000) 3.

49. McCarthy (2000) 6.

50. It should be noted that anxiety itself, springing from deeply-held cultural fears, by definition recognises the *possibility* of subversion, even if such rebelliousness is never made manifest.

51. McCarthy (2000) 211.

52. McCarthy (2000) 18.

53. Even if the theatrical professions were not as despised by the free during Plautus' lifetime as they were in later centuries, when for a free man to act was to risk *infamia*, it is highly likely that actors had never been free Roman citizens, but slaves, freedmen or foreigners. See Brown (2002).

54. McCarthy (2000) 11 n. 17.

55. The farcical mode is characterised by frequent rupture of the dramatic illusion, undermining attempts to focus on a transcendent meaning of the play; by a stream of patterned language, slapstick and stereotyped characters; by trickery; by a fundamental lack of change to the characters' situations by the conclusion; by rebellion for rebellion's sake; by a 'willingness to leave loose ends untied'. It is in the farcical mode that 'the fantasy of slave as hero' appears, reversing normal hierarchies. The slave-hero does, however, ultimately fail to change his status and 'kings remain kings, slaves remain slaves' (McCarthy [2000] 12-14).

56. McCarthy (2000) 11-12.

57. McCarthy (2000) 11-14.

58. McCarthy (2000) 17 n. 26.

59. See Scafuro (1997) 159-60: 'While the presence of Habrotonon carrying the infant and tokens in II and III may have impressed the audience, it is the formality of the arbitration scene that has left its mark on legal historians.'

60. See Konstan (1994) 141-52, Lape (2004) 246-52, Omitowoju (2002) ch. 5.

61. Goldberg (1980) ch. 5.

62. Katsouris (1975); Cusset (2003).

63. Gomme and Sandbach (1973).

64. Until recently the most significant contribution was Post (1938); Hall (2006) ch. 3 discusses the continuity of the motif of childbearing in all ancient genres of theatre.

65. Heap (2002) 99.

66. Heap (2002) 100.

67. Heap (202) 104-6.

68. A goatherd. That the child should be found by a slave whose work necessitates wandering is a commonplace of the foundling-child plot pattern in myth and tragedy.

69. Goldberg (1980) 67 argues the opposite, that the 'arbitration scene is of little concrete significance. The net effect of these one hundred and fifty lines of brilliant dramatic writing is merely to get a ring out where Onesimos can see it.'

70. 'Justice should prevail in all things, to all people and in all places. That's a general rule of life' (232-6).

71. Gomme and Sandbach (1973) 315. Huys (1995) an in-depth study of this plot pattern in Euripides which, however, offers little on its ideological dimensions.

72. Syros actually uses the word *kurios* at one point (306) but this is in a more general sense of 'guardian, trustee' (LSJ definition, with reference to its usage in

this play) and not a reference to the legal institution of the *kurieia* whereby a free man had legal guardianship of the women and children of his household and/or kin and needed, for example, to represent them in court.

73. As I argue in Proffitt (2009). King (1995) has recognised similar attitudes implicit in the distress expressed by American slaves at having to raise children in miserable slavery

74. Although that the slave-born child is dead may also be significant – as I have argued in detail in Proffitt (2009).

75. This characterisation, along with his lack of interest in gaining his freedom, aligns him with the Plautine and American slave characters discussed by McCarthy (2000) 212, who perpetuate the notion that 'slaves were so debased that creature comforts and simple pleasures meant more to them than their freedom'. This places him in opposition to both Onesimos and Habrotonon, who actively strive for it. See below on Onesimos' rejection of the scheming slave archetype.

76. Heap (2002) 101 recognises that 'Syros' respect for the baby as freeborn is confirmed as genuine, despite his own slave status' but, in keeping with her focus on dramatic effect takes this point no further.

77. Goldberg (1980) 70: 'Syriskos' early reference to Neleus and Pelias reminds us not only of the potential significance of birth tokens but also of the fact that they are elements of myth and drama. It is hardly surprising that Charisos should be at first hard to persuade of his paternity, and so is Smikrines.'

78. Omitowoju (2002) 161. Surprisingly, Heap (2002) does not examine this part of the speech, and Gomme and Sandbach (1973) 315 see only that 'there may be a flattering suggestion that that Smikrines is better informed on this subject that Syriskos, who will not have had the same opportunities for seeing tragic acting'.

79. Theophrastus, *Characters* 2.11 (Flattery): 'In the theatre he takes the cushions from the slave and tucks them under his man personally'; see also 9.5 (Sponging) 'When he buys theatre tickets for his guests [with their money], he goes along too, without paying, and the next day takes his children as well as their *paidagogos*' [who would have almost certainly been a slave]. On the importance of acknowledging the possibility of slaves in Greek theatre audiences see Hall (2006) 196-206.

80. 'I'll declaim a whole speech from the tragedy *Auge* if you can't understand it, Smikrines!' (1125-6). On *Auge* see especially Hall (2006) ch. 3.

81. See Huys (1995) 335-60.

82. See Gutzwiller (2000) for a general discussion of metatheatricality in Menander.

83. See Ryan (1989) 91-2, where he cites *Twelfth Night* II.iv.127-8: 'If this were on a stage/I could condemn it as improbable fiction.' This is equivalent to Syros' statement (325-6), 'You've seen the tragedies, I'm sure, and know all this.'

84. Ryan (1989) 91-2.

85. Gomme and Sandbach (1973) 334: 'It is indicative of her values that she gives so much attention to Pamphile's clothes, so little to her misfortune .. Her only deep feelings are for herself.'

86. See Henry (1985) 51-60; Post (1926).

87. More promisingly, Konstan (1994) 141 recognises in all of *Epitrepontes'* characters the 'overdetermination of motives answering simultaneously to the multiple possibilities projected by the contradictions in social values'.

88. Arnott (1979) 354: 'Habrotonon is not blind to the main chance; when she schemes in this play, she makes no secret of the fact that she desires more than anything to be released from the pimp who owns her and achieves her freedom. As

a professional hetaira she rejoices in broken homes and wants men to fall in love with her. Thus Menander hints at the traditional aspects of a hetaira's character without crude or repetitive emphasis.' Within this reading, Arnott is aligning Habrotonon's desire for her own freedom not with a certain unhappiness but with the most negative attributes of the comic-conventional hetaira. For a discussion of Menander's courtesans within the comic tradition see Henry (1985).

89. Arnott (1979) 354.

90. Arnott (1979) 355.

91. Heap (2002) 105.

92. The surviving fragments make it clear that Onesimos is freed during the course of the play; unfortunately any text which might have dealt with Habrotonon's emancipation is lost. Nevertheless, much can be inferred from her perception of the child as a viable means to gaining freedom.

93. Heap (2002) 106.

94. Habrotonon (and to a lesser extent, Onesimos), although formally excluded from any family life of her own, throughout the play actually knows far more about the affairs of the household in which she is currently living and working than do its free members. The slaves effectively control the supply of knowledge to the free; a powerful position indeed, and one perhaps related to the dynamics of many slaveholding households, all over the Greek world, in which long-serving slaves may have had intimate knowledge of the comings and goings (and quite possibly some of the intimate secrets) of their owners' families, perhaps over the course of several generations.

95. Translated by Rackham (1932).

References

Apte, M.L. (1985) *Humour and Laughter: An Anthropological Approach*. Ithaca, NY & London.

Arnott, W.G. (1979) 'Time, plot and character in Menander', *Papers of the Liverpool Latin Seminars* 2, 343-60.

―――― (tr.) (2000) *Menander*, vol. 3, Loeb Classical Library. Cambridge, MA.

Bakhtin, M.M. (1981a) 'Discourse in the novel', in M. Holquist (ed.) *The Dialogic Imagination: Four Essays by Mikhail Bakhtin*, tr. C. Emerson and M. Holquist, 259-422. Austin, TX.

―――― (1981b) 'Epic and novel', in . M. Holquist (ed.) *The Dialogic Imagination: Four Essays by Mikhail Bakhtin*, tr. C. Emerson and M. Holquist, 3-41. Austin, TX.

Bain, D. (ed. & tr.) *Menander: Samia*. Warminster.

Belsey, C. (1985) *The Subject of Tragedy: Identity and Difference in Renaissance Drama*. London.

Brown, P.G.McC. (2002) 'Actors and actor-managers at Rome in the time of Plautus and Terence', in P.E. Easterling and E. Hall (eds), *Greek and Roman Actors*, 225-37. Cambridge.

Cusset, C. (2003) *Ménandre ou la comédie tragique*. Paris.

Easterling, P.E. and Hall, E. (eds) (2002) *Greek and Roman Actors: Aspects of an Ancient Profession*. Cambridge.

Fitzgerald, W. (2000) *Slavery and the Roman Literary Imagination*. Cambridge.

Frost, K.B. (1988) *Entrances and Exits in Menander*. Oxford.

Goldberg, S.M. (1980) *The Making of Menander's Comedy*. London.

Gomme, A.W. (1937) *Essays in Greek History and Literature*. Oxford.

―――― and Sandbach, F.H. (1973) *Menander: A Commentary*. Oxford.

Gutzwilller , K. (2000) 'The tragic mask of comedy: metatheatricality in Menander', *Classical Antiquity* 19, 102-37.

Hall, E. (1997) 'The sociology of Athenian tragedy', in P.E. Easterling (ed.) *The Cambridge Companion to Greek Tragedy*, 93-126. Cambridge.

—— (2004) 'Towards a theory of performance reception', *Arion* 12, 51-89.

—— (2006) *The Theatrical Cast of Athens*. Oxford.

—— (2010) *Greek Tragedy: Suffering Under the Sun*. Oxford.

—— and Harrop, S. (eds) (2010) *Theorising Performance: Greek Tragedy, Cultural History and Critical Practice*. London.

Harris, E.M. (2004) 'Notes on a lead letter from the Athenian agora', *Harvard Studies in Classical Philology* 102, 157-70.

Heap, A.M. (2002) 'The baby as hero – the role of the infant in Menander', *Bulletin of the Institute of Classical Studies* 46, 77-129.

Henry, M.M. (1985) *Menander's Courtesans and the Greek Comic Tradition*. Frankfurt am Main.

Holquist, M. (1990) *Dialogism: Bakhtin and his World*. London.

Howard, J.E. (1994) *The Stage and Social Struggle in Early Modern England*. London.

Huys, M. (1995) *The Tale of the Hero who was Exposed at Birth in Euripidean Tragedy: A Study of Motifs*. Leuven.

Jameson, F. (1981) *The Political Unconscious: Narrative as a Socially Symbolic Act*. London.

Katsouris , A.G. (1975) *Tragic Patterns in Menander*. Athens.

King, W. (1993) *Stolen Childhood: Slave Youth in Nineteenth-Century America*. Bloomington, IN.

Krieter-Spiro, M. (1997) *Sklaven, Köche, und Hetären: Das Dienstpersonal bei Menander*. Stuttgart.

Konstan, D. (1995) *Greek Comedy and Ideology*. New York & Oxford.

Langer, S.K. (1953) *Feeling and Form*. London.

Lape, S. (2004) *Reproducing Athens: Menander's Comedy, Democratic Culture, and the Hellenistic City*. Princeton, NJ.

McCarthy, K. (2000) *Masters, Slaves and the Art of Authority in Plautine Comedy*. Princeton, NJ.

Omitowoju, R. (2002) *Rape and the Politics of Consent in Classical Athens*. Cambridge.

Patterson, O. (1982) *Slavery and Social Death*. Cambridge, MA.

Post, L.A. (1939) 'Dramatic infants in Greek', *Classical Philology* 34, 193-208.

—— (1940) 'A woman's place in Menander's Athens', *Transactions and Proceedings of the American Philological Association* 71, 420-59.

Proffitt, L. (2009) 'Family and Slavery in the Greek Dramatic Imagination', Diss. London (Royal Holloway).

Rackham, H. (tr.) (1932) *Aristotle, Politics*, Loeb Classical Library. London.

Ryan, K. (1989) *Shakespeare*. London & New York

Webster, T.B.L. (1967) *The Tragedies of Euripides*. London.

—— (1974) *An Introduction to Menander*. Manchester.

Wiles, D. (1988) 'Greek theatre and the legitimation of slavery', in L.J. Archer (ed.) *Slavery and Other Forms of Unfree Labour*, 53-67. London.

—— (1991) *The Masks of Menander: Sign and Meaning in Greek and Roman Performance*. Cambridge.

Zagagi, N. (1994) *The Comedy of Menander*. London.

The Slave as Minimal Addition in Latin Literature

William Fitzgerald

The original version of this chapter was written for a conference celebrating the two hundredth anniversary of the Abolition of the slave trade. But in a sense all studies of slavery in the ancient world are written in the context of Abolition. The *OED* tells us that the word 'slavery' first appears with reference to 'the keeping of slaves as a practice or institution' in 1728 ('As slavery was not abolished by the Gospel ... the custom lasted a long time'). The words *servitium* or *douleia* refer to a condition and do not express the modern sense of slavery as a particular institution. But on the subject of slavery our thoughts and feelings are determined by modern events in a different way than they are for other concepts without ancient lexical equivalents ('literature', 'homosexuality' and 'religion', for instance). To perform the thought experiment of projecting oneself back into ancient attitudes to slaves is a more equivocal exercise than doing the same for ancient attitudes to the gods, for instance. For slavery is not just a subject, it is also a practice in which we, as beneficiaries (or victims) of western imperialism, feel implicated. One of the words that was much in the air during the celebrations of 2007 was 'legacy' (as in 'the legacy of slavery'). Abolished though it may have been (and there is room for disagreement on that), slavery is a *legacy*. Classical culture itself is often spoken of as a legacy, and in both cases the word prompts us to ask what we should do with our inheritance. To look at Roman literature from the angle of slavery is to take an eccentric view of familiar texts and to constitute a subject that is never an explicit agenda of those texts. Inevitably, it is to bring to those texts an interest and an urgency that are modern.

An important theme of the celebrations that marked the anniversary of the abolition of the slave trade was a call to redirect our attention from the struggles of a single, saintly white Abolitionist, William Wilberforce, to a broader story that pays due attention to the resistance and the experience of the slaves themselves. When it comes to Latin literature the call to consider the experience of the slaves presents a problem, for erasing or 'consuming' the agency or subjectivity of the slave seems to be what Latin literature does. If the slave comes into focus at all it is usually as a figure through whom the agenda or fantasies of the free can be played out. For the most part, the reader of a classical text is positioned as the slave-owner rather than the abused slave, and one of the roles that classical texts have played in western culture is the promotion of a certain kind of normative subjectivity in which mastery and self-mastery have gone hand in hand.[1] Not surprisingly, the masters have made themselves more interesting to us than their slaves. So, while it might be a salutary reorientation to look at Latin literature through slavery, the opposite is not so clear. Does the study of slavery through Latin literature constitute a step backwards, confirming that it is the experience of the slave-owner that is interesting and significant?

Niall McKeown's *The Invention of Ancient Slavery?*, published in the anniversary year of 2007, ends with a challenge: 'If we simply accept the silences in our sources, we will condemn ourselves to writing (so to speak) the history of the prison-camp guards rather than that of the victims. We must therefore use our imagination to see the other "plot lines". Those plot lines, however, represent only possible readings of the evidence we have. They may be true, but they need not be. We must be careful not to "rescue" the voice of the ancient slave by making it a distorted version of our own.'[2] McKeown has given us a task and made it impossible at one stroke, for what voice can we give to the silent or ventriloquised slaves of Roman literature other than our own, speaking from the position of an abolished slavery, the position from which we refuse to accept the silence of our sources? We seem to be stuck between a rock and a hard place: we can hear, amplify and elaborate the voice of the masters and their ventriloquised slaves or we can listen to our own, post-abolitionist voice. I think we must acknowledge that to read this literature in the context of slavery is to read what the masters have written, provided that we take note of the fact that, for the masters, slavery is a form of blindness. I hope to show that this literature allows itself to be read from the perspective of its own blind-spots. Furthermore, if literary criticism cannot bring the slave into focus, but is reduced to examining the subjectivity of the masters, it can at least show how that subjectivity is marked by the contradictions inherent in slavery as a relation. The ancient texts contain 'other voices' that are waiting to be made to speak, if not those of the slaves themselves, then at least voices that might speak from the other side of the relation as the masters have imagined it.

Let me start by taking advantage of the event which this collection is celebrating to cite an example of how a canonical text might be given another voice by a slave. This example addresses the phenomenon of slave resistance, which has seldom been better articulated than by Milton, or rather than by Olaudah Equiano, who wrote one of the most famous and influential of slave narratives, published in 1789. In an eloquent passage denouncing the cruelty of slave-owners Equiano quotes Milton's Belial as follows:[3]

9. The Slave as Minimal Addition in Latin Literature

No peace is given
To us enslaved, but custody severe;
And stripes and arbitrary punishment
Inflicted – What peace can we return?
But to our power, hostility and hate;
Untam'd reluctance, and revenge, though slow,
Yet ever plotting how the conqueror least
May reap his conquest, and may least rejoice
In doing what we most in suffering feel.

Paradise Lost 2.332-40

Belial is one of the fallen angels and, of course, in Milton's poem his words are specious. He is wrong to call his subjection to God a servitude, as Abdiel explains to Satan at 6.174-80. His punishment is not arbitrary.[4] Furthermore, the struggle Belial articulates will always be unequal: the slave may deny the conqueror a little of his joy but it will be at the expense of a great deal of suffering on his own part. And this gives Belial's argument, in its original context, its perversity. But if what is specious for Belial is true for Equiano, what is perverse for Belial may be sanity for Equiano. Equiano infiltrates Milton's classic with his own narrative of enslavement and gives Belial a very different position to speak from, or perhaps I should rather say that he gives the reader a very different position from which to hear him. The full force of the passage emerges when it is spoken literally rather than metaphorically, by a real slave. But perhaps Milton's text leaves open the possibility of this appropriation when it has Belial claim that he and his fellow slaves feel what the conqueror does more than the conqueror himself, because they are on the receiving end ('may *least* rejoice in *doing* what we *most* in *suffering* feel'). Indeed it is true that Equiano is in a better position to know the meaning of these words than Milton, since in suffering he most feels. I certainly don't want to reduce Equiano's story to his quotations of Milton (of which there are quite a few), since he speaks eloquently in his own voice about, among other things, the continual uncertainty as to whether or not he belongs to the community of those protected by trust. But I take this passage as an example of the way that canonical texts may contain dissident voices, and of the way that, in another sense of the word, they may fail to *contain* them, by leaving open the way to appropriations on the part of those who speak from a different position.[5]

We have no such works by ancient Roman slaves, of course, but just occasionally we may hear a voice that speaks from the position of the slave, as, for instance, in Phaedrus' fable of the ass and the robbers (1.15). An old man kept an ass in his meadow. Hearing the sound of approaching enemies the terrified old man tried to persuade the ass to escape. 'Will they put two packsaddles on me rather than one?' the ass replied. 'No,' said the old man. 'Then what difference does it make to me whom I serve?' Whether or not Phaedrus had himself been a slave, the fable as a genre was associated with slavery, and in Phaedrus' fable there is a real clash of perspective between master and beast of burden.[6] Phaedrus gives his fable a political moral ('in a change of *principatus* the poor change nothing but the name of their master'), though it is the slave-master relationship that provides the metaphor. But there are other, more canonical, texts that leave open a place from which the other position in the relation of slavery may come to be recognised. Let me suggest an analogy to Phaedrus' fable that is a little more questionable since there is no slave figure speaking, though again it involves a fable about an ass. The last epistle of Horace's first book (*Epistles* 1.20) is clearly relevant to slavery since, in this envoi to his first book of epistles, Horace figures the book as a slave eager to leave the family nest. But I want to focus on a passage that is not usually remarked upon. Horace says that when his advice to stay at home is disregarded by the book/slave he, Horace, will laugh

> Ut ille
> qui male parentem in rupes protrusit asellum
> iratus: quis enim invitum servare laboret?
> > *Ep.*1.20.14-16

> Like one
> Who thrusts the recalcitrant ass over a cliff
> Angrily: for who would labour to save one unwilling (to be saved)?

Here Horace alludes to a fable of Aesop in which a recalcitrant ass wanders from the trodden path until it is in danger of falling over a cliff (Aesop 197 Hausrath). The driver tries to pull it back but, faced with the continued resistance of the ass, he finally lets go, saying 'it is a bad victory that you have won'. Let me confess that, as a student, I used to misread the last line of this passage and translate 'for who would labour to serve against his will', as though Horace had written *quis enim invitus servire laboret?* The ass/slave speaks back! One might say that Horace very nearly *did* say that (he was only two letters off!) or that he never came anywhere near saying it (if we consider explicit Roman attitudes, behaviour, environment and indeed the logic of the passage). Or we might say that I read the passage in that way because it made more sense to me. We might, if we want to be bold, attribute these two very different meanings inhabiting virtually the same letters to two different voices in Horace's text. Roman etymology did, after all, connect *servire* with *servare*.[7] Furthermore, the structure of Horace's line might encourage my misreading, for it is held together by the assonance *iratus/invitum*, each of which words is a molossus; *iratus*, we might say, takes us to *servare*, and *invitum* to the forbidden *servire*. But if we want to say that this conflict of senses is part of the meaning of the text then we are reading it as *literature* (which allows words to play) about *slavery* (which is a blindness *to* the other's subjectivity). A minimal modification, a minimal swerve, brings us to the other side of this relationship, so near and yet so far.[8]

But we can get to that other side by less wilful means. Staying with Horace, asses and slaves, I turn now to a passage in which the resentful slave makes another appearance, if only we allow him. *Satires* 1.9 is a well-known anecdote in which Horace has an unfortunate encounter while walking on the Via Sacra, lost in his thought. He is accosted by someone known to him only by name who strikes up a conversation and declares his intention of sticking to Horace as long as he can; it turns out that the Bore (as he is usually known) is hoping to use Horace to gain admittance to the circle of Maecenas, in which the poet moves. Horace tries to shake him off: first he walks faster, then he walks slower and then he whispers something in his slave's ear (*in aurem dicere nescio quid puero*, 9-10). 'Slave'? 'What slave?' we ask. As is often the case in Latin literature, the slave materialises out of nowhere and then disappears again, but his absence from the rest of the epistle is almost palpable. Ears are important in this poem, which describes the unpleasant experience of having one's ear bent, and which ends when deliverance comes from an ear.[9] So the fact that the slave materialises as an ear connects him with the imagery of the poem as a whole. Now there has been much talk of how Horace and the Bore are not as different as we want to believe, but nobody has suggested that we bring the slave into the play of similarity and difference between the characters of this little drama.[10] Can we read this as a poem about slavery as well as ambition? To begin with, we can note that Horace's slave stands in a similar relation to his master as his master does to the Bore: Horace whispers any old thing (*nescioquid*, 10) into the slave's ear in a futile attempt to shake off the Bore, while the latter rattles on about anything that occurs to him (*cum quidlibet ille/ garriret*, 12-13). Once Horace realises that his attempt has been futile, he resigns himself with a bad will to his fate, and once again the focus is on ears (20-1):

> demitto auriculas, ut iniquae mentis asellus,
> cum gravius dorso subiit onus

> I droop my ears, like a resentful ass
> When its back has taken on too heavy a load

Here the poem speaks back to itself by indicating to us precisely what it cannot say: Horace buttonholed by the Bore may be like the burdened ass, but he is also like his own slave, whose ears are constantly at the disposal of his master. Strolling along the Via Sacra, Horace seems to be composing poetry (*nescioquid meditans nugarum*, 2) which, presumably, the slave must remember or record. Horace's slave, for whom carrying burdens is *not* a metaphor, can also be expected to be as resentful (*iniquae mentis*) as an ass, and for the same reason as Horace – he is forced to listen. In the expression *demitto auriculas* the act of listening, of resigning (*dimitto*) the ears to their fate, is also an expression of resentment, as the ears are drooped (*demitto*). With reference to the ass, commentators have been quick to point out that Horace is probably punning on his name, Flaccus.[11] But they are missing something more obvious here if we consider the association between asses and servitude in Phaedrus' Fable (1.15) and *Epistles* 1.20, cited above.[12] Horace may be like the burdened ass, but so, more appropriately, is his slave: no less than the put-upon Horace, he can never shake the bore who is dictating poetry to him. In another respect, though, the slave is like the Bore himself, who sticks to the poet through thick and thin, for that is the duty of a slave. Only *he* can be ignored, unlike the Bore, and *his* presence can be taken for granted. The one thing the master will not do is to set free, or release (*dimitto*) the ear that is (for him) the slave. There is, then, quite a rich drama about slavery going on beneath the anecdote about Horace and the Bore. Insofar as slavery is a relation characterised by blindness to the subjectivity of another human being, this text has much to say about slavery, and it locates the master's blind-spot, from which the slave might speak back, with some precision. If I have conjured a more substantial slave out of this poem, I have done so neither out of the subjectivity of the master nor out of my own, but out of the metaphorical texture of the poem conspiring with the logic of slavery. That logic acknowledges the position from which the slave might appropriate the resentment of the ass with droopy ears as a figure for *himself*, an appropriation that would compare with Equiano's when he transfers the eloquence of Milton's protest against slavery from the misguided demon Belial to his own experience.

Horace's slave, present and available as his master wanders down the Via Sacra, but barely coming into sight, can serve as the anti-Bore in the structure of this poem. The Bore destroys Horace's solitude, whereas the slave could be called 'the minimal addition that *completes* the master's solitude', to borrow a phrase that Ellen Oliensis uses of the slave in Horace, *Odes* 1.38.[13] It is an enigmatic phrase, but entirely appropriate to describe a presence that is so ambiguous. In what sense might the slave *complete* the master's solitude? Does the presence of the slave paradoxically make for a completer solitude (by screening something out, for instance, as a kind of white noise); or does it somehow supplement the solitude to complete what, as solitude, was deficient, lacking? Perhaps just as the ancients shrank from a wild nature that was completely deprived of signs of humanity, so they regarded total solitude as unworthy of a human.[14] Whether as supplement or as screen, the concept of the slave as minimal addition is precarious, implying that slave and master were more than one person, but not quite two.

In *Satires* 1.9 Horace can take the presence of his slave for granted, but in the two poems to which I will now turn the slave is addressed *as* a problematic presence. The first of these is *Odes* 1.38, where Horace the solitary drinker famously tells his attendant slave not to bother with the elaborate preparations that are busying him. He should add nothing (*ad-labores*) to the plain myrtle that will serve as Horace's crown:

Persicos odi, puer, apparatus,
displicent nexae philyra coronae;
mitte sectari, rosa quo locorum
    sera moretur.
simplici myrto nihil allabores
sedulus curo: neque te ministrum
dedecet myrtus neque me sub arta
    vite bibentem.

Boy, I hate those Persian preparations:
crowns woven with bast displease me;
don't bother to look for where
    the late rose lingers.
I care nothing that you labour to improve
plain myrtle: myrtle's not unsuitable
for you who serve, nor for me, drinking
    under the thick vine.

Horace wants to stop somewhere short of two persons, but one person seems to be too few. The poem presents us with an image of ideal closure and self-sufficiency in which the master is solitary because he speaks only to the slave, or rather *past* the slave, for what Horace says to the slave is really said to another audience, with as shadowy a presence as the slave. This being the last poem of Horace's first book of Odes it is often taken as a literary manifesto, an allegory espousing Alexandrian principles of literary style.[15] A manifesto it may be, but it is one which is phrased in terms that are particularly appropriate to a slave-owning society. Horace does not say, for instance, 'I avoid the well-trodden path' but 'I am not the generic master that you think I am'.[16] His poem fine-tunes the slave's presence in a very careful erasure of his initiative, waving away what the slave thinks he wants in order to show that there is, indeed, a Horace.[17] In this poem the slave is established as *minimal* addition by a process of subtraction.

We might posit 'the minimal addition' as an implicit, and asymptotic, ideal of the slave in Latin literature, an ideal never explicitly articulated as such, but no less functional for not being articulated. The minimal addition can be seen as one concept through which the contradictions of the relation between slave and master are played out across Latin literature as a whole. Horace's officious slave has got him wrong, imputing to him desires that he does not have. But suppose that the obsequious slave is all too cognisant of the master's desires. What then? We can supplement Horace's little poem with one that expresses the other half of an inherently ambiguous notion which points to the stubborn refusal of this institution

181

to make sense. 'Minimal addition' is ambiguous in that it expresses both more (addition) and less (minimal) at the same time. Horace protests that his slave's presence is not *minimal* enough, but might a master worry that a slave is not enough of an *addition*? I want to turn now to my main exhibit, a poem in which the minimal addition may be too minimal rather than too obtrusive, a poem in which the presence of the slave as go-between raises the spectre of solipsism. Is there a world out there? Possibly not, if it is only reached and engaged with through a slave.[18]

Propertius 3.6

Dic mihi de nostra, quae sentis, vera puella:
   sic tibi sint dominae, Lygdame, dempta iuga.
num me laetitia tumefactum fallis inani,
   haec referens, quae me credere velle putas?
omnis enim debet sine vano nuntius esse,   5
   maioremque timens servus habere fidem.
nunc mihi, si qua tenes, ab origine dicere prima
   incipe: suspensis auribus ista bibam.
sicin eram incomptis vidisti flere capillis?
   illius ex oculis multa cadebat aqua?   10
nec speculum strato vidisti, Lygdame, lecto,
   ornabat niveas nullane gemma manus?
ac maestam teneris vestem pendere lacertis?
   scriniaque ad lecti clausa iacere pedes,
tristis erat domus, et tristes sua pensa ministrae   15
   carpebant, medio nebat et ipsa loco,
umidaque impressa siccabat lumina lana,
   rettulit et querulo iurgia nostra sono.
'Haec te teste mihi promissa est, Lygdame, merces?
   est poenae servo rumpere teste fidem.   20
ille potest nullo miseram me linquere facto,
   et qualem nolo dicere habere domi!
gaudet me vacuo solam tabescere lecto.
   si placet, insultet, Lygdame, morte mea.
non me moribus illa, sed herbis improba vicit: 25
   staminea rhombi ducitur ille rota.
illum turgentis ranae portenta rubetae
   et lecta exsectis anguibus ossa trahunt,
et strigis inventae per busta iacentia plumae,
   tinctaque funesto lanea vitta toro.   30
si non vana canunt mea somnia, Lygdame, testor,
   poena erit ante meos sera sed ampla pedes;
putris et in vacuo texetur aranea lecto:
   noctibus illorum dormiet ipsa Venus.'
quae tibi si veris animis est questa puella,   35
   hac eadem rursus, Lygdame, curre via,
et mea cum multis lacrimis mandata reporta,
   iram, non fraudes esse in amore meo,
me quoque consimili impositum torquerier igni:

iurabo bis sex integer esse dies.   40
quod mihi si e tanto felix concordia bello
   exstiterit, per me, Lygdame, liber eris.[19]

Tell me truly what you think about our girl:
   So may the mistress' yoke be lifted from you, Lygdamus.
You're not deceiving me, puffed up with false hope, are you?
   Telling me what you think I want to believe.
Surely all messengers should be lacking in deception,
   And a fearful slave should be more trustworthy.
But now, if you have news, tell me from the beginning.
   Start, and I'll listen with ears suspended.
Did you really see your mistress weeping, with hair dishevelled?
   Did tears flow in abundance from her eyes?
Did you look in vain for a mirror on the bed
   Or a jewel on her snowy hands?
Did you see her dress hang sadly from her soft arms
   And her make-up box lie locked at the foot of her bed?
The house was sad, and the slaves were sadly carding their
   Allotted portions; she herself worked in their midst.
She dabbed her wet eyes with the wool
   And replied to my abuse with her complaint.
'Did he promise me this reward and did you witness it, Lygdamus?
   It's punishable to break faith, even when the witness is a slave.
He has the heart to leave me, in my misery, for nothing I have done,
   And keep in his house a woman of a kind I wouldn't mention.
He's happy that I'm wasting away on my lonely bed;
   If he wants, Lygdamus, he can dance for joy over my death.
That wretch has triumphed over me with the help of poison, not her
   charms.
   He's drawn by her magic wheel, spun by strings.
The poison of a monstrous, bloated toad draw him to her,
   and bones picked from gutted snakes;
The feathers of a screech owl found among ruined tombs,
   A woollen head-band that has been draped on a funeral bier.
If my dreams do not whisper empty nothings to me, Lygdamus, I swear
   She will pay the penalty, late but severe, before my feet,
And dusty cobwebs will be woven on his unused bed:
   Venus herself will sleep on their nights together.'
If she made these complaints with real feeling,
   Lygdamus, run back the way you came
And deliver (with plenty of tears) what I now tell you:
   My love is angry, but not deceitful;
I myself have been tortured over a similar fire;
   I will swear that I have been chaste for twelve days.
If peace breaks out after such a conflict,
   Lygdamus, as far as I'm concerned, you will be free.

Evidently there has been a falling out with Cynthia, and Propertius
questions the slave Lygdamus, who has just returned from delivering a
sharp message to his master's beloved. The poem refigures a comic scene

most closely represented in Terence's *Heauton Timorumenos* (263-306), in which the slave Syrus reassures his anxious master that the latter's mistress is pining away without him.[20] Very little has been written on this fascinating poem, and most of what has been written attempts to fill out the dramatic scenario, and in particular the element that is missing in Propertius' version, namely the speech of the slave.[21] Where in this scene are we to imagine Lygdamus speaking? Does the poem actually represent his words and, if so, where? These are the questions that have preoccupied commentators. In my opinion, all of the poem is spoken by a single voice who ventriloquises the others, but the gist of my interpretation does not depend on any particular version of how we 'dramatise' the poem. Rather, I would note the symmetry between the tension in the form and the tension in the fictional situation. The tension in the form derives from the fact that a dramatic scene from comedy has been poured into a lyric poem in which, conventionally, only one person speaks. The tension in the situation is that the master fears that the slave will simply tell him what he wants to hear. On both levels, then, we may wonder whether there is more than one voice, or at any rate, how independent any potential other voice is from that of the main speaker.

When we consider the drama that is being played out between the two lovers, as they are represented by the poem's main voice, we find that Lygdamus plays a crucial, if ambivalent, role. The two lovers communicate through Lygdamus, both witness and conduit of their speech. He is treated as a guarantor of truth inasmuch as he is external to the shadowboxing of the lovers. But is he enough of a 'person' (rather than a mere instrument) to provide the kind of anchor that the lovers' obsessive repetition of his name implies? I don't think that anyone would object to my calling the lovers of this poem anxious, but I want to argue that beneath the lover's anxiety can be heard an anxiety about slavery, or at least about the slave as minimal addition. Of course, this is not explicitly a poem about slavery at all. The presence of the slave Lygdamus enables Propertius to explore a number of related themes: the solipsism of lyric poetry (in which there is only one voice, though here it ventriloquises furiously); the confidence game of love (if I can be sure she feels strongly enough about me, I will tell her how strongly I feel about her and so win her back); and the perverse, even paradoxical ways that lovers send their messages (I declare that I'm through with her in the hope that she will show the anger that will reveal the strength of her love and enable me to state my true feelings). But, rather than taking the line that 'slaves are good to think (about other subjects) with', I would suggest that lyric poetry and love are also good to think with. Reading Roman texts as literature about slavery we may read against the grain so as to make them speak to this different agenda. The elaborate games of love and the no less elaborate games with literary genre in this poem can be connected to the problematic lack of friction in a reality mediated by slaves, to the contradictions of a tool who is a human. So, let us read this poem as a text about slavery.

One could make a first-stage critique of this poem as slave literature as follows: Lygdamus never gets to talk or express an opinion; he is merely a means through which the free communicate, with each other and with themselves, and his freedom is subordinated to the 'bigger' problem of Propertius' amatory 'servitude'. Propertius asks for a full account and promises to listen intently, but what we hear is his version of the scene (*sicin ...?* 9), not Lygdamus', and in this account the poet-lover ventriloquises Cynthia too. All this is compatible with the blind one-sidedness of the practice of slavery itself. But can the text see more than its personae can?

Lygdamus, who crops up again in book 4 of Propertius (7.35 and 8.68-80), both is and isn't an important member of the dramatis personae. Everything in the poem is addressed to him and his name appears seven times in the vocative, while neither Propertius nor Cynthia (if she it is) are mentioned by name. The obsessive repetition of Lygdamus' name is the lovers' way of holding on to a fixed point in their shadowboxing and at the same time a mark of the tenuous nature of their hold on a common reality. Lygdamus is both the potential guarantee of a reality to which the principals can refer and a mirror that stands between them and the possibility of an independent reality. But let us begin at the beginning.

In the second line of this poem a familiar metaphor of love poetry appears, hovering between its metaphorical and literal meanings. The word *domina* in line 2 (*sic tibi sit dominae, Lygdame, dempta iuga*) neatly applies to both Lygdamus' and the poet's relation to Cynthia. The poet-lover has the advantage of a slavery that is metaphorical, a point he rams home when, in the final lines, he promises Lygdamus his freedom just after he has insisted, to Cynthia, that he has himself been *tortured* with a fire similar to hers (*me quoque consimili impositum torquerier igni*, 39). Propertius makes a cruel distinction between the metaphors that he inhabits and the realities that confront Lygdamus. A similarly cruel play on words occurs when Propertius claims that he will listen to Lygdamus *suspensis auribus* (8), for the free hang suspended in a very different sense than do the enslaved. In 4.7, for instance, where Lygdamus next crops up in the Propertian corpus, the dead Cynthia complains that her successor is punishing the slaves who remain loyal to her memory; Lalage hangs by her hair to be whipped (*caeditur et Lalage suspensis torta capillis*, 4.7.45).[22] But this difference in the meanings of suspense for master and slave respectively is not necessarily to Propertius' advantage, since what he wants of Lygdamus is the truth, rather than what Lygdamus thinks his master wants to hear. In the first couplet, Propertius conjures Lygdamus, as he wants his freedom, to tell him the honest truth about his *puella*; but for Lygdamus freedom may be not so much an incentive as a prerequisite for telling the truth: only when free from fear of punishment could he risk an unpalatable truth. Propertius fears that Lygdamus may be pumping him up with false confidence. He declares that every messenger should be reliable (*sine vano*, 5) and that one ought to be able to trust a frightened slave. Line 6 is particularly interesting, since at first glance we take the words *maiorem(que) timens servus* as 'a slave fearing his superior (*maiorem*)', only to find out that *maiorem* modifies *fidem*, 'a fearful slave should command more belief'. But surely a fearful slave is more likely to say what he thinks his master wants to hear, and so command *less* belief.[23] The necessary shift in our understanding of *maiorem* is accompanied by a shift in our attitude to this statement: *servus timens maiorem* has the force of convention, of *doxa*, but *timens servus debet habere maiorem fidem* is, in this case, a paradox. Beneath the idea that can be taken for granted lurks the paradox, and the ground of slavery loses its stability. As the adjective *maiorem* is taken away from the master, it is replaced by *tumefactum* (3): Propertius fears that he may be 'puffed up' by the very servitude of the slave.

The beginning of Cynthia's speech, ventriloquised by Propertius, confronts us with a shift in meaning similar to that undergone by *maiorem*: 'Did he promise me this reward [i.e. rupture] in your presence, Lygdamus? It's punishable to break faith with a slave a witness' (19-20). Once again, *fides* and punishment are related, and once again we have a line that leads us in the wrong direction. *Est poenae servo* (20) we take at first to mean something like 'a slave can be punished if ...', along the lines of the threat implicit in the *timens servus* of line 6. But we are disillusioned when it turns out that *servo* is not a dative but belongs to the ablative absolute formed by *servo teste*, and the punishment is meant for *Propertius'* breach of *fides*. In itself, *est poenae servo* has the swaggering force of the commonplace, the culturally dominant meaning – slaves can always be punished. But *servo teste* carries a note of anxiety: 'it's punishable to break faith *even when* it's *only* a slave who is the witness.' We must ourselves supply the words 'even when' and 'only (a slave)' to the bare ablative absolute: Propertius' Latin forces us to think about the status of the slave and to rummage around in our cultural prejudices. Since in Roman law it is doubtful that a slave could serve as *testis*, we catch some anxiety beneath Cynthia's bluster.[24] She asks, implicitly, if Lygdamus is as minimal an addition as Propertius evidently thinks he is, while, as we know from the beginning of the poem, Propertius is worrying that he may be *too* minimal an addition.

Jumping ahead to lines 31-2, we see the same combination of *testis* and *poena* as in line 20. Cynthia, ventriloquised by Propertius, is declaring to Lygdamus that she will get the better of her rival. Here Lygdamus is a *testis* of Cynthia's words rather than of Propertius':

> Si non vana canunt mea somnia, *Lygdame, testor,*
> *poena* erit ante meos sera sed ampla pedes.

> If my dreams do not whisper empty nothings to me, Lygdamus, I swear
> She will pay the penalty, late but severe, before my feet.

Cynthia calls Lygdamus to witness that her rival will pay the penalty, grovelling before her feet – like a slave, in fact. As in the case of *est poenae servo ...*, the presence of Lygdamus in this scenario gives Cynthia the confidence to speak high-handedly. But is a solemn adjuration effective when the only witness is a slave? As on the previous occasion when Lygdamus served as a *testis*, there is a doubt: *si non vana canunt mea somnia* (31). *Vana* takes us back to Propertius' statement in line 5 that all messengers should be without deception (sine vano). Cynthia's dreams may, like a frightened slave, be flattering her.[25] So, the presence of Lygdamus the slave both encourages a confident, swaggering speech and at the same time raises anxieties that the lovers are talking to themselves in a frictionless world where everything flatters them. The insistent repetition of Lygdamus' name is their repeated attempt to touch a stable reality, though in fact the very stability of that reality is undermined by his presence.

In the final lines Propertius leaves it to Lygdamus to decide whether Cynthia's complaints against him are made from the heart as, presumably, were Propertius' original words, dictated as he now claims by anger, not deceit (*iram non fraudes ...* 38). Propertius asks Lygdamus to make his own judgement: *quae tibi si veris animis ...* (35). If Lygdamus is convinced that Cynthia's anger was heartfelt, then he is to carry Propertius' message to her. The word Propertius chooses to refer to this message is *mandata* (37). Once again, the fact that he is talking to a slave allows him to talk big; in fact, though he has *ordered* Lygdamus to take the message, its content is apologetic rather than imperious. *Mandata* to Lygdamus become, surreptitiously, *mandata* to Cynthia. But not only can Lygdamus not deliver them as *mandata*, he can't deliver them *cum multis lacrimis* either, for that refers to how Propertius spoke them. The combination *cum multis lacrimis mandata* (37) is a striking oxymoron, which reflects the curious status of Propertius' utterance, addressed abjectly to Cynthia by way of an imperious command to his slave Lygdamus. One is reminded here of a passage in Suetonius' *Life of Nero*, in which the revolt of Vindex is surreptitiously welcomed by Romans, who 'pretending to have trouble with slaves at night, repeatedly called for vengeance (or Vindex)'.[26] The slave serves as an alibi for the master who is making a rebellious gesture to *his* master, or mistress as the case may be.

Propertius' poem ends, as it began, with the prospect of freedom for Lygdamus. 'If you think (*tibi*, 35) that she was speaking from the heart then as far as I am concerned/through my agency (*per me*, 42) you will be free.' Whether *per me* means 'through my agency' or, as seems more likely, 'as far as lies in my power', the final couplet creates a triangular relationship in which it is Propertius, not Lygdamus, who is the go-between. We have two three-way relationships in this poem, then: the two lovers have Lygdamus as intermediary between them, and the mistress and her slave have Propertius as intermediary. We can link the two triangles if we

187

remember Cynthia's sarcastic phrase for the angry words Propertius originally sent to her via Lygdamus: *promissa merces* (19), a phrase that might more aptly be applied to Propertius' promise of freedom for the slave. This phrase, then, links the possibility of freedom for Lygdamus to the question of whether the lovers are speaking straightforwardly. Consider the ironies in the situation. Propertius promises to lift the yoke of Lygdamus' mistress from his shoulders *if* Lygdamus is successful in convincing her that Propertius still lives under her yoke (it was merely anger that prompted Propertius to send a message of rupture) and if he is right or reliable in confirming Propertius' hope that she still lives under his (*quae tibi si veris animis est questa*, 35). More ironical still is that fact that Lygdamus is promised freedom if he can convince Cynthia *not* to take what Propertius said too seriously: that *merces promissa* was false, or deceptive, spoken in the heat of the moment. How is Lygdamus to hear the message he is given to convey, and what message does it convey *to him*?

But does it matter if you don't mean what you say when speaking to a slave? Cynthia, as ventriloquised by Propertius, protests that a message of rupture is a breach of *fides* even when spoken to, and delivered by, a slave. Propertius replies, via Lygdamus, that he didn't mean what he said and, as he hands over this message to Lygdamus, he promises to intercede for the slave's freedom. The question of Lygdamus' freedom is a plot line that is not elaborated by the poem, but there is enough about reliable and unreliable speech, about saying what you know the other wants to hear, to allow us to protract the poem beyond its final line, enough to trouble the resounding ending and disrupt its closure.

Lygdamus, in fact, will return to feature in two consecutive poems in the fourth book, where he is still a slave. We must conclude, then, that Propertius' intercession for Lygdamus' freedom, if it took place, has not been successful. In 4.7 the ghost of the dead Cynthia voices suspicions that she has been poisoned and demands that Lygdamus be tortured (*Lygdamus uratur*, 35). In 4.8, which recounts an event before Cynthia's death, Cynthia comes in on Propertius enjoying an orgy and demands that Lygdamus, whom she identifies as the cause of her complaint, be shackled and sold (79-80). Lygdamus appeals to Propertius' *genius*, but he protests to Lygdamus that he can do nothing, for he too is *captus* (70), a 'slave' to his mistress. This throws a retrospective light on the previous poem, where it appears that Lygdamus was not sold in accordance with Cynthia's wishes after the orgy described in 4.8. At the same time, Cynthia's demand in 4.8 suggests that there may be more to the dead Cynthia's wild accusations of murder in 4.7 than we at first thought.

The reappearance of Lygdamus in book 4 seems to be a rare example of a slave with a story, and we might be tempted to fill in the blanks between these three poems to sketch some narrative of his relations with the two lovers. But this may be misguided. In book 4 Lygdamus seems to belong to Propertius and not, as in 3.6, to Cynthia. Perhaps Lygdamus is not a character in the ongoing story of Cynthia and Propertius but a slave conjured up in each case to serve a local purpose. This, at any rate seems to be his role in 3.6, where he enables Propertius to create a dramatic scenario, a little comedy of love, within the compass of a lyric poem. But I have argued that we can hear the insistent repetition of his name by the lovers in 3.6 as an anxious attempt to conjure up an independent presence, a presence that would ward off the spectre of solipsism. Lygdamus, who says nothing, seems to be anything but a resisting slave. But if we listen to this poem from the place that is addressed by his name we hear the frustration generated by the inherent impossibility of this relation, which appears in this case under the guise of the minimal addition, an addition that serves not to complete but to confirm the master's solitude.

Notes

1. Fitzgerald (2000) 34-6.

2. McKeown (2007)162-3.

3. Olaudah Equiano in Potkay and Burr (1995) 221-2.

4. Fallenness, according to Milton, is a cause of slavery not a result. See Jablonski (1997) 182-3.

5. On Milton in Equiano, see Zwierlein (2001) 395-8.

6. Phaedrus' status: Champlin (2005) points out that the evidence for Phaedrus' freedman status is flimsy, but his own argument that Phaedrus must have been a lawyer because his work shows such a command of Roman law is hardly more secure. The fable and slavery: Phaedrus 3 prol. 33-7.

7. Maltby (1991) 564.

8. Compare Terence *Heauton Timorumenos* 356, where a slave makes the point that a minimal change separates the *verba* (reprimands) that are at stake for the comic *adulescens* from the *verbera* that are risked by the slave.

9. In the final lines of the poem the plaintiff of a lawsuit in which the Bore is the defendant appears to arrest the Bore, who has missed his appointment in court, so keen is he to make Horace's acquaintance. The plaintiff asks if Horace will be a witness, to which Horace offers his ear (*oppono auriculam*, 77), a symbol of his agreement.

10. Miller (2004) 160 puts it succinctly: 'Of course, as we know from 1.6, the real social-climber was none other than Horace himself.' Schlegel (2005) 126 comments: 'Shrewd readers (Johnson, John Henderson, Oliensis) observe that Horace has portrayed himself as every bit as vulnerable to the scorn saved for the interlocutor as the interlocutor is.'

11. Parker (2000) discusses, and rejects, suggestions that Horace puns on his name.

12. For more on slaves and domestic animals, particularly asses, see Hall (1995), Fitzgerald (2000) 99-102 and Bradley (2000).

13. Oliensis (1995).

14. On nature, see Beagon (1996) 286-7.

15. See Lowrie (1997) 164-75 for a sophisticated treatment of self-reference in this poem.

16. Or, 'Don't over-interpret me'. Lowrie (1997) 174 puts this well: 'If we

interpreters are the slaves of the poem, the poet on one level tells us not to add by any special labour anything extra to the simple and single myrtle of the poem.'

17. I discuss this poem at more length and with a slightly different emphasis in Fitzgerald (2000)27-30.

18. My analysis of this poem owes much to conversations with Kathy McCarthy, in connection with a course we taught in Berkeley on slavery in Latin literature.

19. I follow the more conservative text of Barber (1960), rather than the recent OCT of Heyworth (2007), which intervenes drastically to give a dramatic scenario that Heyworth considers plausible. Heyworth accepts Housman's transposition of 3-4, but instead of moving it to follow line 8 (assuming a pause after 8 in which Lygdamus repeats his story), he has it follow line 12, after which he posits a lacuna of two lines in which Lygdamus begins to speak. I read the whole poem as spoken by one voice.

20. On the comic aspects of this poem, see Yardley (1986).

21. There is a short but sensitive treatment in Warden (1980) 99-100. See also Butrica (1983); Yardley (1986) and diRienzo (1997).

22. Cf. Plautus *Poenulus* 146, *suspendi, vinci, verbera.*

23. The Roman practice of judicial torture of slaves might seem to suggest otherwise, but see Cicero, *Pro Sulla* 78 and Ulpian (*Dig.* 48.18.1.23-35) for statements that torture of slaves was not conducive to truth.

24. Though a slave could give evidence (only) under torture, Kaser (*RE* Testis, II.1.a) is emphatic that the Romans never used the term *testis* of a slave in a judicial context.

25. *Canunt* (31) means 'prophesy' but also 'to utter in boastful or extravagant language' (*OLD* 4a, s.v.)

26. *Iam noctibus iurgia cum servis plerique simulantes crebro vindicem postulabant* (Suetonius, *Nero* 45).

References

Barber, E. (1960) *Sexti Properti Carmina.* Oxford.

Beagon, M. (1996) 'Nature and landscapes in Pliny the Elder', in G. Shipley and J. Salmon (eds) *Human Landscapes in Classical Antiquity. Environment and Culture,* 284-304. London.

Bradley, K. (2000) 'Animalizing the slave: the truth of fiction', *Journal of Roman Studies* 90, 110-25.

Butrica, J. (1983) 'Propertius 3.6', *Échos du Monde Classique* 2, 17-37.

Champlin, E. (2005) 'Phaedrus the Fabulous', *Journal of Roman Studies,* 97-123.

Di Rienzo, D. (1997) 'Due note Properziane (III 6, 1 e 27)', *Bollettino di Studi Latini* 27, 421-32.

Fitzgerald, W. (2000) *Slavery and the Roman Literary Imagination.* Cambridge.

Hausrath, A. (ed.) (1959-1970) *Corpus fabularum Aesopicarum,* new edn revised by H. Hunger. Leipzig.

Hall, E. (1995) 'The ass with double vision: politicising an ancient Greek novel', in D. Margolies and M. Joannou (eds), *Heart of a Heartless World: Essays in Cultural Resistance in Honour of Margot Heinemann,* 47-59. London.

Heyworth, S. (2007) *Sexti Properti Elegos.* Oxford.

Jablonski, S. (997) 'Ham's vicious race: slavery and John Milton', *Studies in English Literature* 37, 173-90.

Lowrie, M. (1997) *Horace's Narrative Odes.* Oxford.

Maltby, R. (1991) *A Lexicon of Ancient Latin Etymologies.* Leeds.

9. The Slave as Minimal Addition in Latin Literature

Miller, P.A. (2005) *Latin Verse Satire*. London & New York.

McKeown, N. (2007) *The Invention of Ancient Slavery?* London.

Oliensis, E. (1995) 'Life after publication: *Epistles* 1.20', *Arethusa* 28.2-3, 209-24.

Parker, H. (2000) 'Flaccus', *Classical Quarterly* 50, 455-62.

Potkay, A. and Burr, S. (eds) (1995) *Black Atlantic Writers of the Eighteenth Century: Living the New Exodus in England and the Americas*. New York.

Schlegel, C. (2005) *Satire and the Threat of Speech: Horace's Satires Book 1*. Madison, WI.

Yardley, J. (1986) 'Propertius 3.6.9: a weeping mistress', *Phoenix* 40, 198-200.

Zwierlein, A-J. (2001) *Majestick Milton: British Imperial Expansion and Transformations of 'Paradise Lost' 1667-1837*. Muenster.

Slave Agency and Resistance in Martial

Deborah Kamen

This essay has two aims: to read *through* Martial's epigrams to tease out traces of slave agency and resistance, and to illuminate how Martial in turn usurps and neutralizes this agency.[1] Although Martial's epigrams are satiric and (obviously) should not be taken at face value, I argue that by reading his poetry 'against the grain', we can uncover slaves possessing a surprising degree of agency, whether wielding power over the bodies of free people or exercising various modes of resistance.[2] But it is equally important for us to account for the fact that Martial rarely leaves this agency and resistance unconstrained: indeed, he has various strategies for defusing or co-opting behavior that might otherwise be a source of anxiety for free men.[3]

One of the richest areas for the depiction of the 'slave as agent' in the epigrams of Martial[4] is the realm of sexual relations.[5] Sexual roles in antiquity were ideologically mapped onto social statuses[6] – that is, those of higher status were supposed to be active and penetrating, while those of lower status were passive and penetrated. It is perhaps surprising, then, that Martial's slaves are often represented wielding sexual power: sometimes *directly*, by penetrating their masters or initiating sexual relations, and sometimes *indirectly*, through their sexual desirability or their refusal of masters' sexual advances.

Master-slave sex in Martial comes in nearly all permutations,[7] but that between male master and slave-boy is the most frequent. And while the master-on-top model is clearly the norm,[8] on occasion Martial does imagine the slave-boy taking the active, penetrating role.[9] So, one epigram reads, 'Since the boy's cock hurts, and your ass hurts, Naevolus, I'm not a diviner, but I know what you're doing' (*mentula cum doleat puero, tibi, Naevole, culus, / non sum divinus, sed scio quid facias*; III.71)[10] – that is to say, the slave-boy is penetrating the master. At first glance, then, the boy appears to be exercising agency, but his agency is effectively undercut in a couple of ways. First of all, the boy himself is less an agent than his penis is (the *mentula* is the grammatical subject here), and the primary 'agent' in this epigram, in the sense of the one said to be 'doing' something, is the master Naevolus (*facias*). Secondly, the boy is in a way not the point here: he becomes a mere tool – in both senses of the word – in Martial's invective toolkit. Thus, although we get a brief glimpse of the slave-as-active-penetrator, we also find Martial both downplaying and appropriating the slave's agency for his own satiric purposes.

This combination of presenting, co-opting, and neutralizing slave-boys' agency is not unique to III.71. In another epigram, Martial accuses Phoebus of (literally) sleeping with well-endowed slave-boys (*dormis cum pueris mutuniatis*). Martial wants to believe that Phoebus is effeminate (*mollem*)[11] despite the fact that this man is rumoured *not* to be pathic (*cineadum*) (III.73). The *mutuniati* – the well-endowed boys – lurk in the background here as agents – the alleged penetrators of Phoebus – but as with the *puer* in III.71, they are not grammatical subjects, nor is their activity spelled out. Their agency, then, is only hinted at, and even then, it is harnessed in the service of Martial's invective against Phoebus. We find Martial employing some of the same strategies when he responds to Philomusus' insinuations about Martial's well-endowed (*mutuniati*) slave-boys: Martial says he keeps the boys around to bugger (*pedicant*) other people – specifically, nosy people (XI.63). The slave-boys' implied capacity for agency is thus, once again, manipulated by Martial, in this case as a weapon against Philomusus. Finally, in yet another instance, Martial hints that a certain Hamillus, who buggers (*percidis*) well-endowed (*grandes*) slaves when the doors are open, is actually sodomized by these slaves when the doors are closed (*non pedicari se qui testatur, Hamille, / illud saepe facit quod sine teste facit*; VII.62). Thus we see slaves exercising agency once again; but Hamillus, even though he is the 'passive' party in sex (*pedicari*), remains the grammatical subject, literally the agent (*facit ... facit*). The poem's explicit aim is to question Hamillus' virility – what he likes doing without witnesses is also 'ball-less' (*sine teste*)[12] – but a secondary effect is the erasure of the slave-boys' agency.

It is not only slave-boy penetrators who are represented possessing an agency that is then subsequently stripped away. We also find this happening with slaves who initiate or refuse sexual relations with their masters.[13] Describing his ideal slave-boy (*si quis forte mihi possit praestare roganti, / audi quem puerum, Flacce, rogare velim*, IV.42.1-2), Martial writes: 'Let him often force me when I'm unwilling and refuse me when I'm willing, let him often be freer than his own master' (*saepe et nolentem cogat nolitque volentem, / liberior domino saepe sit ille suo*, IV.42.11-12). Indeed, this pretence of slave-as-master, a sort of bedroom Saturnalia,[14] may in part account for the repeated joke we find in Martial of masters addressing their slaves as 'master' (*dominus*).[15] But this apparent role reversal, entailing a 'masterly' slave who compels (*cogat*) his own 'servile' master, is in a sense undermined by the fact that the slave's agency and resistance are themselves demanded. That is, this 'agency' turns out to be something Martial has asked for (*roganti, rogare*).

On occasion, slave-boys in Martial exhibit resistance to their (typical) role as sex objects. Thus, some boys are depicted cutting their flowing locks, a primary marker of their sexual attractiveness and desirability.[16]

Often they do so under the pretext of aiding their master in some way: so, for example, in two epigrams the slave Encolpus vows his hair to Apollo, allegedly so that his master Pudens will attain the rank of Chief Centurion (I.31; V.48). Pudens grants Encolpus permission (*non prohibente ... permisit*, V.48.2-3) – Encolpus is making a vow on his behalf, after all – but he weeps about the end of his slave-boy's sexual availability (V.48.1-3). In the same vein is a series of poems about Earinus, the emperor Domitian's beloved slave-boy. Like Encolpus, Earinus dedicates his hair to a god (IX.16; IX.17), and in a particularly witty epigram, Ganymede points to the newly shorn Earinus and begs Jupiter to let him cut his hair too (*quod tuus ecce suo Caesar permisit ephebo, tu permitte tuo*, IX.36.3-4). In this case, Jupiter, the ultimate master, refuses. Thus, while these poems offer a glimpse of slave-boys exercising resistance, Martial also makes it clear that it is up to the master whether or not to grant permission (*non prohibente, permisit, permitte*). When it comes to this mode of resistance, then, the agency of the slave-boys is shown to be conditional; moreover, it is permitted only when the act also happens to be in the service of a higher authority (whether the master or a god), thereby neutralizing the slave's agency.

A slightly different mode of resistance by slave-boys involves 'cruelly' withholding kisses or sex from their masters. So, in one poem Martial says to the beautiful slave-boy Cestus, who has refused to provide sexual favours: 'You could have succeeded to the bed of Ganymede, but cruelly (*durus*) you would have given your master only kisses' (VIII.46.5-6). Cestus' punishment? 'Happy will your bride who will work on her tender husband, the girl who will first make you a man' (*felix, quae tenerum vexabit sponsa maritum / et quae te faciet prima puella virum!*, VIII.46.7-8). The bride may be *felix*, but Cestus certainly won't be: the verb *vexabit* implies that the woman will tire him out without much sexual satisfaction on his part.[17] Thus, in return for Cestus' cruel (*durus*) withholding, Martial threatens a life of sexual dissatisfaction.[18] In another poem, Martial catalogues a number of sweet fragrances, ending with, 'Your kisses, harsh (*saeve*) boy Diadumenus, smell like this. What if you should give them in their entirety, ungrudgingly?' (*quid sit tota dares illa sine invidia?*, III.65.10). This last line has been taken, I think correctly, as a 'veiled imperative';[19] that is to say, Martial is not really *asking* Diadumenus to deliver so much as *commanding* him, thus effectively overruling the boy's resistance.

This type of response by Martial is common. About the slave-boy Telesphorus, Martial writes: 'When you see that I want it and sense that I'm taut, you make big demands: Suppose I want to refuse, is that allowed? And unless I say, under oath, "I'll give it", you withdraw those buttocks which allow you much power over me (*permittunt in me quae tibi multa*)' (XI.58.1-4). Thus, the slave has power over his master (or at least his buttocks do, since they *permittunt*),[20] but as we have seen before, the master – while acknowledging the boy's capacity for agency – still has the final word: 'To you I will do nothing, but my cock, [wiped clean] with a washed piece of wool, will tell your eager greediness to blow me (*tibi nil faciam, sed lota mentula lana / λαικάζειν cupidae dicet avaritiae*)' (XI.58.11-12). These lines have been interpreted in various ways: One scholar has argued that the wiped-clean penis indicates that 'intercourse has taken place', in which case we are to imagine that Martial has forced himself on the boy, cancelling out any (temporary) power the slave had over him. Another interpretation is that Martial resorted to masturbation, which explains his words 'I will do nothing to you', and also the necessity to clean up.[21] Either way, I think the final line is significant: even if the Greek verb *laikazein* was, in general, bleached of its full sexual meaning,[22] in this context (a poem about master-slave sex) I think it must have had some of its original sense of performing fellatio. And so, whether or not we are to understand that Martial penetrated the boy, we should nonetheless see a threat of (future) *irrumatio*.

In a similar example, Martial writes that whenever he asks his slave-boy Lygdus to come meet him, Lygdus agrees, setting a time and place; but the boy often (*saepe*) resists by not showing up for their rendezvous, leaving Martial to resort (perhaps as in XI.58?) to masturbation (XI.73.1-4). But yet again, Martial has the last word, punishing Lygdus with a curse: 'May you carry an umbrella for a one-eyed mistress' (*umbrellam luscae, Lygde, feras dominae*) (XI.73.6). We could take this threat literally – that Lygdus will have an ugly mistress someday for whom he will perform particularly demeaning tasks – or, I think more likely, figuratively. That is to say, the 'one-eyed mistress' is likely Martial's penis; and it has even been suggested that the umbrella is to be taken as the boy's open mouth.[23] Thus, XI.73.6 may represent a threat of *irrumatio*, in which case the poem ends on a similar note to XI.58. Such instances of slave resistance and agency, then, are ultimately overturned when the master exercises his (much greater) power over the slave's body.

In other poems, Martial essentially fetishizes the slave's resistance.[24] We have already seen an example of this in IV.42, where Martial's dream boy refuses (*nolit*) his advances. In a similar instance, Martial tells his slave-boy Diadumenus: 'I don't want any kisses, except those resistant (*luctantia*) ones which I've snatched' (V.46.1). And in a further epigram, Martial says to his slave-boy Dindymus: 'You pursue, I flee; you flee, I pursue; this is my intention. I don't want your willingness, Dindymus, I want your unwillingness (*velle tuum nolo, Dindyme, nolle volo*)' (V.83). The thrill of the chase is what turns Martial on: Dindymus' unwillingness (*nolo ... nolle*) is far from being an obstacle; his resistance is instead embraced (as is the boy himself) by Martial (*velle ... volo*). In all of these cases, then, slave resistance – whether feigned or genuine – is framed as part of an 'erotic game', with the master in charge.[25]

Let's turn now to the male master-female slave pairings in Martial, which entail power dynamics slightly different than those discussed thus far. Because the female slave, unlike her male counterpart, was (presum-

195

ably) always the penetrated party in sexual relations with her master, she is for the most part represented as a sex object, available at any time for the taking[26] – albeit a sex object less appealing than either a freeborn woman (III.33) or an attractive slave-boy. On occasion, however, Martial does imagine the female slave using her sexual desirability to exercise a degree of agency.[27] In a couple of poems (VI.71, XIV.203), he describes female slaves who, with their wanton gestures and sexy dance moves, can arouse anyone, from old men like Priam to paragons of chastity like Hippolytus. As such, these girls are seen to exercise power over free men's bodies. But, as with the slave-boys, this agency is ultimately undercut: the point of VI.71 is that the girl and her master have switched places – the master is mocked for selling his slave girl and buying her back as his 'mistress' (*vendidit ancillam, nunc redimit dominam*; VI.71.6) – and it is the master's voluntary subjugation that is attacked. XIV.203 is an *apophoreta* poem, meant to be attached to this girl as a gift-tag, and so despite her apparent agency, she is explicitly labelled here as a commodity.[28]

And what about the agency of male slaves who have sex with their mistresses? As 'penetrators', these slaves are by definition active, and the problematic nature of this agency may be one reason that slave-mistress sex is represented so infrequently in Latin literature.[29] Concern about paternity was surely another.[30] Nonetheless, at least some of Martial's epigrams do depict free women having sex with male slaves.[31] So, for example, in VI.39 (seemingly) all of Cinna's male slaves have had sex with his wife Marulla, a fact that could be threatening both to Cinna and to the social order as a whole. However, Martial ameliorates this threat by not focusing on the slave-mistress sexual relations as such: none of the seven named slaves is explicitly said to have done anything to Marulla (she herself disappears after the first line of the poem); indeed, none is even the subject of a verb. Instead, the poem's real subject is Cinna, who is mocked for being too dense to realize that 'his' children are not really his own.

While sex is the realm in Martial in which slaves are most frequently depicted possessing agency – even if that agency is ultimately stripped away – we also find slave-agents in number of non-sexual capacities. It was the case, in Martial's poetry as in reality, that certain occupations granted slaves power over their masters' bodies, which was a necessary, but also potentially troubling, arrangement.

The tools of the slave-barber, for instance, could easily be put to less-than-innocuous purposes.[32] One poem describes (hyperbolically) the brutality of the slave-barber Antiochus, saying, for instance, that Prometheus would prefer to have the vulture tear out his liver than have this man cut his hair (XI.84). Particularly striking in this poem is Martial's use of the word *stigmata* to describe the marks on his own chin inflicted by Antiochus (XI.84.13): the word calls to mind the marks a master inflicts on his slave as punishment,[33] and in this way, Antiochus' actions represent a reversal of normative master-slave power relations. In another epigram,

Martial jokingly asks Gargilianus, a man who depilates himself, whether he is afraid of the barber (*numquid tonsorem, Gargiliane, times?*, III.74.1). But while Martial insinuates in both of these poems that slave-barbers are capable of exercising (dangerous) agency, the unnamed barber in II.74 is deprived of agency – he is only the direct object of Gargilianus' hypothetical fear – and the thrust of the invective is an attack on effeminate grooming practices. In XI.58, the poem discussed above in which Telesphorus makes demands on his master (*rogas*, XI.58.2), Martial draws an analogy with a hypothetical situation in which a slave-barber, his razor above Martial's neck, asks (*roget … rogat*, XI.58.6, 8) for freedom and wealth. Fear (*timor*, XI.58.8) would drive Martial to agree to the demands, but once the razor was put away, he would use his regained authority to break the barber's legs and hands (XI.58). That is, the barber, just like Telesphorus, would be made to pay for his (attempted) agency.[34]

Another slave occupation entailing power over the free man's body, not to mention his mind, was that of the pedagogue.[35] Pedagogues – who were almost always of servile background, whether slave or freedman – were custodians of both free and slave children in Rome. In this capacity, they could exercise close supervision over their charges: Martial describes his own pedagogue Charidemus as unnecessarily strict, denying him entertainment, love affairs, fancy clothes, lavish food and drink, and even inflicting physical violence (XI.39).[36] The pedagogue's potential for violence, like that of the barber, was particularly problematic, from an ideological perspective: slaves' bodies were supposed to be at the disposal of the free, not vice versa. Thus, Martial's strategy for countering the pedagogue's agency is to assert his own authority: in XI.39, he closes the poem by telling Charidemus to stop (*desine*, XI.39.15) and proclaiming, 'My girlfriend will tell you that I'm a man (*virum*) now' (XI.39.16). This proclamation has two implications: that Martial is an adult Roman citizen (*vir*), with bodily inviolability; and that he is a proper male with a capacity to penetrate (to which the *amica* can attest) – underlying which might be a veiled threat to penetrate Charidemus if he doesn't lay off.[37]

Slave-cooks, like slave-barbers and pedagogues, are also depicted by Martial as potentially wielding power over their masters' bodies. Indeed, Martial represents cooks with a great deal of independence in the kitchen, preparing dishes unsupervised.[38] Because of the nature of their work, cooks could easily exercise mastery over free men's bodies, potentially – whether deliberately or not – preparing bad or even poisonous food. In Martial's poems, this culinary agency is frequently countered with physical violence. Thus, in one epigram, Martial addresses his friend Rufus, saying, 'You say the hare isn't cooked (*esse negas coctum leporem*) and ask for a whip. Rufus, you'd prefer to cut up your cook than your hare' (III.94). Unsurprisingly, the agency of the cook is elided here – we don't hear 'the cook didn't cook the hare' but 'the hare isn't cooked' – and his agency is further erased by Rufus' response: namely, to exert his physical authority over the slave's body. Similar responses to Rufus' are seen in a couple of other poems as well (III.13.3-4; VIII.23).

Finally, yet another profession granting slaves power over their masters' bodies was that of the doctor. One way in which slave-doctors are imagined exercising their authority is by controlling their patients' consumption of alcohol.[39] This may seem like trivial point, but it reflects a larger power imbalance: after all, it is the master who is supposed to limit the slave's consumption, not the other way around. Slave-doctors are also depicted exercising agency through their intimate access to free women's bodies: Martial and presumably other Roman men feared that these slaves might be having sex with their wives.[40] Finally, and perhaps most significantly, the doctor, like the barber, was equipped with sharp tools, and therefore had the capacity to inflict violence on his patients, again intentionally or otherwise.[41] Indeed, doctors in Martial are represented as making patients sicker, prolonging painful deaths, even killing their patients outright.[42] However, although Martial's slave-doctors are not fully stripped of agency, their power is nonetheless weakened by the nature of their portrayal: namely, as greedy, incompetent, or sexual tools – all common stereotypes of the 'bad slave'.[43]

In this chapter, I have examined the various ways in which Martial represents – and then restricts – the agency of slaves in sexual relations with their masters, as well as the power of slave-barbers, pedagogues, cooks, and doctors over their masters' bodies. I should add that Martial also portrays slaves in other contexts possessing some degree of agency. This agency generally comes in the form of what James C. Scott calls, in the context of peasant communities, 'everyday forms of resistance',[44] which include acts like gossiping,[45] complaining,[46] lingering,[47] neglecting duties,[48] stealing from masters,[49] and running away[50] – all of which Martial mentions slaves doing, if only in passing. Martial, then, does not imagine slaves as 'wholly passive':[51] he portrays slaves not only resisting but even exercising power over their masters. Significantly, however, Martial rarely presents slave agency and resistance unchecked. In the realm of sexual relations, the agency of slaves is often fetishized, commodified, or co-opted. Thus, the slave initiating or resisting sex is made less a real threat than a desirable sex object, and in some cases, his or her agency is erased altogether. In other, non-sexual realms, where slave agency is potentially more dangerous to the master,[52] Martial responds by asserting the slave's natural inferiority, stressing his object status, or employing (or having his characters employ) physical violence. In all cases, what we find is that Martial, after hinting at slave agency, redraws the line between slave and free in an attempt to right the (threatening) imbalance of 'normative' power relations.[53] Slaves in Martial, then, are represented as simultaneously – or at least consecutively – active and passive, subject and object, as is perhaps inevitable given their dual status as both human and property.[54]

Notes

1. On Martial and slavery, see, e.g., Barbu (1963) on Martial and Juvenal; Garrido-Hory (1981), which catalogues slaves, freedmen, and the relations of slaveholding in Martial; Fitzgerald (2000) *passim*; Fitzgerald (2007) 97-105 and *passim*.

2. On slave resistance in Rome, see Bradley (1984) 26-33, (1989) and (1994) ch. 6. On various forms of slave resistance in modernity, see, e.g., Hartman (1997), Camp (2004), Alpers et al. (2005) and Alpers at al. (2007).

3. On free people's fear of slaves in Greco-Roman antiquity, see most recently Serghidou (2007). See also Thalmann (1996), McCarthy (2000), and Fitzgerald (2000) on the ideological work that Latin literature does to relieve free people's anxieties about master-slave relations. But cf. the critique of this kind of scholarship in Bradley (2001) 476, which involves, in his words, 'the mechanical attribution of "anxieties", as a sort of post-modernist "party line", to every piece of imaginative literature in the Roman repertory' (2001).

4. Throughout this chapter, I refer to both poetic persona and poet as 'Martial'. I do not mean to imply, however, that the two are one and the same.

5. On slaves and sex in Marital, see Garrido-Hory (1981) ch. 6. See also Panciera (2001) 121 n. 14, in the context of sex with *pueri* in Martial: 'It is too large a subject to examine here, but it is worth contemplating the possibility that master-slave sexual relationships could be more complex than the usual dynamic between master and slave.' Cf. the construction, in nineteenth-century America, of female slaves as simultaneously subject and object, active and passive, in sexual relations with their masters (see Hartman (1997) ch. 3).

6. See, e.g., Dover (1978), Winkler (1991), Halperin (1991), Williams (1999), among others.

7. On the permutations of sex in the Roman imaginary more generally, see Parker (1997).

8. For slaves as (penetrated) *cinaedi*, see, e.g., II.43.13; VI.39.12; IX.90.7; X.98.2; XII.16.2; XII.75. For indirect references to masters penetrating slaves, see, e.g., II.60.2; IV.52; XII.33; XIII.26.

9. As Richlin (1992) 43 remarks, these instances represent 'a complete reversal of the norm in Greek and most Latin poetry'.

10. In this essay, I use the text of Shackleton Bailey (1993).

11. On *mollitia*, see Edwards (1993) ch. 2 (she argues that *mollis* means not simply sexually 'passive' but 'like a woman').

12. On this double meaning of *sine teste*, see also Galán Vioque (2002) ad loc.

13. Cf. Parker (2007) 285: 'Slaves are always depicted as the passive instrument of a master's or mistress's lust. I know of no case where the slave is depicted as initiating the affair.'

14. The Saturnalian aspect of Martial's poetry is well recognized: for the argument that many books of Martial's epigrams (not only the *Xenia* and *Apophoreta*) were published and meant to be circulated during the Saturnalia, see Citroni (1989); on the Saturnalian motif as it relates to Martial's self-representation as an epigrammist, see Roman (2001) 130-38. Perhaps we should view slave agency as one facet of Martial's Saturnalian poetics. (I thank Stephen Hinds for suggesting this idea to me.)

15. For slaves as *domini*, see, e.g., XI.70.2; XII.66.8. Howell (1995) 140 thinks that *dominus* is simply a standard mode of address, whereas Shackleton Bailey (1993) 405 argues that it carries erotic overtones.

16. For masters paying for long-haired boys: XII.70.9; XII.97.4. See also groups of desirable slave-boys with flowing locks: II.57.5; III.58.31; XII.49.1. Cf. the comparative unattractiveness of short-haired slaves: X.98.8-10; XI.11.1-3; XIV.158.

17. For this meaning of *vexo*, see also XI.81.1. On the sexual sense of *vexo* more generally, see Adams (1982) 200.

18. Cf. Martial accusing the slave-boy Hyllus of 'cruelly' (*durus*) refusing today what he granted yesterday; the boy claims as his excuse 'beard and years and hair' (IV.7.1-3). The beard, like the cutting of long hair, marked the end of the boy's sexual availability. As such, we find masters in a number of poems either praying that their beloved's beard come slowly (V.48.7-8; IX.56.11-12; XI.22.5-8), or bemoaning the latter's growth of facial hair (VIII.52.10; X.42).

19. Watson (2003) ad loc.

20. On Telesphorus' simultaneous possession and lack of power, see Fitzgerald (2000) 47, and (2007) 124.

21. For both interpretations, see Kay (1985) ad loc. (the former is favoured by Kay, among others; the latter suggestion is Scaliger's).

22. On the meaning of *laikazein* see Bain (1992) 74-7 (but cf. Henderson (1975) 153). On the sense of *laikazein* (as used in Latin) as a 'generalised expression of contempt', see Adams (1982) 132.

23. For both readings, see Obermayer (1998) 83-5. Obermayer (1998) 85 n. 289 cites, as the earliest interpretation of the umbrella as a mouth, Domizio Calderino's 1474 Venice commentary on Martial.

24. For the observation that slave agency is fetishized, I thank Sarah Levin-Richardson (personal communication). For slavery in general as the fetishized commodification of human beings, see, e.g., Baptist (2001).

25. For an excellent treatment of this 'erotic game', see Fitzgerald (2000) 47-9.

26. For the female slave as sex object, see IV.66.11-2. See also Patterson (1982) 173: there is 'little variation among slaveholding societies with respect to the sexual claims and powers of masters over female slaves: I know of no slaveholding society in which a master, when so inclined, could not exact sexual services from his female slaves.'

27. See Sullivan (1991) 165, who says that Martial opposes master/female-slave sexual relations for precisely this reason, 'because amorous passion subverts the hierarchical order by enslaving the master to his natural and social inferior, a female slave'. Cf. Stallybrass and White (1986) ch. 4 on the power of female servants over their Victorian masters.

28. On women (in general) as objects of exchange, see, most famously, Rubin (1975).

29. Parker (2007) proposes a handful of reasons for the relative silence of our sources on this topic: sex between free women and slaves probably did not happen often; if it did, no one talked; and slaves were (in general) considered tools, passive instruments, not sexual agents. See also Saller (1996) 127, who suggests that mistress-slave sex was considered particularly problematic because it 'violated the social order by placing the matron in a position of subordination to a slave'.

30. It was presumably this concern that prompted a legal prohibition against mistress-slave sex: *Dig.* 48.5.25.

31. For free women having sex with male slaves, see, e.g., II.60; III.39; V.61; VI.39; VI.67; VII.14; X.91; XII.58; XII.91.

32. The tools of the barber's trade are catalogued in an epigram entitled 'barber's metal gear': see XIV.36. On slave-barbers in Martial, see Garrido-Hory (1981) 142-3, and Fitzgerald (2000) 49: 'One can well imagine that the experience of being shaved by a slave might give rise to horrible imaginings in the master.

After all, here is the slave he had beaten applying a (reasonably) sharp blade to his throat!'

33. See also Fitzgerald (2000) 49 on this point; on *stigmata* in antiquity, see Jones (1987).

34. Martial has a slightly different approach to slave-boy barbers, who appear either as deceased (VI.52) or as sex objects (VIII.52); in both cases, he neutralizes their potential for violent agency.

35. On the role of pedagogues in Rome, see Bradley (1991) ch. 3. For pedagogues in charge of free boys, see, e.g., VIII.44.2; IX.27.11; in charge of slave boys, see III.58.30-31; XII.49.1.

36. The *topos* of the strict, and sometimes abusive, pedagogue is seen throughout Latin literature: see, e.g., Bradley (1991) 53-54. For pedagogues inflicting violence, see also X.62.10.

37. On the *vir* as impenetrable, see, e.g., Walters (1997).

38. For slaves having control in the kitchen: V.50.7-8; VII.27; XI.31; cf. XIV.220.

39. For doctors controlling alcohol intake: VI.78; VI.86.1-2; IX.94; IX.96.

40. For doctors having sex with patients: VI.31; XI.60.5-6; XI.71.

41. For fear of doctors' brutality: XI.74; XI.84.5-6. This fear of slave-doctors appears to be widespread among slaveholding societies: In eighteenth-century Virginia, for instance, black slave-doctors treated white patients until 1748, when whites' fears led to laws curbing this practice (see Genovese (1974) 224).

42. For doctors making patients sicker: V.9; prolonging painful deaths: X.77. For doctors killing patients: I.30; I.47; VI.53; VIII.74.

43. For the 'suspicious model' of slavery in the Roman imaginary, see Thalmann (1996).

44. See Scott (1985). See also Bradley (1994) 125: 'Beneath the surface calm which elitist writings evince, however, there was a constant ferment of defiant activity as slaves, of every description, ran away, stole, cheated, damaged property and shirked work, or as they directed violence against themselves or their owners, all in an effort to withstand the cruelty and deprivation slavery heaped upon them.'

45. For the fear of slaves overhearing (and then gossiping): II.82; VII.62.3-4; XI.38; XII.24.4-8.

46. For complaining slaves: I.92.1-2; IX.92.1-2.

47. For lingering slaves: XII.29.11; XIV.119 (cf. lingering/playing permitted during Saturnalia: XIV.1.3; XIV.79). See further Bradley (1994) 115.

48. For (allegedly) negligent slaves: VII.86.11; XII.87.1-2.

49. For thieving slaves: VIII.33.5-6; X.37.12 (cf. masters enlisting the aid of their slaves in thievery: II.37.8; III.23.1). See further Bradley (1994) 115-16.

50. For runaways: III.91.3; XI.6. See further Bradley (1994) 120-1.

51. I borrow this phrase from Orlando Patterson (1984) 173, who says that the slave is not a 'wholly passive entity'.

52. As Joshel (1992) 86 says: 'The complaints about doctors killing their patients and teachers corrupting their students do not belittle these professionals; quite the reverse, they indicate some fear about what the doctor or teacher could do.'

53. For a similar argument about the ideological work done by Plautus, see McCarthy (2000).

54. On this dual status, see, e.g., Arist. *Pol.* 1.1253b32, Varro *RR* 1.17.1. For very helpful comments on this paper, I thank Stephen Hinds, Sandra Joshel, Sarah Levin-Richardson, and the organizers and participants at the 'Imagining Slavery: "Celebrating Abolition" Conference 2007' conference at Royal Holloway, University of London. All errors are of course my own.

Deborah Kamen

Bibliography

Alpers, E.A. et al. (2005). *Slavery and Resistance in Asia and Africa*. London & New York.

—— et al. (2007). *Resisting Bondage in Indian Ocean Africa and Asia*. London & New York.

Bain, D. (1991) 'Six Greek verbs of sexual congress', *CQ* 41, 51-77.

Baptist, E.E. (2001) '"Cuffy", "Fancy Maids", "One-Eyed Men": rape, commodification, and the domestic slave trade in the United States', *American Historical Review* 106.5, 1619-50.

Barbu, N.I. (1963) 'Les esclaves chez Martial et Juvénal', *Acta antiqua Philippopolitana*, 67-74. Sofia.

Bradley, K. (1984) *Slaves and Masters in the Roman Empire: A Study in Social Control*. Brussels.

—— (1989) *Slavery and Rebellion in the Roman World, 140 BC-70 BC* Bloomington, IN & London.

—— (1991) *Discovering the Roman Family: Studies in Roman Social History*. New York.

—— (1994) *Slavery and Society at Rome*. Cambridge.

—— (2001) 'Imagining slavery: the limits of the plausible', *JRA* 14, 473-7.

Camp, S. (2004) *Closer to Freedom: Enslaved Women and Everyday Resistance in the Plantation South*. Chapel Hill, NC & London.

Citroni, M. (1989) 'Marziale e la Letteratura per i Saturnali (poetica dell'intrattenimento e cronologia della pubblicazione dei libri)', *ICS* 14, 201-26.

Dover, K.J. (1978) *Greek Homosexuality*. New York.

Edwards, C. (1993) *The Politics of Immorality in Ancient Rome*. Cambridge.

Fitzgerald, W. (2000) *Slavery and the Roman Literary Imagination*. Cambridge.

—— (2007) *Martial: The World of the Epigram*. Chicago, IL & London.

Galán Vioque, G. (2002) *Martial, Book VII: A Commentary*, tr. J.J. Zoltowski. Leiden.

Garrido-Hory, M. (1981) *Martial et l'esclavage*. Paris.

Genovese, E.D. (1974) *Roll, Jordan, Roll: The World that Slaves Made*. New York.

Halperin, D.M. (1990) *One Hundred Years of Homosexuality: And Other Essays on Greek Love*. New York.

Hartman, S.V. (1997) *Scenes of Subjection: Terror, Slavery, and Self-Making in Nineteenth-Century America*. New York & Oxford.

Henderson, J. (1975) *The Maculate Muse: Obscene Language in Attic Comedy*. New Haven.

Howell, P. (1980) *A Commentary on Book One of the Epigrams of Martial*. London.

Jones, C.P. (1987) 'Stigma: tattooing and branding in Graeco-Roman antiquity', *JRS* 77, 139-55.

Joshel, S.R. (1992) *Work, Identity and Legal Status at Rome: A Study of the Occupational Inscriptions*. Norman, OK & London.

Kay, N.M. (1985) *Martial Book XI: A Commentary*. London.

McCarthy, K. (2000) *Slaves, Masters, and the Art of Authority in Plautine Comedy*. Princeton, NJ.

Obermayer, H.P. (1998) *Martial und der Diskurs über männliche 'Homosexualität' in der Literatur der frühen Kaizerzeit*. Tübingen.

Panciera, M.D. (2001) *Sexual Practice and Invective in Martial and Pompeian Inscriptions*. PhD Diss., UNC Chapel Hill.

Parker, H.N. (1997) 'The teratogenic grid', in J.P. Hallett and M.B. Skinner (eds) *Roman Sexualities*, 47-65. Princeton, NJ.

—— (2007) 'Free women and male slaves, or Mandingo meets the Roman Empire', in Serghidou (ed.) 281-98.

Patterson, O. (1982) *Slavery and Social Death*. Cambridge, MA.

Richlin, A. (1992) *The Garden of Priapus: Sexuality and Aggression in Roman Humor*. New York.

Roman, L. (2001) 'The representation of literary materiality in Martial's "Epigrams"', *JRS* 19, 113-45.

Rubin, G. (1975) 'The traffic in women: notes on the "Political Economy" of sex', in R.R. Reiter (ed.), *Toward an Anthropology of Women*, 157-210. New York.

Saller, R. (1996) 'The hierarchical household in Roman society: a study of domestic slavery', in M.L. Bush (ed.), *Serfdom and Slavery: Studies in Legal Bondage*, 112-29. London & New York.

Scott, J.C. (1985) *Weapons of the Weak: Everyday Forms of Peasant Resistance*. New Haven, CT.

Serghidou, A. (ed.) (2007) *Fear of Slaves – Fear of Enslavement in the Ancient Mediterranean. Peur de l'esclave – Peur de l'esclavage en Mediterranee ancienne (Discours, représentations, pratiques)*. Actes du XXIXe Colloque du Groupe International de Recherche sur l'Esclavage dans l'Antiquité (GIREA). Rethymnon, 4-7 November 2004. Paris.

Shackleton Bailey, D.R. (ed. & tr.) (1993) *Martial Epigrams*, 3 vols. Cambridge, MA.

Stallybrass, P. and White, A. (1986) *The Politics and Poetics of Transgression*. Ithaca, NY.

Sullivan, J.P. (1991) *Martial: The Unexpected Classic. A Literary and Historical Study*. Cambridge.

Thalmann, W.G. (1996) 'Versions of slavery in the *Captivi* of Plautus', *Ramus* 25, 112-45.

Walters, J. (1997) 'Invading the Roman body: manliness and impenetrability in Roman thought', in J.P. Hallett and M.B. Skinner (eds) *Roman Sexualities*, 29-43. Princeton, NJ.

Watson, L. and P. (eds) (2003) *Martial: Select Epigrams*. Cambridge.

Williams, C.A. (1999) *Roman Homosexuality: Ideologies of Masculinity in Classical Antiquity*. New York.

Winkler, J.J. (1990) *The Constraints of Desire: The Anthropology of Sex and Gender in Ancient Greece*. New York.

Playing Ball with Zeus: Strategies in Reading Ancient Slavery through Dreams

Edith Hall

> In dreaming,
> The clouds methought would open and show riches
> Ready to drop upon me, that, when I waked,
> I cried to dream again.
>
> Caliban in *The Tempest* Act III sc. 2

> Who is so alienated from human experience that they have
> not on occasion noticed some truth in a dream?
>
> Tertullian, *De anima* 46

It is Sicily in the 130s BCE. The large numbers of newly imported slaves are being badly treated: branded, starved, inadequately clad, and savagely beaten. They discuss rebellion although they do not yet implement it. But a Syrian slave named Eunus encourages them by reporting oracles and messages from the gods about the future. He has received these both in dreams and waking visions. Heartened by Eunus' special foreknowledge, the slaves rise up, kill their masters, found a new kingdom and oppose the might of the Roman army.

The source for this remarkable series of events, the Sicilian historian Diodorus, thinks that Eunus invented his dreams in order to exert power over the other slaves (*Library* 34/35.2.4-5). Since Diodorus was writing a century after the events in question, we might question the reliability both of his sources and his moralistic judgement of the authenticity of Eunus' dreams. But there are two undeniable truths underlying Diodorus' narrative: he assumes that his readership will find it entirely plausible both that slaves can dream of self-emancipation, and that slaves can believe in the predictive power of dreams enough to start a mass revolt.

Recorded dreams of slaves in Carolina show that they often concerned the dreamers' ancestors, and it has been suggested that this was a 'coping mechanism' for dealing with trauma that presented in the form of a psychological residue from ancestor veneration in their indigenous African religions.[1] Studies of such dreams are part of the recent interest in the psychological damage caused by slavery.[2] Some psychoanalysts have argued that the psychological damage inflicted by the removal of kinship ties, identity, and sources of support, as well as by ongoing trauma, can be handed down over many generations within families descended from slaves.[3] Even for the distant descendants of slaves, 'confrontation of the internalised slaver is just as important as it is ... to confront the external slaver'.[4] A man originally born a slave, Samuel Ward, wrote as early as 1855 that although he had no conscious memories of slavery, it remained 'among my thoughts, my superstitions, my narrow views, my awkwardness ... Ah, the infernal impress is upon me, and I fear I shall transmit it to my child, and they to theirs! How deeply seated, how far reaching, a curse it is!'[5] In records of ancient dreams involving slavery we therefore potentially have a source of exceptional value for its psychological effects in that society. If there are any ancient records of specific dreams experienced by individuals enduring servitude, they might offer the type of insight into their subjective psychological lives which the essays in this volume have demonstrated are so hard to identify in other sources. Predictably, few of the dreams recorded in most ancient texts were created in the psyches of slaves, since the dreams of heroes, magistrates, king and generals, as well as their elite womenfolk, were of course far more likely to be recorded, or fictively imagined, by historiographers, poets and playwrights. But the evidence for slave dreamers is augmented substantially by one remarkable ancient source, the five-book *Interpretation of Dreams* (*Oneirocritica*) written in the second century CE during the age of the Antonines by Artemidorus of Daldis in Lydia (Asia Minor), in which the dreaming slave, and dreams about slaves, are staple features of the discourse.

In this chapter I take it as self-evident that in a field where revealing materials are so difficult to come by, we can't afford to dispense with any type of source just because it presents hermeneutic challenges. I argue that Artemidorus' dream book does something to which no other pagan source from the ancient Greek and Roman worlds can remotely lay claim: it treats the subjectivity of slaves with *exactly* the same seriousness as the subjectivity of the free. Some scholars have argued that in his desire to cater for the 'sophisticated elite' of the eastern provinces of the Roman empire Artemidorus actually differed from other, more socially downmarket oneirocritics.[6] But this is to obscure altogether the startling fact that when Artemidorus discusses the meaning of a dream symbol, he frequently and dispassionately tells the reader precisely what it signifies for a rich man, a poor man, and a slave, or for a free woman and a slave woman respectively.[7] Sometimes he even distinguishes between its meanings for different types of slave: 'White clothes are auspicious for those accustomed to wear them and Greek slaves ... In the case of Roman slaves they are good only for those who are well behaved. For other Roman slaves, they mean bad luck' (2.3). Slaves in some fictional, imaginative sources, especially drama, had of course sometimes been allowed a degree of psychological interiority by ancient playwrights,[8] although to a much lesser degree than high-status characters. But when it comes to the 'real', everyday slaves of antiquity, Artemidorus' acknowledgement that they had an inner psychological life, as susceptible to interpretation as anyone else's, is a wholly exceptional phenomenon.[9] Even within the genre of dream interpretation it is remarkable, as can be seen from a comparison with the Hippocratic *Regimens* 4, which is devoted to what different dream images signify for a person's health. The many dreams there analysed never refer to the status of the dreamer and take it for granted that he enjoys sufficient money and control over his own time to make elaborate provision for diet, exercise, relaxation and sleeping arrangements. Artemidorus, in contrast, offers us an exceptional opportunity to 'brush history against its grain' by disinterring not the experiences of the ruling class, but the experiences of those who, as Walter Benjamin categorised them in his justly famous *Theses on the Philosophy of History* (number 7), performed the 'nameless drudgery' that allowed history to take place at all.[10]

Since Foucault drew attention to Artemidorus in *The Care of the Self*, the third volume of his *The History of Sexuality*, first published in French in 1984, several scholars have stressed the significance of Artemidorus' substantial text for the study of ancient psychosexual ideologies,[11] and indeed for the study of ancient slavery.[12] Kudlien's study of some aspects of dream divination in relation to his central topic of interest, which he calls the *Sklaven-Mentalität*, carefully uses Artemidorus to build a picture of the emotional tensions that underlay ancient slave-owning households – the fear, distrust, paranoia, sexual strain, and suppressed as well as enacted violence.[13] Yet by apparently abandoning the hope that we can access the experience of slaves themselves, rather than the general psychological ambience of households, Kudlien is not being as respectful to ancient slaves as Artemidorus himself seems to have been. Bradley, on the other hand, who is laudably open to the possibilities even unconventional source materials offer to the historian of slavery, devotes an important section in *Slavery and Society at Rome* (1994) to Artemidorus. Yet he seems to me to have been so understandably struck by the 'uniformly negative' associations of slavery in Artemidorus' semiotic system, and by the slaves' own apparent acceptance of the ideology that construed them as 'in all senses a naturally inferior species', that he cannot be sensitive to the startling *contradictions* inherent in the dream-book's configuration of slaves' psychological humanity.[14]

Artemidorus's findings are largely organised according to categories of phenomena that appear in dreams – parts of the body, items of clothing, types of weather and so on. The book is designed to make it possible to consult it in order to look up the meaning of a particular dream, as well as to be read straight through by a trainee dream interpreter like Artemidorus' own son, to whom part of the work is addressed. Artemidorus claims to have been given his good grasp of the subject of dreams from 'experience' (*peira*, 1.1); he has 'not only taken special pains to produce every book on the interpretation of dreams', but has also 'consorted with the much-despised diviners of the market-place', professionals often dismissed as charlatans or buffoons. He has 'patiently listened to old dreams and their consequences in the cities of Greece and at religious festivals there, in Asia, in Italy, and in the larger islands' (see also the prologue to book 5). He offers the reader excellent evidence on his profession generally, warning, for example, that fraudulent dream interpreters make false claims, such as that the whereabouts of runaway slaves can be deduced from elaborate quotations of poetry in dreams (4.63).

Artemidorus thinks within a broadly Stoic tradition of dream analysis, and therefore does not accept that dreams may have an origin external to the soul, for example in the special homeland of dreams which features in some ancient literature (*Odyssey* 24.12, Hesiod, *Theog.* 212, Ovid, *Met.* 11.613-15).[15] The most important concepts underlying his work are, first, that dreams are predictive not retrospective (like most people in antiquity he saw dream analysis primarily as a form of divination). Secondly, his theories result from a combination of personal experience, transmitted experience (*historiê*), and the application of the basic principle that dream interpretation 'is nothing other than the juxtaposition of similarities' (2.25, i.e. analogy, *hê tou homoiou metabasis*); a slave, for example, might be represented by a mouse because he lives with the householder, and eats his scraps. Thirdly, it is crucial for the interpreter to know the dreamer's 'identity, occupation, birth, financial status, state of health, and age' (1.9). This is because Artemidorus has a sensibly relativist model of human happiness, and is well aware that the same symbol might mean different things in different minds, especially minds belonging to people of radically different status: 'Olive trees whose fruit has been gathered up mean good luck for all but slaves, for whom it signifies thrashings, since it is by blows that the fruit is taken down' (2.25). Another example is the apparently common dream experienced by pregnant women that they give birth to a snake. In a free woman this dream can often have a positive predictive force, but in a slave woman it can only mean that the child will become a runaway, 'because a snake does not follow a straight path' (4.67). Artemidorus is also clear that a single event which would benefit one person would injure another, for example, the death of a slave owner, which would be bad for him but could be good for his slaves (4.81). He is also aware that ethnicity will affect the sign system used in any one individual's dreams (1.8); the first example he gives here is that, among the Thracians, tattoos mean good birth to one tribe and slave status to another.

Lastly, Artemidorus believes that there are fundamentally two types of significant dream. Those which are allegorical substitute one image for another (e.g. a mouse or a foot for a slave). But some dreams, those that are *theorematic*, are in 'realist' rather than allegorical mode, since what you see is what you get. Sometimes in dreams a mouse is just a mouse. In the prologue to book 4, Artemidorus writes:

The masses do not have the same dreams (*enhupnia*) as men who know how to interpret dreams. The masses see exactly what it is they desire or dread in dreams, whereas experts dream symbolically ... A frightened man who knows about dreams and is a runaway slave will not dream of the actual man, but that he is e.g. escaping from a wild animal. And a dream that you find a runaway slave (4.1) can be *theorematic* (i.e. literally true), or *allegorical*.

That is, a runaway slave may or may not be an expert in oneirocriticism, but his degree of expertise will determine whether he dreams he is being pursued by his furious owner or by a wild animal. Equally, someone who dreams that he finds a runaway slave may be about to find a runaway slave, or to experience something which, in the language of dreams, the runaway slave symbolically replaces.

This introduction to Artemidorus, however brief, still shows that slaves play a prominent part in his discussion even of general principles, that he can conceive of a slave with expertise in dream interpretation, and that his work assumes that slave dreams merit analysis alongside those of higher-status individuals. This assumption is in itself significant, since in Homer only persons of royal status dream, a tradition that continued into Latin epic,[16] while in Greek tragedy, with one exception, only aristocrats' dreams merit discussion.[17] Moreover, the content of such dreams does not feature such under-privileged persons as slaves. This elite bias stands in marked contrast to the class-conscious dream experienced in Sumerian legend by Sharrumkin (later Sargon of Akkad) when he was lowly cup-bearer to the king of Kish, a dream in which his master was drowned in a river of blood. This foretold accurately that Sharrumkin would replace the king on the throne.[18] Yet the exclusively aristocratic focus of the Greek epic and tragic presentation of dreams is certainly not evident in Artemidorus' dream book, in which well over one hundred of the dreams are of direct relevance to the perception of slavery in the second century CE, at least to the perception of domestic slaves, living cheek-by-jowl with their master's families, who are the only slaves whose precise role is discussed. Although 'captives' feature generically in his writing, he does not refer specifically either to agricultural slaves on large estates, or to industrial slaves working in, for example, mines. It was presumably easier for domestic slaves living near urban centres or in attendance at festivals to be in a position, financial and physical, to consult a dream critic in the first place.

In his fifth and final book, Artemidorus offers short accounts of ninety-five dreams which he knows have actually come true. Three of them were dreamt by slaves. In these three cases we may therefore be in the most unusual position of being able to enjoy direct access to images produced in the minds of ancient slaves, as well as the manner in which their dreams were interpreted. The first reads as follows (5.23)

A man dreamt that one star fell out of the sky while another star ascended into the sky. The dreamer was someone's house-slave (*oiketês*). When his master died, he thought he was free and without any master. But it came to light that his former master had a son, and he was forced to become his slave. The fallen star therefore stood for the man who died, while the one that ascended into the sky signified the one who would control him and be his master.

These few unadorned sentences of Greek prose record a desperately sad little story of one slave's temporarily held belief that he had become a free man. His disappointment on discovering that he was legally compelled to serve another man, much younger than his previous owner, can only be imagined. For a rare, brief moment we may be in intimate touch with the inner psychological world of an actual ancient slave owned by men of two different generations of a family somewhere in the Roman empire. But his predictive dream of the simultaneous falling and rising stars also presents a stubborn knot of problems to the historian of slavery. It is with defining and addressing four of the headings under which these fundamental problems fall that this article is primarily concerned: (1) the status of dream as evidence, (2) the hermeneutic problems caused by our different, culturally determined ideas about dreams, (3) the generic features of the dream-book, and (4) the difficulty in disentangling the subject-object relationships in the process of dream interpretation.

The first issue is simply the ontological and epistemological status of any dream as 'historical' evidence.[19] Dreams do not have a material form, at least until they are written down by a dream interpreter like Artemidorus. Dreams, as records of the non-conscious or subconscious activity of the mind, do not relate to truth and experience of the world in the same way as, for example, memories, experienced when the subject is conscious and reprocessing images of empirically discerned reality and occurrences. In terms of affinities with types of literature, the content of a narrated memory has more in common with historiography and biography, since the 'rules' governing the physical laws of the remembered world will exclude the paranormal or supernatural, while the content of a narrated dream shares much with myth and fiction. Although the dreams recorded by Artemidorus are for the most part remarkably free of surreal or paranormal features, which he indeed (in marked contrast to modern psychoanalysts) regarded as of little value and not qualified for use in divination,[20] the third of the specific slaves' dreams that were proven to be prophetically correct in Artemidorus' fifth book certainly contains imagery that is reminiscent of the world of mythical prodigies (5.91):

> Someone dreamt that he had three penises. He happened to be a slave and he was freed and acquired three names instead of one, adding the two names of the man who had freed him.

Here, the subconscious mind of the slave in question is said to be working through the very real specifics of how his identity, on his release in his imperial city, would be created anew by formal means of nomenclature. But this question of identity politics is expressed in a somatic prodigy (see also 1.45, where Artemidorus says that this dream was very rare and to his knowledge had only ever been experienced on this one occasion). Indeed, Artemidorus acknowledges elsewhere in the book that the imaginative landscapes and events of dreams are often closely related to people's knowledge of myths, and even to their knowledge of specific works of literature: the deterioration in a relationship between a woman and her slave girl was presaged, for example, by her dream about the conflict between Hermione and her slave Andromache in Euripides' *Andromache* (4.59).[21]

Yet it could be argued that it is not in the content of the dream, in terms of imagery and its relationship with empirical reality, that its importance as historical evidence lies. Perhaps it is in the psychological *concern* that the dream addresses, or at least is interpreted as addressing. Both the 'stars' dream and the 'penises' dream are interpreted by Artemidorus and/or his source, who may or may not have been the slave dreamer himself, as directly addressing the slave's status as slave. One dream predicts that the slave will falsely believe himself to have been freed, while the other predicts that the slave will actually be freed, as the dreams Eunus reported to his Sicilian fellow-slaves presumably did. On this evidence, the subconscious mental activity of at least some slaves was (unsurprisingly) preoccupied with the fact of their servitude and their hopes for release from it. The third slave's dream in Artemidorus' fifth book is not, however, about liberation (5.85).

> A slave (*doulos*) dreamt that he received a cooked egg from his mistress, and that he threw away the shell while keeping the yolk. His mistress happened to be pregnant. She subsequently gave birth to a baby. While the mistress herself died, the child was brought up, on the orders of her husband, by the man who had experienced the dream. Thus the container was thrown away and of no value, while the contents provided a livelihood for the man who had experienced the dream.

The dream, like the 'stars' dream, does involve the question of a drastic change in a slave's status caused by his owner's death. But the change in status is not from slavery to freedom. The implication seems to be that the slave, although not emancipated, was not unhappy to be trusted sufficiently to be awarded means of subsistence for himself as well as the dead woman's baby, along with, perhaps, a degree of independence.

Curiously, the image of the hard-boiled egg occurs in another ancient dream about child-rearing and a trusted slave. No scholar has, to my knowledge, doubted the authenticity of the story, since it is recorded autobiographically by the canonical classical writer Aelius Aristides. On one his travels in pursuit of health, he dreamt that he saw his nurse (*trophos*) with his foster sister Callityche, and she brought him what he first thought were apples but later saw were boiled, peeled eggs (*Sacred*

Tales 1.45). He later says that says that no one was dearer to him than this aged nurse, and that her name was Philoumene (1.78). The owner-slave relationship is, by this free dreamer, couched in the language of affect and sensibility. But in Artemidorus, beneath the apparently happy outcome and the quaintly culinary image, there lurk the menace of economic reality and the dependence of many slaves, regardless of whether they were freed or not, on the continued economic wellbeing and goodwill of their owners or former owners. It is not clear from the information provided what would have happened to this slave dreamer on the demise of his mistress otherwise.

Indeed, the 'sources' from which Artemidorus provided these fleeting glimpses into the psychosocial consequences of slavery are always precarious. The treatise includes discussions both of what an object might signify in a hypothetical dream and records of actual dreams that have either been told to Artemidorus himself or that he has learned about from other sources. He uses several different linguistic formulae to introduce his account of a dream, for example *'edoxe tis'*, 'it seemed to someone' [sc. e.g. 'that he was flying'], without specifying from what source he, as dream interpreter, knows about this dream. An example here is one of the numerous dreams recorded in the treatise that presage enslavement in a free dreamer (4.65),

> Someone dreamt (*edoxe tis*) that he had sexual intercourse with a piece of iron just as you would with a woman. He was condemned to slavery and was enchained in iron, and had, as it were, intercourse with it.

The dream is unlike any other in the treatise, and the concreteness of the image combined with its distinctiveness, despite the vagueness of the introductory formula, may suggest that Artemidorus is drawing on an experience recorded by another dream interpreter even if not by Artemidorus himself. But in another common formula, 'I know someone to whom it seemed' [that he was, for example, flying], where the Greek formula is *oida tina hos edoxen*, it is perverse to deny that Artemidorus has personal knowledge of the dreamer, since that is indeed the normal meaning of *oida* with the accusative of a person.[22]

Two dreams which do fall into this category, fascinatingly, reveal two free men whom Artemidorus knows and who have clearly been concerned about the sexual status (and availability to women) of male slaves in their possession, or rather about the consequent erosion or eradication of the hierarchy dividing free from slave. In the first example, Artemidorus says (1.26),

> I know someone who dreamt his eyes fell out and dropped to his feet. Nevertheless, he did not go blind. Instead, he married his daughters to his slaves, and in this way the better was mixed with the worse.

Two body parts – eyes and feet – signify this free man's daughters and slaves respectively, and their unnatural proximity in the dream symbolises what, it is implied, is an inappropriate mating in reality. In the second instance, the man whom Artemidorus says he knows (3.51) 'was crippled in his right foot. He dreamt that his slave was crippled in the same foot and limped in the same fashion. He caught his slave with his own female lover (*erômenê*) ... The dream was telling him that his slave would err in the same way as he did.' The ever-present potential for slaves to become sexual partners, and discomfiture with the idea that they might have sexual feelings towards women with important roles in their owners' lives, are thus acknowledged in their owners' dreams. It is important to notice this alongside and as a partial corrective to the pervasive elision of masters with the 'masculine' penetrative agency in sexual relationships, and slaves with the 'feminine', penetrated passivity, an elision brilliantly documented by Winkler in a pathbreaking article.[23] Among the dreams described by Artemidorus, none can easily be seen as expressing such desire, from the *slave's* point of view, as the story of the slave Aesop's affair with his master's wife in the ancient biography of Aesop may well do, if that tradition did indeed emerge from an oral tradition of story-telling at the lower end of the social spectrum.[24] Yet the best evidence for a slave dream articulating such a desire comes in a Christian text written in the same century as Artemidorus' book, the *Shepherd* of Hermas. Hermas opens this visionary work by relating a dream he has experienced. In the dream, there appeared to him a woman named Rhode. Hermas tells us that long ago he had felt aroused by this woman when he was her slave at Rome, and he had helped her out of the Tiber after she had been bathing (*Vis.* 1.1.4-9).[25]

The few dreams recounted in some detail and over more than one sentence form another category where either direct experience or anecdote has played a role. In one outstanding dream of this kind (4.69), the dreamer's desire to 'talk back' to his master is interpreted as having been given only thinly veiled expression:

> A slave dreamt that he was playing ball with Zeus. He quarrelled with his master, and, since he took certain liberties in his speech, he antagonised the man. For Zeus signified the master. The ball-playing indicated both the exchange of words on an equal footing and the quarrel itself.

When combined with the provision of proper names, detail may indeed suggest that we should take the slave's dream seriously. In a section on dreams whose predictive force could not have been diagnosed at the time the dreams occurred but was later validated, for example, he offers 'Syros, the slave of Antipater', who 'dreamt that he had no soles on the undersides of his feet. He was burnt alive' (4.24). Here neither the nomenclature nor even the status of slave is strictly speaking relevant to the point at issue.

11. Playing Ball with Zeus

Since Artemidorus has just been talking about Alexander the Great, perhaps this Syros was the slave of Antipater of Sidon, and Artemidorus had found the dream in the historiographical tradition that had built up around Alexander. Dream accounts which concretely mention a particular place also suggest that a real dream (or at least one believed to be real) ultimately lies behind a record in Artemidorus' dream-book, especially since he insists that the dream interpreter needs expert local knowledge. Artemidorus, who was himself born in Ephesus, records that a prostitute of slave status was freed and became able to give up the sex trade after she dreamt that she had entered Artemis' temple there (4.4), 'for she would not have been allowed to enter the shrine if she had not given up prostitution'.

A further group of dreams whose authenticity we ought not be too quick to dismiss is constituted by those which Artemidorus says 'many people' have experienced. A striking case here is the dream of decapitation (1.35). Artemidorus discusses what it means if a slave dreams that he is beheaded. If he falls into the category of slave trusted by his master (a category which looms large in the dream book, as we shall see further below), then this dream foretells that he will lose that all-important trust, since condemned men are said to be 'headless' (*akephalos*) and nobody trusts such a person:

> But to all other slaves the dream signifies freedom. For the head is master of the body, and when it is cut off, it signifies a slave separated from the master who will be free. But many (*polloi*) who have had this dream have only been sold.

The terse final sentence here is suggestive. Many slaves have dreamt that their masters were decapitated (and some modern dream analysts would certainly infer that this was an articulation of the suppressed rage that slaves must have had to deal with on a permanent basis). But in Artemidorus' day the headless master offered the slave dreamer the hope that he would be freed. Unfortunately, he seems to have heard of 'many' cases in which these hopes were frustrated. Perhaps the psyches of slaves who knew something about dream interpretation could even subconsciously produce optimistic dreams, apparently predicting their liberation, far more often than such aspirations were ever likely to be fulfilled.

There is one more category of dream which does not deserve undue scepticism on the part of the modern scholar, and that is the type of dream common enough to have attracted, by Artemidorus' day, a large bibliography. In the course of his treatise Artemidorus mentions a substantial number of other dream critics, from the classical period to his own day; the interpretation of certain dreams had attracted a considerable controversy. The dream of a thunderbolt strike, Artemidorus tells us (2.9), has always been held to predict a change in status and fortune, since 'whatever has been struck by a thunderbolt loses its characteristic properties'. But then he says that later writers including 'Alexander of Myndus and Phoebus of Antioch' have discussed what such a dream might mean to a slave. Some maintained that it was a good sign, and would signify that they would no longer have masters and would no longer toil; this interpretation was based on the (fascinating) tradition that slaves struck by thunderbolts were allowed to wear the clothes of the manumitted and to be honoured like freedmen on the ground that Zeus had honoured them. But the debate has never been resolved, says Artemidorus, who proposes the following solution: the dream signifies freedom for slaves who are not trusted or honoured by their masters. But for those that are, it means that they will lose the trust, honour, and possessions that flow from that trust.

Three things of interest emerge here. First, the subtlety of these distinctions implies that slaves had become discontented when predictions of imminent liberation based on their dreams had failed to be fulfilled. Secondly, we see Artemidorus falling back, as often, on his favourite distinction between the distrusted slave and his trusted counterpart (who may of course have been relatively well treated and less desperate to be freed). And thirdly, we have lost a substantial ancient literature on slaves and society in the form of earlier dream-books, a literature of which Artemidorus' work must only represent the tip of a very interesting iceberg.

Artemidorus' interest in dreams, and the skill in interpreting them on which he prided himself, have produced extreme reactions in some recent scholars. These seem to be related to each scholar's own preparedness to take the practice of psychological analysis of any kind at all seriously. Harris dismisses him 'a man of monumental gullibility',[26] an assessment forged in opposition to Miller's admiration for his conscientiousness and 'associative genius'.[27] Bowersock thinks that he is a 'snob', while Walde regards him as 'very erudite'.[28] But fighting about Artemidorus' intellect and social pretensions means forgetting entirely the dreamers about whom he writes, which is simply to compound the neglect suffered by slaves at the hands of history. Given that we have no particular reason to doubt the authenticity at least of the dreams which have been discussed so far, our time is better spent in addressing the second acute problem that ancient slave dreams, in common with all ancient dreams, present to the modern scholar. This problem is actually a magnified version of the fundamental methodological challenge besetting the practice of all ancient history – can we discuss a past culture in contemporary conceptual language at all? In one sense, it is easier to discuss ancient practices which no longer exist today (for example, divination from the livers of sacrificial animals) precisely because there are no intrusive contemporary prejudices about what mottled splodges mean on a liver to obscure our understanding of what mottled splodges might have meant to someone in the second century CE. We are inclined to try to analyse ancient dreams according to our own beliefs about dream symbolism, since very great importance has been attached to dreams over the last century or so by psychoanalysts and those who popularise their work. But Sigmund Freud did not write an *Interpretation of Liver Markings* that can stand between us and ancient hepatoscopy.

For Freud's *Interpretation of Dreams* (1900) and its epigones themselves bequeath two huge and inter-related problems to the aspiring user of Artemidorus as a document of social history. The first is the misconception that because Freud thought that dreams expressed unconscious desires, or rather discharged primitive impulses (many of them erotic) in veiled form, an ancient dream-book will tell us a good deal about the primitive impulses revealed in ancient psyches.[29] The characterisation in Plato's *Republic* of the 'animal' part of the soul getting the better of our self-control and reason while we are asleep, and having licentious flings which include incest and murder, is likely to encourage such an expectation (9.571b-c). On one level this is true, since a substantial proportion of the dreams described by Artemidorus, especially but not exclusively in the section on sex in his first book (1.78-82), do indeed involve erotic activity. Artemidorus envisages the possibility of men dreaming about sexual intercourse with wives, prostitutes, siblings, parents, sons, daughters, older men, younger men, gods, goddesses, corpses and animals as well as both male and female slaves. Almost every sexual position is discussed, along with masturbation and oral sex. But the *meaning* of all these erotic dreams, like the meaning of the dreams in all the other categories, is hardly ever about sexual activity: it is about changes in *power* relative to other individuals, or in status, health, wealth, domicile, and about the outcome of lawsuits or other business negotiations. Even a dream about a penis can indicate 'poverty, slavery, and bonds, because it is also called "the obligatory thing" (*anagkaion*) and is a symbol of necessity (*anagkê*)', the cosmic principle which had always been associated with slavery in the Greek mind.

People *may* have had a good deal of erotic dreams in antiquity, but they did not, apparently, think that these dreams had much to do with eros. Typically, to dream of having sexual intercourse with one's own slave, male or female, signifies that the dreamer will take pleasure in his possessions (*ktêmata*), because slaves are one kind of possession. If the slave is the figure in the dream who sexually penetrates his owner/the dreamer, then this will mean a shift in the balance of power in which the slave comes to look down on the master (1.78). The ancients had sexual dreams, which *we* may be tempted to interpret as being about intimate libidinal urges, but *the ancients* interpreted them as referring to relative status, power and wealth in a much more widely defined and often public sphere. The Presocratic Heraclitus may famously have said, 'The waking have one world in common, whereas each sleeper turns away into a private world of his own' (89 B 15 DK), but Artemidorus interprets dreams emphatically in terms of the power structures in the world experienced in common by people when awake.

The temptation to interpret ancient dreams as evidence of the ancient subconscious rather than evidence of the ancient preoccupation with social status, a preoccupation of which the dreamers were presumably perfectly conscious in their *waking* lives, points to the second hazard presented by the Freudian legacy. We may even be unaware of the interference in our thinking about ancient dreams caused by Freud's writings, since despite 'sporadic attempts to reinstate a nineteenth-century scientific disdain of dreams, Freud's influence is now so pervasive as to be almost invisible'.[30] We need to be very careful not to read ancient dreams in the hopes of acting as a psychoanalyst who can reveal what the ancient subconscious mind indicated, as some Freud-influenced scholars have (with very little success) been tempted to do.[31] This is more difficult than it sounds, since so many of the ancient dreams do seem to contain the kind of imagery in which Freudian analysts have traditionally been interested, for example the dreams about eggs and penises, as well as the several dreams in Artemidorus about flying, birth, death, houses, significant numerals, and verbal puns. We know, admittedly, that Freud had studied Artemidorus, along with nineteenth-century classical scholarship on the ancient dream tradition,[32] and therefore may therefore have been prompted by contact with the ancient source to 'look for' eggs, penises, flying and puns in his clients' dreams. But the appearance of such content in Artemidorus makes it quite impossible to evade the thorny question of the extent to which, if at all, the experience and content of dreams are universal, transcending cultural and historical differences.

Our very word *dream* – Freud's titular *Traum* – does not mean the same as Artemidorus' titular *oneiros* or indeed the other terms, such as *onar*, *hupar* and *opsis*, which he uses from time to time.[33] By *oneiros* Artemidorus seems to mean a particular subcategory of significant dream, with predictive force, which he in turn distinguishes from the *enhupnion*. This is what he holds to be an insignificant dream about the dreamer's immediate (rather than future) experiences, especially bodily ones to do with food, illness, and very intimate relationships (1.1). There are also passages in the treatise where he seems to acknowledge little difference between dreams experienced while asleep and visions experienced when awake. But even more significant than the lexical issue is the question of the universality or otherwise of the *content* of dreams. We dream about receiving messages on the telephone, which had not been invented in Artemidorus' day, while his clients dreamt about being visited by Apollo. Dreamscapes are clearly susceptible to absorbing images from the contingent, historically specific culture of the dreamer: the question, therefore, is whether *any* of the symbols in dreams, let alone their meanings, remain unchanged across time and culture. When it comes to a peculiar institution such as slavery, of which most of us will thankfully today have no direct personal experience, but which might be expected to have profound psychological implications, what are we to make of its relation to dreams reported from many centuries ago? It is vital to keep an open mind about the type of content and interpretation Artemidorus offers, even when the dreams seem bizarre or disproportionately focussed on non-surreal elements which can seem 'undreamlike' to us.

Even among modern psychoanalysts, there is very little agreement about the correct way to interpret dreams, or even about their actual significance.[34] Although some analysts believe that dreams can reveal impulses dating back to the analysand's infancy, and are thus in a sense retrospective, there are others who believe that dreams process the events merely of the previous day, or address immediate anxieties, or even that under some circumstances they can be predictive insofar as the preconscious mind can pick up signals invisible to – or evaded – by the conscious mind: Budd cites a patient who dreamt of a multitude of red soldiers fighting the night before being diagnosed as suffering from leukaemia.[35] When it comes to pre-Freudian traditions of dream interpretation in civilisations other than the Greek and Roman worlds, we also, inevitably, find major differences.

Yet in the Chinese dream tradition, for example, we find a tendency, similar to that of Artemidorus, to interpret the meaning of dreams as completely dependent on the social status of the dreamer: in a text from the same century as Artemidorus, which includes a long discussion of dreams compiled during the Eastern Han Dynasty, the author Wang Fu stressed that the content of dreams was heavily influenced by the dreamer's social status and role.[36] A statement almost identical to Artemidorus' programmatic comment on status in 1.9 (see above, p. 207) also appears in Chen Shiyan's treatise on dream interpretation *Mengzhan yizhi*, completed in around 1562, which includes nearly seven hundred dreams collected over a period of many centuries.[37] Moreover, the dreams which talk about slavery reflect very similar concerns as those from the Antonine world. The slave-owner Mr Yin of Zhou ran a large estate:

> Among his workers was someone who would dream at night of being the ruler of a state whose happiness was beyond compare. Yet Mr Yin would dream at night that he had become a slave who was ordered to every kind of task while suffering no end of beatings.[38]

In the first century CE, the tyrannical wife of a self-proclaimed provincial governor named Peng Chong was plagued by nightmares adumbrating the couple's brutal assassination by three of their household slaves.[39] It seems that in ancient China as well as the ancient Mediterranean, slaves dreamed of freedom and high status, slave-owners expressed their own terror of enslavement in dreams, and drastic falls from high estate were heralded by dreams involving slaves. Perhaps reading ancient dreambooks in search of information about slavery is better served by comparative evidence from other slave-holding societies than the psychoanalytical couches of the post-Freudian Western world.[40]

The third serious set of problems facing the historian using Artemidorus is generic. These problems are created by the assumptions and conceptual framework underlying his genre. Even these formal, literary issues do not allow us to stray far from the question of social class, however. It is essential to address the fundamental issue of the readership to which Artemidorus must have supposed the genre of dream-book would appeal, and his wider constituency both in terms of the people whose previous dream experiences have ended up in his book, and the people whose dreams may be subsequently be interpreted, directly or indirectly, with its help. Here the evidence is certainly confusing, but Artemidorus' systematic inclusion of what certain types of dream might mean for slaves, people whose ubiquity in the ancient world is routinely ignored in so many other types of ancient writing, simply can't be dismissed. It seems quite certain to me, from the evidence in Artemidorus alone, that ancient slaves wanted to have their dreams interpreted, and that the scores of references to them in the dream book is a reflection of this historical reality. Perhaps the aspirational attitude of slaves which the book implies, as well as their personal and financial freedom actually to consult an oneirocritic, is related to the specific historical times. Artemidorus travelled throughout large areas of the Roman empire during a period of relative peace and prosperity, when legislation had curtailed some of the very worst atrocities that could be committed against slaves. Hadrian had put a stop to penal servitude for both slaves and freedmen, prohibited the sale of both male and female slaves to the gladiatorial schools, and had decreed that masters no longer had the right to punish their slaves with death.[41]

Alternatively, we could see slaves' interest in dreams as a more long-standing historical phenomenon. Although, as we have noticed, certain genres such as epic and tragedy associate dreams with upper-class people, in other, less elevated genres, the class associations of an interest in dreams are very different. Aristophanes' *Wasps* notoriously opens with two slaves, Sosias and Xanthias, decoding what is signified by the animals and birds they have seen in their dreams in ways that are startling (given the speakers' non-citizen status) for the acuity of their insights into Assembly politics. One of the great strengths of Harris' recent book on dreams in antiquity is that he demonstrates the diversity of ancient opinions on the value (or insignificance) of dreams and the intellectual respectability (or dubiousness) of interest in their contents. There were many highly educated writers, for example Polybius, who considered dreams to be entirely worthless, and people who concerned themselves with dreams to be either womanish or extremely vulgar.[42] The Epicurean Lucretius chides the superstitious for setting any store by the dreams with which soothsayers terrorise them (*De rerum natura* 1.102-6). As we saw at the opening of this chapter, Diodorus regarded the dreams with which

Eunus aroused his fellow slaves to revolt as the cynical inventions of a man manipulating the passions of some of the most wretched and least educated people imaginable. This seems to present the political use of dreams in a similar light as the passage in Aristophanes' *Knights* where the rival demagogues compete in trying to win the support of the demos through dream prophecies (1090-5).[43] On the other hand, wisdom figures of great authority sometimes treat dreams with respect, from the moment when Socrates tells Crito that a beautiful woman announced to him in a solemn dream that he would die (*Crito* 44a-b), apparently the first ancient Greek epiphany dream afforded to an individual of less than royal status.[44] Aristotle, who is clear that dreams are not created by the intellectual or rational or even the cognitive parts of the soul (*On Dreams* 1.459a 8-11), says without any apparent derision that prescient and vivid dreams are often experienced by very 'common or garden' (*euteleis*) sorts of men because they are communicative and emotional and therefore susceptible to stimuli (*On Prophecy in Sleep* 2.463b15-18).

Taking dreams seriously, then, was perhaps a phenomenon that had always had a tendency to cross class boundaries. At one end of the spectrum there may always have been many high-minded Platonists like Synesius of Cyrene, in whose *Concerning Dreams* it is argued dreams can put one in touch with the eternal world of ideas, while at the other perhaps there is truth in the implied customer-base in Artemidorus' text – drawn from across the socially diverse, and highly aspirant, populations inhabiting all kinds of different households in busy imperial cities. We saw earlier that Artemidorus entertained seriously the concept of a runaway slave who was knowledgeable about dreams (4.1, see above, p. 208), and this accords with the assumption in several other ancient sources, for example Plautus' comedies, that anyone can learn to interpret dreams,[45] and in which dreamers include a pimp, a prostitute, and a *senex comicus*.[46] A dream of a Roman peasant about a ritual involving a slave was part of the aetiological tradition surrounding the Ludi Votivi Maximi (Cicero, *On Divination* I.xxvi.55-6).[47] The fragmentary eighth *Mimiamb* of Herodas seems to involve a woman waking up her female slaves and telling one of them her dream. Perhaps the dream experienced by the lowly slave Aesop at the beginning of his ancient *Life*, in which the goddess Isis appears with the Muses to him in a parodic refashioning of the epiphanies traditionally experienced by great canonical authors, crystallises the class tensions underpinning the phenomenon of ancient dream interpretation.[48] This would apply especially if this story of social rise of the clever slave, a poor man's folk hero, were a product, as many scholars believe, of an oral tradition that had developed among the very lowest echelons of society (see above, p. 212). And it is just possible that some people in antiquity associated excellence at dream interpretation with the exoticised 'barbarian wisdom' that also associated some kinds of magician and herbalist with the foreign lands that happened to produce many slaves (see Cicero,

On Divination I.xxiii.46-7). In nineteenth-century North America dream books were sometimes deliberately marketed as having particular mystical authority because written 'antebellum' by women 'of color'.[49]

A further genre-based hazard affecting the way we read Artemidorus is that his approach is conditioned by the widespread second-century penchant for writings of an encyclopaedic nature, and he is keen to offer a comprehensive account of the types of image that appear in what he regards as significant dreams.[50] In order to impose an intelligible order on his subject-matter, and presumably one which would enable a reader to locate a discussion of a particular dream-image quickly and easily, Artemidorus uses a taxonomy which arranges the images a dreamer might experience into certain empirical categories – types of animal or bird, for example, or epiphanies of particular gods. This means that we are given a grid of the world as seen by Artemidorus' contemporaries. Within this grid, large areas of experience are organised into relations with each other in ways that were felt to be equivalent to a sliding scale of social statuses from king down to poor man, prisoner and slave. In dreams where the symbolism pertains to the body, for example, the head indicates a father, the foot indicates a slave, the right hand indicates a father, son, male friend, or brother; the left hand a mother, mistress, daughter, or sister; the penis indicates parents, wife or children, and the shin indicates a wife or mistress (1.2).

In the animal world, masters are unsurprisingly represented by traditionally regal creatures such as lions and eagles, while donkeys and timorous little birds signify slaves. Such symbols are, in isolation from other symbols, often said to mean the same to free people and slaves, underlining that the fundamental semiotics of dreams transcend class boundaries. For Artemidorus (2.68), flying with wings is auspicious for all men alike. 'The dream signifies freedom for slaves, since all birds fly without a master and have no one above them ... For slaves, dreaming that one is flying up into the heavens always signifies that they will pass into more distinguished homes, and frequently even into the court of a king.' Similarly, a dream of being harnessed to a cart like a four-footed animal, regardless of the dreamer's current status, foretells slavery, drudgery, and illness (3.18).

Yet there is a limit to slave's comparability with free people, expressed in another, altogether contradictory assumption that the inner world of slaves was so extremely distorted by their 'social death' that some dream symbols signify the *exact opposite* in the psyche of a slave and a free person. Thus (2.54) for a rich man dreaming of fighting wild beasts is bad, but for slaves it signifies freedom, provided that they are killed by the beasts, thus annihilating their incomplete personhood under slavery. It is usually bad to dream that you are carried, but it *is* auspicious for a house slave to dream he is being carried by his master (2.56). Dreaming of a shipwreck portends harm for all but those who are being forcibly detained or slaves, to whom it indicates that they will be released from those who detain them (2.23). The yoke is a good sign for all but slaves, for whom it means an obstacle to their freedom (2.24). The life of a slave is so very distorted, so out of kilter with 'normal' human experience as rationally intuited, that images which in dreams almost universally have negative meanings sometimes become positive for slaves, and *vice versa*. This is most conspicuous of all in dreams involving sex roles, especially the dream of a man that he changes into a woman (1.50). For a rich man or a statesman this dream augurs ill, because women stay at home and it will signify the end of his public life. But since slaves have no access to public life anyway, it can actually mean 'a less painful servitude, since women's labours are less arduous'.[51]

These fundamentally contradictory messages mirror the contradictions inherent in the status of slave, understood as a human with a subjective viewpoint on relationships and with similar aspirations to social ascent as a free person, but whose personhood is also compromised in fundamental ways. Yet, taken as a whole, the most noticeable thing about the slaves' dreams in Artemidorus is the degree to which their interpretations are *circumscribed*. If we are to believe Artemidorus' analyses, the dream life of slaves was under unremitting pressure from their waking status. One of the most unpleasant features of the dream-book is the number of different symbols that predict to a slave dreamer that he or she will suffer violence from his master: this applies to beef, because both straps and whips are made of oxhide (1.70); to dancing, because a beating sets a slave's body in motion (1.76); to being aroused to an erection by one's master, because a flogging 'extends' the body (1.78); to harvested olive trees 'since it is by blows that the fruit is taken down' (2.25), and to hemp because 'it is cut down and twisted' (3.59), as well as to mountains, glens, valleys, chasms, and woods (2.28 etc.).

On a more optimistic note, there are no fewer than twenty-six slave dreams, besides the 'three penises' dream discussed above, portending freedom. Freedom could also be suggested by a dream in which a slave serves as a soldier (1.5), is awarded the free status of ephebe (1.54), that he has one or no ears (1.24), since this signifies release from the demands of authority, or no teeth (1.31), since the teeth represent both the master who provides the nourishment to his slave and, paradoxically, the nourishment that a slave's labour can provide to a master. Other emancipation dreams include those in which the dreamer is turned into brass (1.50), sees a statue of himself erected in the market-place (1.50), blows on a sacred trumpet, acts as a herald (1.56), rides through the city on horseback, runs the sprint in the athletics competition (1.58), is crowned as victor in the pancration (1.62), garlanded with date-palm or olive (only permitted to free men, 1.77), enjoys fellatio from a rich free woman (1.79), or practises fellatio on himself (1.80). Wearing a purple robe (2.3) means good luck for both slaves and for rich men. For slaves, it signifies freedom, since slaves are not permitted to wear it.

Freedom was also predicted for a slave who dreamt that he was dead, or being carried out for burial, provided that he was not a slave entrusted with the care of the house (2.49). Yet for a slave who is trusted with supervision of the house, the dream is not so propitious, for it signifies loss of the trusteeship. One of the interesting things about the accounts of dreams experienced by slaves is, in fact, the degree to which the subconscious mind was felt to carry over intra-household distinctions between higher and lower status slaves. Everyone who has ever had any dealings with captivity of any kind will understand the importance that the pecking order assumes where access to ordinary freedoms and pleasures is curtailed. The most disturbing example is 2.15, in which Artemidorus reports that he knows of a household slave who dreamt that he struck some frogs with his fist. The man became overseer of his master's house and took charge of the other slaves in the house. For the pond represented the house; the frogs, the other slaves; the punch, his command over them. The complexity of the pecking order in the average household is best illustrated by the murder dreams in 4.64. A slave who dreamt that that he was murdered by his master was in fact freed by him. But another man, who dreamt that he was murdered by a fellow slave, was not freed, because the slave, unlike a master, did not have the power to set him free. Chillingly, Artemidorus adds that these two fellow slaves grew to hate each other, for 'murderers are not on friendly terms with their victims.'

Even within the complex generic structure and formal taxonomy of Artemidorus' dream-book, therefore, it is possible to detect subtle contradictions in the logic, narrow circumscription of aspiration, and telling gradations of domestic hierarchy that offer us a fuller and more detailed picture of the ancient slave's psychosocial horizons than any other ancient document. The last problem on which I would like to focus is, however, is not a matter of the formal expectations of the dream-book at a type of writing, but would apply equally to authors in most other genres. This is the question of the degree to which we are entitled to believe that we are achieving access, in relation to a book written by a free man, to the subjectivity of the people about whom he writes at all. A sceptic would certainly stress that the dream interpreter is 'already working with a mediated and rationalized construct', the form and content of which depend 'on the competence and credibility of the narrator'.[52] On the other hand, subject/object relations in texts dealing with voices and subjectivities erased from the literary and historical record have in recent years become extremely controversial under the influence of feminist and postcolonial theorisation of literary narrative.[53] Artemidorus, as we have seen, offers interpretations of the symbolism in slaves' dreams which overwhelmingly relate to the possibility of emancipation or being sold, the likelihood that they will suffer physical punishment, and the state of their relationships with their owners. It might be argued that far from being in contact with slaves' subjectivity, we are in contact with a man who, since he enjoyed the privileges of liberty, *assumed* that these issues are the only things slaves ever think about.

Such an argument would be the geneaological descendant of the conventional, Hegelian opposition of subject and object, which virtually defined consciousness as the incisive, masterful, knowing subject's experience of the passive, known object. It would certainly apply to the longsuffering, passive, and often dying slaves and slave dreamers that emanated from the psyches of some eighteenth- and nineteenth-century Abolitionists. A famous example is the old slave who is hanged because he is too old to labour, while a white woman continues impassively drinking tea, in the 1770 dream experienced by the New Jersey Quaker and abolitionist John Woolman and recorded in his diary.[54] A similar masterful authorial subject imagining an unfortunate slave object narrates Longfellow's 1852 poem 'The slave's dream' (1842), even though the 'object' is the dreamer whose 'subjective' memories of his 'native land' are described in the stanzas introduced by these lines:

> Beside the ungathered rice he lay,
>   His sickle in his hand;
> His breast was bare, his matted hair
>   Was buried in the sand.
> Again, in the mist and shadow of sleep,
>   He saw his native land.[55]

Another example is the dream experienced by the dying Soudi, an African boy abducted by slavers in a story by the Victorian reformer Helen Pease.[56] But in texts from the same era dealing with 'real' slaves, the contribution of the slave 'objects' in texts by free 'subjects' has recently been radically reassessed, under the influence, primarily, of African American scholars. Of particular significance here is Robert Burns Stepto's study of black narrative, *From Behind the Veil* (1979). By analysing the biographical accounts of nineteenth-century slaves, and the ways in which these narratives were indeed paternalistically framed, doctored and generally interfered with by white emancipationist writers and promoters, Stepto develops a critique of the whole notion of narrative control, a critique in which objects become subjects and subjects interact with other subjects.[57]

With this in mind, we might more fruitfully read the apparently restricted psychological scope of Artemidorus' slave dreamers as both illuminating the brutal circumscription of their subjectively experienced lives, and demonstrating the plausible assumption that the slaves who took their dreams to interpreters articulated their own agency in pressing for answers which would relate to precisely these issues. This seems to me to be supported particularly by the extraordinary presence in the dreambook of two dreams that would actually encourage a slave who was thinking about running away, or indeed had already done so: non-migratory birds, such as the swallow and the house martin, signify that runaway slaves who were originally freeborn will return to their native land (4.56),[58] while a cuttlefish symbolises benefits for runaways because of the thick inky fluid that it often employs to make its escape (2.14).

What Artemidorus had to say about the dreamlife of slaves, which according to him focused (like everyone else's) on improvements in status and the avoidance of suffering, is – if nothing else – a demonstration of his unusual premise that all humans are psychologically the same, regardless of their current position on the social scale. This assumption must have been reinforced by his experience of real people, slave and free, in the real world. But Artemidorus' text is, of course, like all pagan Greco-Roman writing, informed by the fundamental intellectual contradictions which could never be resolved for as long as it was necessary to justify some individuals being possessed and oppressed by others. He is – although actually quite infrequently – happy to reflect back on some free dreamers the extreme prejudices about the intellectual capacities of slaves that the dreamers' own self-interest required, for example the advice that pelicans signify that a runaway slave will be found near a river or pond, since pelicans 'represent senseless men who act without reason or reflection' (2.20). In an even more striking example of recycled prejudice, he reproduces the widely held dualistic assumption that slaves analogically represent crude matter to the master's spirit, as beings of the physical world in relation to the transcendent, cerebral world of ideas represented by the slave-owning class. Artemidorus claims that one of the things that slaves can mean in a dream is the body of their owners (*to sôma tôn despotôn*, 4.30):

> The same man who saw his slave in a high fever became ill himself, as might be expected. For the relationship of the slave to the man who had this dream is analogous to the relationship of the body to the soul (*to sôma pros tên psuchên*).

But this abstract principle, however callous and commonplace,[59] is everywhere in Artemidorus simultaneously undermined to the point of effective cancellation by his actual *practice* of taking slave dreams seriously. The egalitarian form of many passages in the ancient dream book implicitly dismantles its hierarchical content. The soul – or psyche – of the ancient slave was really there all the time.

Notes

1. Fairley (2003).
2. See e.g. Black (1997) and Akbar (1984).
3. Barbara Fletchman Smith, a psychoanalyst who was worked with Caribbean people and their descendants in the UK, is convinced that slavery in the Caribbean and American society caused 'trauma on a massive scale' that 'has been handed

down through the generations, is still being handed down, and is hard to express and conceptualise' (see Fletchman Smith (2000) 8). Among the legacies of slavery she includes fear. Fear is distinct from anxiety 'because it is likely to relate to a real rather than a phantasised past' (p. 9).

4. Fletchman Smith (2000) 9.

5. Ward (1970 [1855]) xiv.

6. Grottanelli (1999) 147; see also Bowersock (1994) 79-87.

7. On masculine and feminine roles and conceptual categories in Artemidorus see especially MacAlister (1992).

8. See Hall (2010) 11-26, 148-55.

9. Pack (1955) 287-9 showed considerable insight in commenting, however briefly, on the ethical 'neutrality' of Artemidorus, and his tacit assumption that prostitutes, fugitives and thieves have as good a right as anyone to learn what the future may hold for them.

10. See further Hall (2009) 32-5.

11. Winkler (1990) ch.1.

12. On the utility of Artemidorus for the social historian of slavery, see especially Kudlien (1991) 68-81 and Bradley (1994). An important article by del Corno published in a prominent reference work in 1978 certainly helped to draw attention to ancient dream interpretation, even if his description of Artemidorus' work as offering 'a mirror of reality' needs considerable modification in the light of the methodological problems I am trying to explore here.

13. See specially Kudlien (1991) 72-7, 151.

14. Bradley (1994) 142-4.

15. Husser (1996) 23; Harris (2009) 50-1.

16. Husser (1996) 82; Bouquet (2001).

17. The exception is the charioteer's dream in the Euripidean *Rhesus*, on which see Kessels (1973) 32-3. In Homer the dream is experienced by King Rhesus (*Iliad* 10.494-7).

18. See Husser (1996) 38. The *Legend of Sharrumkin* is published with commentary in Cooper and Heimpel (1983).

19. Harris (2009) 93.

20. Artemidorus stresses this point in 1.1-2, where he also implies that the topic had been discussed at length by his professional predecessors.

21. See further Hall (2006) 16-17.

22. See LSJ under **eidô* B1.

23. Winkler (1990) ch. 1; see also MacAlister (1992).

24. Translation in Daly (1961) 67.

25. See the translation of Joseph Marique in Glimm, Marique and Walsh (1947) 233-4. See further Miller (1994) 131-47, Harris (2009) 69, and the acid comments of Brown (1988) 70 on Rhode's casual insensitivity towards her slave's sexual feelings.

26. Harris (2009) 114.

27. Miller (1994) 91.

28. Bowersock (1994) 81; Walde (1999) 124.

29. The excellent study of Price (1986) illuminates the depth and nature of the impact of Freud on classical scholars' discussion of dreams during the twentieth century.

30. Ferguson (1996) 3.

31. See e.g. the rather reductive interpretations in Kurth (1950).

32. Above all Büchsenschütz (1868). Artemidorus was very familiar in German-

speaking intellectual circles, having been printed in a German edition by Philipp Melanchthon, no less, as early as 1597. See Walde (1999) 126-7.

33. Kessels (1973) 121-78.

34. Hamilton (1996); Budd (1999).

35. Budd (1999).

36. Strassberg (2008) 12.

37. Strassberg (2008) 84: 'Emperors and kings have dreams proper to them, sages and worthies have dreams proper to them, and workers and servants have dreams proper to them. Whether these indicate failure or success, poverty or abundance, every dream derives from the nature of the particular person.'

38. Strassberg (2008) 87 n. 14.

39. Strassberg (2008) 247-8 n. 15.

40. A promising experiment in bringing transhistorical and transcultural discussions of dreams together is constituted by the collection edited by Shulman and Stroumsa (1999).

41. *Digest* 29.5.1, 48.8.4.2, 48.18.1.

42. Compare the eighteenth- and nineteenth-century suspicion of dream-books as the province of irrational and under-educated women and plebeians, documented in Perkins (1999).

43. Harris (2009) 150.

44. Harris (2009) 25.

45. Traill (2004); Harris (2009) 166.

46. Harris (2009) 178-9.

47. See Cancik (1999) 169.

48. Translation in Daly (1961) 7-8.

49. See Gardner (2005).

50. Miller (1994) 77.

51. See MacAlister (1992) 147.

52. Walde (1999) 131.

53. Hall (2007).

54. Woolman (1971) 161.

55. First published in Longfellow (1842).

56. Pease (1893) 34.

57. See further Hall (2007).

58. With the apparent nostalgia for the slave's native land expressed in this dream interpretation cf. the graffito inscription found in an excavated house on Delos, first published by Couve (1895) 474, in which a slave recalls the figs and water of his homeland, Antioch on the Maeander.

59. It is taken as a conceptual starting-point by Glancy (2003) 9-10 in the fine first chapter 'Bodies and Souls' of her study of slavery in early Christianity.

References

Akbar, N. (1984) *Chains and Images of Psychological Slavery.* Jersey City, NJ.

Black, D. (1997) *Dismantling Black Manhood: An Historical and Literary Analysis of the Legacy of Slavery.* New York & London.

Bouquet, J. (2001) *Le Songe dans l'épopée latine d'Ennius à Claudien.* Brussels.

Bowersock, G.W. (1994) *Fiction as History: Nero to Julian.* Berkeley, Los Angeles & London.

Bradley, K. (1994) *Slavery and Society at Rome.* Cambridge.

11. Playing Ball with Zeus

Brown, P. (1988) The *Body and Society: Men, Women, and Sexual Renunciation in Early Christianity*. New York.

Büchsenschütz, B. (1868) *Traum und Traumdeutung im Alterthume*. Berlin.

Budd, S. (1999) 'The shark behind the sofa: the psychoanalytic theory of dreams', *History Workshop Journal* 48, available online at http://www.psychoanalysis.org.uk/budd.htm.

Cancik, H. (1999) '*Idolum* and *imago*: Roman dreams and dream theories', in Shulman and Stroumsa (eds) 169-88.

Cooper, J.S. and Heimpel, W. (1983) 'The Sumerian Sargon legend', *Journal of the American Oriental Society* 103, 67-82.

Couve, L. (1895) 'Fouilles de Délos', *Bulletin de correspondance hellénique* 19, 460-516.

Daly, Ll.W. (1961) *Aesop without Morals: The Famous Fables, and a Life of Aesop, Newly Translated and Edited*. New York & London.

del Corno, D. (1978) 'I sogni e la loro interpretazione nell'età dell'Impero', *Aufstieg und Niedergang der Römischen Welt* II, 16.2, 1610.

Fairley, N.J. (2003) 'Dreaming Ancestors in Eastern Carolina', *Journal of Black Studies* 33, 545-61.

Ferguson, H. (1996) *The Lure of Dreams: Sigmund Freud and the Construction of Modernity*. London & New York.

Fletchman Smith, B. (2000) *Mental Slavery: Psychoanalytical Studies of Caribbean People*. London.

Gardner, E. (2005) ' "The Complete Fortune Teller and Dream Book": an antebellum text by Chloe Russel, a woman of colour" ', *New England Quarterly* 78, 259-88.

Geer, R.M. (1927) 'On the theories of dream interpretation in Artemidorus', *Classical Journal* 22, 663-70.

Glancy, J.A. (2003) *Slavery in Early Christianity*. Oxford.

Glimm, F.X., Marique, J.M.-F. and Walsh, G.G. (1947) *The Apostolic Fathers* [= *Fathers of the Church*, vol. 1]. New York.

Grottanelli, C. (1999) 'On the mantic meaning of incestuous dreams', in Shulman and Stroumsa (eds), 143-68.

Hall, E. (2006) *The Theatrical Cast of Athens*. Oxford.

—— (2007) 'Subjects, selves, and survivors', *Helios* 34, 125-59.

—— (2009) 'Greek tragedy and the politics of subjectivity in recent fiction', *Classical Reception Journal* 1, 23-42, available online at http://crj.oxfordjournals.org/cgi/reprint/1/1/23.

—— (2010) *Greek Tragedy: Suffering under the Sun*. Oxford.

Hamilton, V. (1996) *The Analyst's Preconscious*. New York.

Harris, W.V. (2009) *Dreams and Experience in Classical Antiquity*. Cambridge, MA & London.

Husser, J.-M. (1996) *Dreams and Dream Narratives in the Biblical World* (English translation by J.M. Munro). Sheffield.

Kessels, A.H.M. (1973) 'Studies on the dream in Greek literature', PhD Diss. Utrecht.

Kudlien, F. (1991) *Sklaven-Mentalität im Spiegel antiker Wahrsagerei*. Stuttgart.

Kurth, W. (1950) 'Das Traumbuch des Artemidorus im Lichte der Freudschen Traumlehre', *Psyche* 4, 488-512.

Longfellow, H.W. (1842) *Poems on Slavery*. Cambridge, MA.

MacAlister, S. (1992) 'Gender as sign and symbolism in Artemidorus' *Oneirokritika*: social aspirations and anxieties', *Helios* 19, 140-60.

McKibben, D.B. (1949) 'Negro slave insurrections in Mississippi, 1800-1865', *Journal of Negro History* 34, 73-90.

Miller, P.C. (1994) *Dreams in Late Antiquity: Studies in the Imagination of a Culture*. Princeton, NJ.

Oppenheim, A.L. (1956) *The Interpretation of Dreams in the Ancient Near East* [= *Transactions of the American Philosophical Society* 46.3, 179-373]. Philadelphia.

———— (1966) 'Mantic dreams in the ancient Near East', in R. Caillois and G.E. von Grünebaum (eds) *The Dream and Human Societies* 341-50. Berkeley, CA.

———— (1969) 'New fragments of the Assyrian dream book', *Iraq* 31, 153-65.

Pack, R. (1955) 'Artemidoros and his waking world', *Transactions and Proceedings of the American Philological Association* 86, 280-90.

Pease, H. (1893) *Soudi: A Story of African Slave Life*, LSE Selected Pamphlets.

Perkins, M. (1999) 'The meaning of dream books', *History Workshop Journal* 4, 102-13.

Price, S.R.F. (1986) 'The future of dreams: from Freud to Artemidorus', *Past & Present* 113, 3-37.

Rousseau, G.S. (1963) 'Dream and vision in Aeschylus' "Oresteia"', *Arion* 2, 101-36.

Scheidel, W. (1993) 'Slavery and the shackled mind: on fortune-telling and slave mentality in the Graeco-Roman world' [review essay on Kudlien (1991)], *Ancient History Bulletin* 7, 107-14.

Shulman, D. and Stroumsa, G.G. (eds) (1999) *Dream Cultures: Explorations in the Comparative History of Dreaming*. New York.

Strassberg, R.E. (2008) *Wandering Spirits: Chen Siyuan's Encyclopedia of Dreams*, translated with an introduction. Berkeley, Los Angeles, CA & London.

Traill, E. (2004) 'A haruspicy joke in Plautus', *CQ* 54, 117-27.

Walde, C. (1999) 'Dream interpretation in a prosperous age? Artemidorus, the Greek interpreter of dreams', in Shulman and Stroumsa (eds), 122-42.

Ward, S.R. (1970 [1855]) *Autobiography of a Fugitive Negro*. Chicago, IL. Reproduction of the original edition published in London.

Winkler, J. (1990) *The Constraints of Desire: The Anthropology of Sex and Gender in Ancient Greece*. New York.

Woolman, J. (1971) *The Journal and Major Essays of John Woolman*, ed. P.P. Moulton. Richmond, IN.

Index